Ngũgĩ

Reflections on his Life of Writing

Ngũgĩ

Reflections on his Life of Writing

Edited by
Simon Gikandi & Ndirangu Wachanga

JC JAMES CURREY

James Currey
is an imprint of
Boydell & Brewer Ltd
PO Box 9, Woodbridge
Suffolk IP12 3DF (GB)
www.jamescurrey.com
and of
Boydell & Brewer Inc.
668 Mt Hope Avenue
Rochester, NY 14620–2731 (US)
www.boydellandbrewer.com

British Library Cataloguing in Publication Data
A catalogue record for this book is available on request from the
British Library

ISBN 978-1-84701-214-2 (James Currey paperback)

ISBN 978-1-84701-223-4 (James Currey Africa-only paperback)

Contents

References

Preface

This started as a work of commemoration and celebration. The two of us had been working on Ngũgĩ's works for many years from different directions— Simon Gikandi as a literary critic and historian; Ndirangu Wachanga as a journalist and documentarist. In the course of our lives and work, we had had many encounters with Ngũgĩ and knew him well in different contexts. On January 5, 2018, the author, one of the most eminent writers to have come out of Africa in the modern period, would be celebrating his 80th birthday. We thought it would be a good occasion to reflect on Ngũgĩ's life in writing, and to think through his work from the perspective of those who had known him either personally or through reading and commenting on his texts. Our goal was to put together a collection of short essays, poems, and stories that reflect on the life of the writer, his world, and his works. We were particularly interested in imaginative pieces that would reveal the different, and sometimes complex, layers that had gone into the making of the writer; and we wanted to go beyond his well-established institutional image and to probe how what might initially have appeared to be minor episodes in his life provided vistas into his coming into being as a writer, as an intellectual of decolonization, and a major figure in conversations about human rights and justice in the long twentieth century and the beginning of the twenty-first century. We were also interested in Ngũgĩ's role outside the academy in the world of education, the mass media, community theater, and activism, places where we had encountered him many times. The works collected here are reflections of this desire to celebrate the writer in his prime.

The story of Ngũgĩ's life and its intersection between his experiences and education is well known. His interviews over the years, and his memoirs in late career, have given us a complex image of the writer in his various iterations; but what we see in this collection is both an extension and complication of this well-established narrative. Ngũgĩ means different things to different people, but one of the themes running through the collection is how he is both rooted in a very specific Gĩkũyũ and Kenyan realm from which he has spread his wings to the world. The first introductory essay by Gikandi tries to negotiate the local events that went into the making of the author; the second essay by Wachanga documents how Ngũgĩ's life and work has emerged against a background of global transformations in time and space. In the section titled 'Serenades & Beginnings' we have represented essays that capture the essence of Ngũgĩ's life in writing through poetic experimentation: Mĩcere Gĩthae Mũgo's experiments with African orature and technologies of performance to rehearse and embrace, in language, Ngũgĩ as an age mate and a figure of his time; Tsitsi Jaji turns the writer into a figure of modernist experimentation; and Charles Cantalupo elevates him to a figure of epic. In this section, we are taken through the hidden transcripts of Ngũgĩ's beginnings, from his undergraduate days at Makerere University College and the University of Leeds (Susan Kiguli and Roland Nasasira), the impact of *Weep Not, Child* on a generation of readers (Gikandi and Peter Kimani), his dramatic rejection of the Church (Ime Ikiddeh), and the surveillance of the state that sought to contain him (Levin Opiyo).

The second section of the book, 'Memories, Recollection & Tributes', provides us memories and encounters with Ngũgĩ from both familiar and unexpected sources. Bernth Lindfors was one of the first witnesses to Ngũgĩ's emergence as a writer, and his recollection of early conversations sets the tone for this section. In this section we also have accounts from witnesses to Ngũgĩ's role as a major figure in the transformation of what would come to be known as postcolonial criticism at the University of Nairobi in the 1970s (Eddah Gachukia and Margaretta wa Gacheru) and accounts of how his project of radical pedagogy would continue to influence younger writers and critics across geographies and time zones (Grant Farred and Chege Githiora). But there are also unexpected stories of what Willy Mutunga calls 'inspiring encounters' in his contribution to this volume. Indeed, 'encounter' is a key word in this section, and in others. Whether these encounters take place in Kenya (Mutunga), Yale (Ann Biersteker), or Asmara and Leeds (Jane Plastow), they are all recalled as unforgettable and transformative. But these encounters also call attention to certain elements of Ngũgĩ's life that are not always talked about. From Mutunga we learn of the novelist's deep involvement in the radical underground movement at the University of Nairobi in the 1970s, and of the influence of his work on Kenyan jurisprudence. And we also learn of the price he had to pay for his commitment including detention and exile. One of the most touching moments in the book is Rhonda Cobham-Sander and Reinhard Sander's account of Ngũgĩ's struggle to find a philological home in German, his vulnerabilities, and the destructive effect of his exile on those close to him.

In the third section of this collection, 'Working with Ngũgĩ', we have accounts of what it meant to collaborate with Ngũgĩ from the perspective of his publishers (James Currey and Henry Chakava). The lessons provided here are crucial to understanding Ngũgĩ's influence outside the academy. As Currey notes, Ngũgĩ was a central figure in the decolonization of publishing and, as we can see from Chakava's account, there was an important interplay between his work at the University of Nairobi and the transformation of the publishing scene in Kenya. Publishing Ngũgĩ was a risk that Chakava took, but it could also be said it was the risk that enabled the emergence of an indigenous publishing scene. Indeed, Ngũgĩ has often acted as an agent of institutional change in unexpected places such as the work of a curator or designer turned activist (Sultan Somjee) or in the conception of *Mūtiiri* as a scholarly journal in Gĩkũyũ setting out to invent new vocabularies (Kimani Njogu).

What about Ngũgĩ the theorist? In the fourth section of the collection, 'The Writer, the Critic & the World', we have accounts of Ngũgĩ as a writer and critic who has shaped the discipline of literary studies in ways that have been clear to many of us but has perhaps not been entirely acknowledged in the wider world of global literary studies. Ngũgĩ has made memory and recollection a central part of debates about African pasts and futures (Emilia Ilieva); he has brought a new dimension to our conversations about the autobiographical contract in fiction (Gĩchingiri Ndĩgĩrĩgĩ); and he has added to our understanding of the idea of return in postcolonial practices (James Ogude). In this section, we have a reappraisal of Ngũgĩ's intervention in the debate on language in African literature and his quest for a new linguistic paradigm (Alamin Mazrui) and the challenge he has presented to both writers and readers in regard to African languages (Kĩariĩ Kamau). Most of the essays in this section affirm the transformative role Ngũgĩ has played in transforming the idea of World Literature inherited from the German romanticists (Anne Adams), in challenging the epistemological organization of knowledge (Boyce Davies), and in the creation of an African public sphere (Grace Musila).

The last section of the collection contains samples of what we call the 'other Ngũgĩ'. Here, we reproduce some texts by Ngũgĩ that add another layer to our institutional image of him. These included two addresses given at the University of Dar es Salaam. The first essay is a commemoration of Grant Kamenju perhaps one of the best critics of African literature and culture, a figure who remains unknown to many. The second piece is an address Ngũgĩ delivered on his award of an honorary Ph.D. at the University Dar es Salaam. He used this momentous occasion to reflect on the signature role played by the university in the transformation of African knowledge. The ideas contained in these essays are familiar to readers of Ngũgĩ's work, but the mode of address, the fact that both speeches were given in Kiswahili, was unique. The same can be said about 'Asia in my Life', where Ngũgĩ pays tribute the Asian cultures that influenced his childhood and found echoes in his education and writing, reminding us that his formation as a subject was not caught between the binary opposition of a European colonizer and an African colonized, but was mediated by a third party—that of the Asian in East Africa. We end the collection with Ngũgĩ's Gĩkũyũ poem, 'A Riddle of Love'. This is from a cycle of love poems Ngũgĩ wrote for his wife Njeeri published in *Mūtiiri*. It is a poem that uses all the resources of the language to express the author's love, betrothal and marriage to Njeeri; but it is also a display of his love of the Gĩkũyũ language. We end the collection with this poem because it brings together the many Ngũgĩs that we have known over the years—the writer, the theorist, the activist, the friend of many, and the lover.

Simon Gikandi & Ndirangu Wachanga

Acknowledgements

In putting this work together, we have accumulated a lot of debts. We thank Ngũgĩ for being able to answer our questions even when we pretended he didn't know what we were up to, and Mĩcere Mũgo for providing us with a perfect serenade to her age mate even as she struggled with some health challenges. Mũkoma wa Ngũgĩ facilitated the re-publication of some texts, and we thank him for that. We owe immense thanks to Abdul Abdilatif Abdalla for providing help with the Dar es Salaam addresses and, in general, for providing us with crucial background to Ngũgĩ's period in London. We thank our friends at various organizations, including the Nation Group of Newspapers and East African Educational Publishers, for their behind-the-scenes support. As we worked on this project, we were inspired by Willie Mutunga, former Chief Justice of Kenya, who has been an example of how literature and jurisprudence can speak to each other and of the significance of justice in the African imaginary. His long friendship with Ngũgĩ is also a model of a rare politics of friendship and a culture of generosity. The editors would like to thank Princeton University for providing funds, through the Princeton African Humanities Colloquium, for research, travel and editorial services.

Chronology

1938	Born in Kamĩrĩĩthũ, Limuru on 5 January to Thiong'o wa Ndũũcũ and Wanjikũ wa Ngũgĩ.
1947–48	Attends Church of Scotland Mission at Kamaandũra, Limuru.
1948–55	Attends Manguũ Karing'a (Gĩkũyũ independent) school.
1952	Governor Baring declares State of Emergency in Kenya.
1954	Manguũ is closed as an independent school; it becomes part of the Kĩnyogoori District Education Board (DEB).
1955–59	Studies at Alliance High School, Kikuyu.
1955	Family home razed and rebuilt as part of the colonial government's villagization project.
1957	Publication of 'I Try Witchcraft' in Alliance High School magazine.
1959–64	Studies at Makerere University College, Uganda.
1960	End of State of Emergency in Kenya; publication of 'The Fig Tree' in *Penpoint*.
1961–64	Columnist for *Sunday Post*, then for *Daily Nation* and *Sunday Nation*.
1961	*The Rebels* is broadcast on Uganda Broadcasting Service; submits 'The Black Messiah' (published in 1965 as *The River Between*) for a competition sponsored by the East African Literature Bureau.
1962	Attends Conference of African Writers of English Expression at Makerere; *The Black Hermit* produced at the Ugandan National Theatre, Kampala.
1962–64	On Editorial Board of *Penpoint*.
1963	Kenya becomes independent; *The Black Hermit* published by Makerere University Press.
1964	Graduates from Makerere, B.A.; enters Leeds University; begins writing *A Grain of Wheat*; publication of *Weep Not, Child*.
1965	Publication of *The River Between*.

1966   *Weep Not, Child* wins first prize for Anglophone fiction at first
            World Festival of Negro Arts at Dakar; attends International PEN
            Conference in the United States.

1967   Attends Third Afro-Asian Writers Conference in Beirut,
            Lebanon; returns to Kenya; 'This Time Tomorrow' is broadcast
            on BBC Africa Service; publication of *A Grain of Wheat*; attends
            first African-Scandinavian Writers' Conference, Stockholm.

1967–69   Appointed Special Lecturer in English at University College,
            Nairobi.

1968   Together with Henry Owour Anyumba and Taban lo Liyong
            presents a memo to the University College Senate proposing
            the abolition of the Department of English; Ife Conference
            on African Writing in English, Ife, Nigeria; visiting lecturer,
            University College, Dar es Salaam.

1969   Resigns from his teaching position to protest violations of
            academic freedom at the University, including the barring of
            Oginga Odinga, the opposition leader, from speaking at the
            University.

1969–70   Fellow in Creative Writing, Makerere University College.

1970   Publication of *This Time Tomorrow*.

1970–71   Visiting Associate Professor at Northwestern University,
            Evanston, Illinois.

1971   Returns to University of Nairobi.

1972   Publication of *Homecoming*.

1973   Promoted to Senior Lecturer and Head of the Department of
            Literature at the University of Nairobi; awarded the Lotus Prize
            in literature at 5th Afro-Asian Writers' Conference in Alma Ata,
            Kazakhstan.

1974   With Mĩcere Gĩthae Mũgo begins *The Trial of Dedan Kimathi*.

1975   *Publication of Secret Lives*; completes *Petals of Blood* in Yalta at a
            Guest House of the Soviet Writers Union

1976   Becomes chairman of Kamĩrĩĩthũ Community Education and
            Cultural Centre's cultural committee; attends international
            Emergency Conference on Korea in Tokyo; *The Trial of Dedan
            Kimathi* performed at the Kenya National Theatre, Nairobi.
            Promoted to Associate Professor of Literature at the University of
            Nairobi.

1977   *The Trial of Dedan Kimathi* is performed at FESTAC 1977 in
            Lagos, Nigeria; publication of *Petals of Blood*; legally changes
            name to Ngũgĩ wa Thiong'o; *Ngaahika Ndeenda* is performed
            at Kamĩrĩĩthũ; license for further performances of the play is
            withdrawn; arrested and detained at Kamiti Maximum Security
            Prison.

1978   Death of President Jomo Kenyatta; Ngũgĩ released from
            detention; denied position at University of Nairobi.

1979   Ngũgĩ and Ngũgĩ wa Mĩriĩ are arrested under false charges for
            drinking after hours; he is defended by Willie Mutunga and
            others; charges are dismissed; 400 academics sign a petition
            asking for his reinstatement at the University of Nairobi.

1979–82   Involved in the revision of Gĩkũyũ orthography.

1980   *Mzalendo Kimathi*, the Kiswahili translation of *The Trial of
            Dedan Kimathi*, is performed at the University of Nairobi; gives
            talk at Africa Centre, London; publication in Gĩkũyũ of *Caitaani
            Mũtharaba-ini* and *Ngaahika Ndeenda*.

1981   *Caitaani* receives Special Commendation by the Jury of the
            Noma Awards for Publishing in Africa; rehearsals for *Maitũ
            Njugĩra* begin at Kamĩrĩĩthũ Community Education and Cultural
            Centre; publication of *Detained*.

1982   Denied permission to produce *Maitũ Njugĩra* at the Kenya
            National Theatre; government de-registers the Kamĩrĩĩthũ Centre
            and bans all theater in the region; publication of English editions
            of *Devil on the Cross* and *I Will Marry When I Want* in London;
            attends launch of *Devil on the Cross* in London; remains in exile
            in London; publication of *Njamba Nene na Mbaathi ĩ Mathagu*
            [Njamba Nene and the Flying Bus] in Nairobi; with other Kenyan
            exiles in London, forms Committee for the Release of Political
            Prisoners in Kenya.

1983   *Njamba Nene na Mbaathi i Mathagu* receives Special
            Commendation in the Noma Award for Publishing in Africa;
            publication of *Barrel of a Pen*.

1984   Guest Professor, University of Bayreuth; delivers Robb Lectures,
            University of Auckland, New Zealand; delivers papers at
            University of Zimbabwe and Institute for Development Studies,
            Harare; publication of *Bathitoora ya Njamba Nene* [Njamba
            Nene's Pistol].

2002	Mwai Kibaki's National Rainbow Coalition (NARC) wins the December elections ending twenty-four years of Daniel arap Moi's presidency.
2003	Conducts the 6th Annual William H. Matheson Seminar in Comparative Arts, Washington University, St. Louis; as guest of the Steve Biko Foundation he delivers lecture to commemorate the deaths of Steve Biko and Robert Sobukwe.
2004	Returns to Kenya, after twenty-two years of exile, for a one-month visit. The first of three projected volumes of the Gĩkũyũ novel *Mũrogi wa Kagogo* is published in Nairobi.
2005	Publishes *African Intellectuals: Rethinking Politics, Language, Gender and Development*.
2006	Publishes *Wizard of the Crow*, the English translation of *Mũrogi wa Kagogo*; delivers McMillan-Stewart Lectures at Harvard University.
2009	Shortlisted for the Man Booker International Prize; delivers lecture at the University of Nairobi to commemorate the publication of the East African edition of *Wizard of the Crow*.
2010	Publishes his first memoir, *Dreams in a Time of War*.
2012	Publishes his second memoir, *In the House of the Interpreter*; finalist for the National Book Critics Circle Award following the publication of this memoir.
2013	Awarded Honorary Doctorate in Literature from the University of Dar es Salaam.
2014	Awarded Honorary Doctorate by Bayreuth University; receives Nicolas Guillen Lifetime Achievement Award for Philosophical Literature from the Caribbean Philosophical Association; publishes *Globalectics*.
2015	Hosted at State House by the Kenyan president, Uhuru Kenyatta; guest (with Mĩcere Mũgo) at the re-opening of the refurbished Kenya National Theatre; delivers 'The Chinua Achebe Legacy Series' at The City College of New York.
2016	Wins Park Kyong-ni Prize; delivers the Neville Alexander Memorial Lecture at Harvard University's Center for African Studies.
2017	Awarded Honorary Doctor of Letters by Yale.
2018	Celebrates 80th birthday; publishes *Wrestling with the Devil*, a new edition of *Detained*.

Introduction
Ngũgĩ wa Thiong'o:
Reflections on His Life of Writing

Simon Gikandi

I Becoming a Writer

If one was looking for that moment that encapsulates Ngũgĩ wa Thiong'o's entry into the edifice of African letters—and hence the institution of modern authorship—it is probably that day in May, 1964, when his first novel, *Weep Not, Child* is published by Heinemann Educational Books in London. We have at least two images of this moment: the first one is Ngũgĩ's now famous interview with John de Villiers for the mass circulation *Daily Nation* newspaper in Nairobi. The young author was introduced to his new public as follows:

> Slightly built James Ngũgĩ spoke slowly, earnestly. Only his hands were restless, seeming to flay the air in frustration when his command of the English language, as spoken, left him groping for the word or phrase that would express exactly his meaning. 'I was trying', he said, 'to express the feelings of a small village community in Kenya during the Emergency. The terror, the fear of the unknown in which so many of the little people lived. The setting is a local one, which I know and have lived in, but the feeling, I think, is universal: the feeling of the little man, a child, in a world at war. He is caught in a situation he cannot control; he can only live it'. He was talking about his book, *Weep Not, Child*, which is being published in Britain this week by William Heinemann. ('The Birth of a New East African Author'; reprinted in Sander and Lindfors 7)

Here, there is the often-forgotten combination of the moment of arrival of the artist, of his uncertain entry into the culture of letters, and, with it, some hesitation, perhaps doubts about his own capacity to carry the burden thrust on him by history as the first East African novelist. In the interview itself, we can see Ngũgĩ making the first tenuous step into the public sphere that will come to define the rest of his life, drawing adulation from generations of readers, but also the enmity of an insecure postcolonial state. For the literary historian, there isn't much information to be gained from this interview: apart from the usual comments on the authors who have influenced him, his education, and his aspirations, Ngũgĩ does not tell us much about his coming into being as an artist. In fact, apart from the introductory comments, we have few insights into what pushed the young undergraduate from Makerere University College in Kampala to the aspiration of becoming an author, nor do we have much insight into what it means to inaugurate what will turn out to be a seminal moment in the making of Africa literature. What does it feel to be a writer? What brought this child of 'Mau Mau' to writing as, not merely a vocation, but as the mark of a will to overcome the constraints of a childhood lived under the shadow of empire, the promise of freedom, and what will turn out to be betrayal? The de Villiers interview is scant on details—both interviewer and interviewee seem unsure about what this moment means. And if Ngũgĩ seems to be reticent about his achievement, it is not because he hasn't mastered the language of self-expression; rather, it is because he himself is yet to realize how momentous and inaugural this occasion will become.

It will take almost fifty-two years for Ngũgĩ to take a measure of his own feelings about the business of becoming a writer. This is how he recalls this moment in *Birth of a Dream Weaver*:

> It's hard to capture in words the sensation at seeing an advance copy of my first novel to be published: *Weep Not, Child*. I rushed home to show it to my mother and Nyambura and my immediate brothers and sisters. The kids, Thiong'o and Kimunya, were too young to care, but I showed them anyway and made them hold it. My mother wanted to know if that was the best I could have done and was satisfied when I told her I had done my best. I didn't know how the neighbors would take it. The image of a successful graduate was a black gown, a flat cap with tassels, and a rolled something in his hands, not a guy in regular wear holding a book in his hands, claiming authorship. But they received it well, and though they could not read it, they couched it reverently ... A Nairobi bookshop run by Marjorie Oludhe Macgoye arranged for me to sign books, and I couldn't believe that people would actually line up to have me sign their copies of *Weep Not, Child*. (204–5)

It would be easy to assume that the contrasts here are between the representation of the actual event of writing as it was taking place and the recollection of the event in tranquility, if I may borrow from William Wordsworth's famous terms in the Preface to the *Lyrical Ballads*. The difference between the Ngũgĩ of the early interviews and the memoirist, I contend, is not about the time that separates the author from the event, but the tone he adopts to describe it. In his early interviews, Ngũgĩ tends to be formal and succinct, working hard to repress the emotions which, as we will discover later in the memoirs, have been the engine driving his works. He seems to conceive his coming into being as an artist as the logical extension of his education in the canon of English letters. In almost all the interviews conducted in the 1960s and 1970s, most of them collected in *Ngũgĩ wa Thiong'o Speaks*, edited by Reinhard Sanders and

Bernth Lindfors, the question of literary influence seems to provide the code for explaining the unprecedent act of authorship. An identification with the works of Joseph Conrad or D. H. Lawrence is assumed, either by Ngũgĩ or his interlocutors, to be the point of entry into writing. The life that might have gone into this writing—the violence of colonialism or the aspiration for an education—are made secondary to this colonial *Bildung*.

Consider this 1967 exchange between Ngũgĩ and fellow students at Leeds University:

> **Marcuson**: James, where were you born?
>
> **Ngũgĩ**: I was born in Limuru, Kenya, in 1938. I come from a large peasant family. My father had four wives. I was the fifth child of the third wife. In all there were about twenty-eight children. My father was a tenant farmer on the farm of an African landowner.
>
> **Marcuson**: At what age did you go to school?
>
> **Ngũgĩ**: Nine, to a primary school near our village for about two years. Then I moved to another primary school, part of what was called Gĩkũyũ Independent Schools. These were schools which belonged to people who had rebelled against missionary influence, so they wanted the kind of education that belonged to the people.
>
> **Marcuson**: What did you think of the missionary schools?
>
> **Ngũgĩ**: As I see them, you know, in their historical role, they have been the forerunners of colonialism—the John the Baptists preparing the way for Christ—the colonial administration. (*Ngũgĩ wa Thiong'o Speaks* 25)

Notice how the kernel of Ngũgĩ's early life, the things that are intimately connected to his coming into being as a writer—his childhood and his education—are truncated. The author provides nothing but the bare details. Yet, as we will discover as we delve deeper into his life in writing, the sketch that Ngũgĩ provides here is the peg on which his imagination hangs. There is the place in a particular time: 'Limuru, Kenya, in 1938' is a supplement, a stand in as it were, of the long struggle between Gĩkũyũ squatters and white settlers leading toward a bitter and violent conflict. 'Gĩkũyũ Independent Schools' is a synecdoche of the long and painful struggle by Gĩkũyũ nationalists to find a space in which they can imagine modernity outside colonial control. And, of course, the missionary schools represent the compromised space in which African subjectivity is imagined and elaborated. Ngũgĩ's succinct, yet trenchant responses, reveal as much as they conceal. It is not until the memoir that we will come to discover the complex family history and the turmoil surrounding it, the things that make the imaginative a tool of coping with the dissonance of the times.

Readers who are intimate with the cultural context of Ngũgĩ's novels have always suspected that they were always underwritten by an autobiographical register. I speculated on this in my monograph, *Ngũgĩ wa Thiong'o*; Evan Mwangi hinted at it in 'Contextualizing Untranslated Moments'; and Gĩchingiri Ndĩgĩrĩgĩ confirms it in his contribution to this collection. It is, however, in reading Ngũgĩ's memoirs that we come to realize how what Sigmund Freud famously called the family romance was, indeed, the condition of possibility of Ngũgĩ's life in writing. In 'Family Romances', Freud calls attention to the experiences of a growth in which children become dissatisfied with the images of their parents and seek to replace them imaginatively with an alternative family, one of 'higher social standing' (239).

If one is born, as Ngũgĩ is, into a family of landless peasants in a culture that values land ownership more than anything else, you are bound to always feel out of place and to aspire for an alternative family. For Ngũgĩ, the alternative family is made up of a new social class associated with colonial culture. This is the family that Njoroge sees when he peeks through the fence that separates the landed from the landless in *Weep Not, Child*:

> The path he followed passed just below Mwihaki's home. The houses were hidden by a big hedge of growing fir trees that surrounded the household. You could see the corrugated iron roof and the wooden walls of the imposing building through an opening or two in the hedge. Njoroge had been there, out in the courtyard, a number of times when he and others went to collect money for picking pyrethrum flowers for Jacobo. The place looked like a European's house, and Njoroge was always overawed by the atmosphere around the whole compound. He had never been in the big building and he was always curious to know what the inside looked like. (17–18)

Later, in *Dreams in a Time of War*, Ngũgĩ will recall the alternative family, the one authorized by colonialism, embodied by the homestead of the Reverend Stanley Kahahu, who 'exuded modernity in person and in family':

> Their homestead, however, remained a mystery to me ... I had never been beyond the outer gates. A thicket of pine trees surrounded the homestead, and I could only get glimpses of the house through gaps in the trees. But this changed when one day his wife, Lillian, invited the children of the families that worked on their land to a Christmas party. (79–80)

Ngũgĩ's life in writing will be informed by the colonial romance and haunted by its powerful patriarchal tropes; in a world divided in two, the fate of the family, an essential condition for imagining communities, is tied to the fortune or misfortune of fathers. And as often happens in the postcolonial text, the children of peasants are condemned to perpetual orphanage; that is, unless, they break away from their fathers and seek sanctuary in the world of the mother. For Ngũgĩ, the scene of writing is associated with maternity, the realm that the colonial family romance seeks to repress. Rejected by his father, Ngũgĩ is baffled: 'The move deepened my sense of myself as a stranger, a feeling I had harbored since I learned that the land on which our homestead stood was not really ours', he recalls in *Dreams* (97). Ironically, it is this sense of not belonging to a place that propels him into the world of dreams, a world initiated by the mother who sends him to school: 'My father had no say one way or another in this enterprise. It was my mother's dream and her entire doing' (60). The authority of this new world, the world of stories, will be enhanced by a half-sister:

> She was disadvantaged in every possible way but had remained optimistic about life, dwelling in the world of songs and stories, becoming the collective memory of the community. I grew up with her stories. She was the only one who could conjure them up in daytime. She could not see the daylight; she felt it in her trembling hands. She had molded my world in ways that only I could understand. She had made me want to become a dream weaver. (*Dreams* 204–5)

Orality provides the first step in Ngũgĩ's aesthetic education; the colonial school and university will come later.

Yet it could be said that colonial institutions ultimately enable Ngũgĩ to become a writer. For not only do Alliance High School and Makerere University College provide Ngũgĩ with access to literary culture, but also a sanctuary in which he can imagine life outside the violence of history and the fears rooted in his sense of dispossession and displacement. But these institutions do not provide any guarantees. Indeed, the triumphant tone that the author adopts in *House of the Interpreter*, his second memoir, conceals the tenuousness of his position and deep doubts about his location and identity. The tenuousness of Ngũgĩ's position is most apparent when his aspiration to enter the house of culture comes up against the brutal realities of colonial governmentality. Even as he makes his boisterous journey through Englishness, mastering the canon of English letters, Ngũgĩ cannot escape the shadow of being the colonial outlaw. He shuttles between the colonial fortress with its 'threatening tower' looming 'larger and larger' over him (69) and the embrace of Shakespeare (177). When it comes to Ngũgĩ's life in writing, we cannot avoid the intersection between the self that turns to writing in order to make sense of the violence of its history and the institution of the author as a product of that history.

II A Life in Writing

Although he is not born until 1938, Ngũgĩ's work cannot be separated from the foundation of the Kenyan Crown Colony in 1900, the turmoil engendered by white settlement during this period, the establishment of imperial governance, and the introduction of colonial culture. Colonialism may now appear to some readers to be part of a diminished—or diminishing—past but for Ngũgĩ and his generation it is the condition of possibility of their making and being as modern subjects. And perhaps there is no generation that experiences colonialism as a form of trauma than that born in the 1920s and 1930s, for, unlike their elders who can remember a time before colonialism, this generation lives under the totality established by empire and the pain and loss that it generates. Someone born in the 1890s, let's say Jomo Kenyatta, can still look back to a time when colonialism did not formally exist, or when it existed as a minor intrusion in the social organization of communities. The generation that is born before formal colonialism can turn to the work of memory to gird themselves against the changes taking place in colonial Kenya. But for those born in the 1920s (Dedan Kimathi's generation) or the 1930s (Ngũgĩ's generation), the memories of the past are just sharp reminders of multiple losses—the loss of land, the denigration of custom, and the deligitimation of the authority of the elders.

A settler colony like Kenya is defined by violence in its various manifestations. There is the violence that comes with the alienation of African land to cater for the interests of white settlers; there is the violence of new institutions of governmentality, including policing, tax collection, and even the inoculation of cattle; and there is the hidden violence involved in the project of creating new subjects. Colonial attempts to transform local society are often contested and resisted, and this, too, creates its own dialectic of violence. Ngũgĩ's generation cannot escape from the hard power of imperialism, nor can they live outside the orbit of colonial cultural institutions, so they are bound to carry the burden of this history. Colonial institutions, especially Protestant Missions and their schools, will mold Ngũgĩ. In fact, Ngũgĩ does not need to be conscripted into colonial institutions because, as he reminds us in his memoirs, they are his only conduits for social mobility and improvement. Still, as he makes his way through colonial institutions, academically gifted and determined, he is constantly reminded of the pressures put on the colonized generation by the unfulfilled promises of the colonial mandate.

Ngũgĩ lives under the shadow of the colonial promise and the nationalist demand. His older brothers belong to the generation of the 1940s (a reference to their years of coming of age rather than birth). This is a generation of young men, some of them returning from the European wars, who discover that the fight against fascism has no dividends for the African. This generation (apart from Kimathi, it includes the radical Gĩkũyũ writer, Gakaara wa Wanjaũ) are often renegades from the Christian missions who find themselves marginalized in the native reserves, with limited opportunities for land ownership, a key measure of adulthood, or with no job opportunities in spite of their relatively-good education. The generation of the 1940s is an unhappy genera-tion. They have two fathers who fail to live up to their expectations: there is the colonial father, who will not stomach any questioning of his authority (both Kimathi and Gakaara are kicked out of mission schools for questioning the colonial order); and then there is the African father who appears helpless in the face of European power. The result is the confrontation between fathers and sons that runs through most of Ngũgĩ's early fiction.

The drama played out between fathers and sons first appears in *Weep Not, Child* where Njoroge's older brother, Boro, seethes in anger when he real-izes that not only was the family land stolen by the settler Howland, but that their father is impotent in the face of the theft. The story of the stolen lands comes into Boro's mind 'with a growing anger. How could these people have let the white man occupy the land without acting?' (27). Colonial power has, of course, neutered the traditional father and replaced him with a white father, a torturer with no legitimacy. Njoroge's tragedy arises from the fact that the African father cannot protect him from the white, colonial father who seeks to castrate him. For Ngũgĩ, then, writing is born out of violence, both the vio-lence inherent in the colonial event itself and its cultural texts.

There is no doubt that Ngũgĩ comes of age in one of the most violent peri-ods in Kenyan history. By the end of the 1940s, responding to demands for land rights and political representation, the militant generation has taken up arms and set up fighting units in the mountains and forests; prominent colo-nial chiefs have been assassinated; the government cannot guarantee security to a panicked settler class. On October 20, 1952, the governor, Evelyn Baring, declares a state of emergency in Kenya, setting off a series of events that are going to mark Ngũgĩ's life and creative work deeply. Nationalist leaders are arrested and taken to remote districts for what will turn out to be mock trials or none at all; emergency laws and regulations are put in place; reinforcements are flown in from Britain and soldiers march down the streets of Nairobi in a show of force. This is just the beginning. Under the state of emergency, the colonial government is allowed to 'repatriate' all members of the Gĩkũyũ, Meru, and Embu ethnic groups from cities and settled areas to what are known as native reserves, places that many of them had left because of lack of land or work. In cities, towns, and villages, sympathizers of the nationalist movement are arrested without trial, subjected to detention orders, and sent to camps in places that are inhospitable and inimical to people from the highlands. The names of the detention camps will become legendary: Manyani, Hola, Mada Island. The Gĩkũyũ call detention *ithamĩrio-inĩ*—a place of no return.

At the same time, the government also embarks on a process of what will come to be known as villagization: all people living in the native reserves are to be moved from the scattered hills and hamlets that have always constituted their homesteads into new fortified villages surrounded by trenches, spikes, and armed guards on towers. In a bid to isolate the fighters in the forest, the government also cuts off local populations from their farms leading to severe hunger and malnutrition. This period will come to be known as *hingo ya thiina*, the time of suffering.

For Ngũgĩ, this time, the time of what is sometimes called 'Mau Mau', will be inscribed in writing as a turning point in the narrative of his life and the history of his country. The meaning of 'Mau Mau' or the Land and Liberation Army will change as the author's understanding of the historiography evolves or as he seeks an alternative lexicon and account for the past. *In Weep Not, Child*, the young hero, subjected to torture and deprived of his dreams of an education because of his brother's involvement in the movement against colonialism, will encapsulate the fear and terror of that moment. In *A Grain of Wheat*, the movement will be treated as the mark of a stillborn narrative of decolonization. By the time we get to *Petals of Blood*, 'Mau Mau' will have come to be seen, through a Marxist perspective, as the coming into being of the radical history of nationalism in Kenya. In *The Trial of Dedan Kimathi*, it will be shown to be nothing less than the totalized moment of the narrative of liberation itself. In *Matigari*, the movement will have the power of the historical repressed waiting for the moment of its return and restitution. Whatever language we develop to explain these transformations, there is no doubt that hidden beneath the rhetoric, whether it is that of the romance of nationalism or revolution, 'Mau Mau' is an important part of Ngũgĩ's political consciousness and unconscious. Leaving aside his own political transformation, we are left to wonder what mark it left in him.

Like many members of his generation, Ngũgĩ cannot escape from the troubles of the time, but he has the opportunity for momentary refuge in the house of culture, which he finds at Alliance High and Makerere University. And if the voraciousness of his consumption of culture at these citadels of high learning is anything to go by, the aspiring writer seems to invest heavily in the idea, promoted by English writers and critics since Matthew Arnold in the nineteenth century, that culture has the capacity to ward off anarchy (see *Culture and Anarchy*). When he is confronted by the reality of the state of emergency, or the iron heel of colonial power, Ngũgĩ turns to culture for rescue.

This point is illustrated well by an encounter in *Dreams in a Time of War*: finding himself in the front of white power in the form of a policeman interrogating 'Mau Mau' suspects and their sympathizers, and knowing that one of his brothers is a member of the organization, Ngũgĩ trembles with terror, and then, seeking to understand his narrow escape from the bond of the law, he goes in search of his primary school teacher, Samuel Kibicho, hoping he could lend him books to ward off the dangers around him. Ironically, it is at this moment—one of deep fear—that Ngũgĩ discovers that he has been admitted to Alliance High School (*Dreams*, 242). He never seems to doubt that books and the institution of the school will protect him from the terrors of history and the lived experience.

Often, as we see in in the *House of the Interpreter*, the only thing standing between Ngũgĩ and imprisonment is the uniform of Alliance High School. His life at Alliance becomes 'a series of crossings between the conflicting realities of the school and the new village' (73–4). At Alliance, Ngũgĩ sometimes wishes that he could unburden his deep fears to his teacher Joseph Kariuki, newly arrived from Makerere, but the terror of the times remains unspoken even to the man who embodies a black presence: 'neither in the classroom nor outside did he openly discuss the parallels between the music and the terror in the country. Neither did we. We kept our thoughts to ourselves, confining our musings to matters of meter and melody' (62). Arriving at Makerere at the end of June 1959, Ngũgĩ seems relieved that he has left a wounded country— 'the colonial Kenya of terror and uncertainty' (*Birth* 17) behind him; his life at Makerere will be recalled primarily in terms of his educational achievements and his coming into being as a writer. At Makerere, the troubles seem to belong to a remote past. Still, the state of emergency means that those subjects closely identified with the troubles—the Gĩkũyũ, Embu, and Meru communities—are vulnerable outside the boundaries of the university college, the city of Kampala, and the country of Uganda. They live under the shadow of the wounded country and its uncertain future.

And, then, almost overnight, the suffering is over. In 1960, the state of emergency ends, and after what oral history will come to represent as many years spent in the wilderness, Kenyatta, the symbol of anti-colonial resistance, himself a weaver of dreams, returns to his ancestral village of Ichawerri. It is the beginning of scores of such returns, many of them captured in Ngũgĩ's stories and, most vividly in *A Grain of Wheat*. Peasants confined to villages return to their homes; workers and traders make their way back to the hitherto forbidden towns and cities; and detainees, like Gikonyo, begin their journeys from their places of banishment to old dispensations. The crowning point seems to be that evening on December 12, 1963, when the Union Jack comes down, and a soldier called Kisoi Munyao raises the new Kenyan flag—black, red, and green—captured in a popular song from the period:

Mũnyao haicia bendera
Haicia bendera

Nĩ ya marũri matatũ
Haicia bendera

Mũtune thakame iitũ
Haicia bendera

Na mũiru gĩkonde gitũ
Haicia bendera

Ngirini nĩ ithaka ciitũ
Haicia bendera

Munyao raise our flag
Raise our flag

It has three colors
Raise the flag

Red for our blood
Raise the flag

Black for our skin
Raise the flag

Green for our land
Raise the flag

'It felt good to hear that song and anthem', Ngũgĩ will recall in *Birth of a Dream Weaver* (189).

Beneath the bravado of the new national song, however, there is deep anxiety, which is best captured toward the end of *A Grain of Wheat*: 'Everybody waited for something to happen. This "waiting" and the uncertainty that went with it—like a woman torn between fear and joy during birth motions—was a taut cord beneath the screams and the shouts and the laughter' (220). Soon, the dream of independence will fade; and the author, a product of 'Mau Mau', of radical nationalism and its promises, will recalibrate his fiction to make sense of a situation in which, as he puts it in a note to *A Grain of Wheat*, decolonization has created problems that are 'sometimes too painfully real for the peasants who fought the British yet who now see all that they fought for being put on one side'. This note sets the mood for Ngũgĩ's writing from 1967 onwards, a mood of disenchantment and betrayal.

As we move into the later novels, *Petals of Blood*, *Devil on the Cross*, and *Matigari*, the autobiographical register, which defined the author's beginnings as a writer, disappears, giving way to collective histories of loss and displaced identities. Previously authorized by the author's subjective sense of displacement in what should have been the spaces of his mooring and a concurrent desire to claim kinship with family, community, and ethnos, writing is now asked to bear witness to the birth pains of a nation and its troubled history. As Ngũgĩ's career progresses, we begin to notice that narratives are no longer about vulnerable subjects alienated from their communities, but stories of what Georg Lukács, in *The Historical Novel*, calls world historical individuals

(127), figures such as Kimathi in *The Trial of Dedan Kimathi*. By the time we get to the literature of late postcoloniality, the author has shifted his audiences from the interiorized fears and anxieties of Njoroge (*Weep Not*) or Muthoni (*The River Between*) to the affirmative world of Karega (*Petals*), Wariinga (*Devil*) and Matigari (*Matigari*).

The transformation taking place in Ngũgĩ's oeuvre cannot, however, be explained simply in terms of his disenchantment with the terms of decolonization, or even his own troubled relationship with the Kenyan state (which leads to a period of imprisonment without trial and eventual exile), nor can it be explained simply by tracing a shift from the liberalism cultivated by colonial Englishness to Marxism or black radicalism. Ngũgĩ's transformation as a writer is also motivated by his expanding audience, his identity as an important modern writer, and his identification with what we may call the cause of the international avant-garde. All the works Ngũgĩ writes in the 1980s and after are driven by a fundamental belief that the role of art is not merely to explain the world, but to change it. The work of art is hence called upon to not simply capture the moods and feelings of the colonized, or the disenchantment of the postcolonial, but to intervene in the arena of politics and culture, to will new subjects and agents of social transformation into being. The avant-garde idea is demonstrated most vividly in the project of the theater at Kamĩrĩĩthu, where Ngũgĩ and his compatriots seek to nurture an open theater in which local peasants are asked to enact their histories and everyday experiences as an alternative to the narrative of development promoted by the state and the ruling class.

This is the project that is interrupted when Ngũgĩ is first imprisoned and then exiled, effectively cut off from the audiences whose desires he sought to transform. Produced in exile, *Mũrogi wa Kagogo* (*Wizard of the Crow*) invites a reading that is deceptive—it wants to be read as a global novel and, indeed, points readers to Ngũgĩ's expanded world from New Jersey and New York to India. Beneath this appeal to a global audience, however, *Mũrogi* is Ngũgĩ's attempt to continue the political project of the avant-garde away from the audience and polity he left behind. But how can an author, now ensconced in the privileged halls of American academia, claim to intervene in the lifeworld of the postcolony? Does the Kenyan state care about allegories of its corrupt politics and sartorial narratives about its failure? The proof of the pudding is in its eating. In August, 2004, the author returns to Kenya after twenty-two years of exile to launch *Mũrogi*.

But what was supposed to be a triumphant return turns tragic: Ngũgĩ and his wife, Njeeri, are brutally attacked; she is sexually assaulted. There is bewilderment everywhere. Who could have done this? After all, the old dictatorship, the one satirized in *Mũrogi*, has been defeated; the residence where the author was attacked was supposed to be well guarded; a security detail was close by;

it does not make sense. Or does it? Was this attack the deep state's revenge for what they considered to be the author's arrogation of the rule of judgment in *Mūrogi*? In a perverse way, the attack confirmed the power of the literary text to intervene in the lived experience and to challenge the authority of the state and other institutions of domination.

Let me end by noting that although I have written considerably on Ngũgĩ's works as a novelist, a theorist, and as a teacher, and I have talked at length (in *Ngũgĩ wa Thiong'o*) about his influence on me as a young student, an aspiring editor, and an academic, I can say that the most important gift he gave me (apart from *Weep Not, Child*) was what is broadly called a politics of friendship and hospitality. Through his works, he connected me to a generation of fellow students and activists and at a time when literary scholarship was scorned as the lowest of the low faculties, he energized and authorized many of us to pursue our dreams and to live out the conviction that language and the imagination mattered even in the age of technology and bureaucracy. He established cultural lines that connected us to other sites of literary scholarship in East and West Africa, the north of England, and the Caribbean. He brought the black diaspora home to us. And above all, he put language at the center of our preoccupations. In 1980, as I sat at what was then Heinemann Educational Books editing *Ngaahika Ndeenda* and *Caitaani Mũtharaba-inĩ* line by line, debating matters of orthography with Ngũgĩ, I felt that something new was about to happen. Exile was to change everything, but in the back of my mind, I could not forget his insistence that the work we were doing had to measure to the highest standards of the time—that the Gĩkũyũ text should have the same quality of paper and print and design as any other text. And that was a time when a text mattered not just as a scriptural mark but also as the embodiment of a certain mode of learning and of being in the world.

Ngũgĩ at Work

Ndirangu Wachanga

In 2010, Ngũgĩ wa Thiong'o authorized me to document his life and work in form of a documentary film. Looking at his life and his intellectual biography provides a window into an understanding of the major debates on African languages and literatures, the role of writers and intellectuals in political, social, and cultural transformation, on colonialism and decolonization, on the pain and melancholy of exile, diasporic privileges and displacements, and on the memory of the colonized. It is instructive that Ngũgĩ turned 80 when his country, Kenya, was celebrating 55 years of political independence. The coincidence is insightful because Ngũgĩ's biography and intellectual career are emblematic of Kenya's complex process of becoming a nation, its political and cultural challenges, as well as its intellectual history. His biography provides revealing insights about the deployment of memory, and the role of memory in the evolution of the African nation states, allowing us to evaluate the relationship between the state and the African memory project. If the process of becoming of most African nation states continues to been defined by an unofficial program of forgetting, Ngũgĩ's biography invites the public to resist the urge to forget—rather to re-member.

This documentary project is motivated by a belief that the preservation of memories and experiences through visual and audio technology has a number of advantages over written materials: it enables representation and subsequent preservation of raw voices. While the objective is to produce a feature film documentary on Ngũgĩ, all the footage captured during the production process will be thematically archived in an open access repository. For more than half a century, he has been an eloquent voice championing human rights and a leader in global cultural criticism and political activism. Because of his longevity, Ngũgĩ's life and writings connect readers to an East African history that they only read in history books. In the following discussion, I organize my reflection on Ngũgĩ's life and his works around four distinct stages.

Phase I—Growing Up (1938–1959)

Born on January 5, 1938, Ngũgĩ grew up during the most violent period in Kenya's history, and came of age at the end of British occupation in East Africa. This phase of Ngũgĩ's growth is now documented in his first two memoirs:

Dreams in a Time of War and *In the House of the Interpreter*, confirming what critics have speculated about the autobiographical nature of his early creative works, particularly *Weep Not, Child*. In these memoirs, we encounter a young Ngũgĩ who is a victim of overlapping national and global events, including the tragedy of the Second World War, the Mau Mau war, the impact of the independent school movement, and the declaration of the State of Emergency in 1952.

The estrangement of his mother from his father when he was very young serves as a critical turning point in his biography, and it is in *Dreams in a Time of War* that he introduces himself as Ngũgĩ wa Wanjiku. His mother, like Nyokabi in *Weep Not, Child*, became the undying oasis of sanguinity at a moment of crisis that was defined by private mourning and collective suffering. When his mother decided that he would go to school, it was 'the offer of the impossible that deprived me of words' (*Dreams* 59), promising to never 'bring shame' to her 'by one day refusing to go to school because of hunger or other hardships' (60). During this period (the 1940s) opportunities for education are limited, and Ngũgĩ is the first one in his family to go to school, like others of his generation in similar circumstances leaving behind a dispossessed community that regarded education as a path to freedom. But it is also a traumatic period because everyone in his village had lost a family member either to the war, in the forest, or to the detention camps.

While attending one of the best schools in Kenya, Alliance High School, Ngũgĩ is educated in English and a certain kind of Englishness but haunted by his own relationship with his mother and the slipping connectedness to his community. This absence is important because it allows us to examine the way he captures that history in his works, particularly when he was guarded against physical colonial violence by Alliance High School's perimeter fence. This phase marks the beginning of Ngũgĩ's journey toward a discovery he makes while attending Makerere University College in Uganda: education, which was supposed to liberate him and empower his family, was also a form of alienation. While Ngũgĩ's attempt to reconnect with his mother through the figure of Nyokabi in *Weep Not, Child* is powerful, it falls short of curing his sense of alienation, particularly because he is aware that his mother could not read or write. It is Nyokabi who carefully weaves the processes of seeking education and growing up into an intricate lump in which the violence of colonialism and the resilience of resistance to it is ensnared with private mourning and collective melancholy. When many years later Ngũgĩ decided to write in Gĩkũyũ, it seems he was in search of new resources of language that could reconnect him to the mother and the community that he had left behind.

It makes sense at a functional level that Ngũgĩ turned to writing in Gĩkũyũ for ideological reasons—to raise the consciousness of the people he worked with at Kamĩrĩĩthũ Community Education and Cultural Centre. But at a deeper level, especially when we examine what happened when he first wrote in Gĩkũyũ, we note that Ngũgĩ did something he had never done before: he began to draw on oral resources. Looking at Ngũgĩ's work written in English, we don't find Ngũgĩ using devices rooted in orality such as proverbs, sayings, or folktales—they are conspicuously absent. His work is fashioned after the European novel. When he started to write in Gĩkũyũ, we find the influence of a very localized culture. It seems Ngũgĩ could only access oral tradition through Gĩkũyũ. English had given him a new model of expression. Gĩkũyũ opened up localized resources.

In my interview with Henry Chakava in 2016, the legendary publisher said that Ngũgĩ's use of oral tradition was one way of considering an alternative kind of novel instead of emulating inherited models. According to Chakava, *Matigari*, in which the oral narrative serves as the foundation of the story, is the novel Ngũgĩ should have written in 1964. In *Matigari*, the oral narrative fuels Ngũgĩ's certain fluency in Gĩkũyũ, a mood, which he rarely captures when he writes in English. Still, Ngũgĩ's *Dreams in a Time of War* provides us with a child's image of the leitmotifs that powerfully permeate his adult writings: colonialism, Christianity, culture and tradition, land, and more importantly, the pains of dispossession and the resilience of resistance against it.

Phase II—Early Writings (1960s)

From Alliance High School, Ngũgĩ joined Makerere University College where, in addition to studying the classics of British literature, he encountered African, Indian, and Caribbean writing. It was during his Makerere days as an under-graduate student that he wrote his first two novels: *Weep Not, Child* (1964), and *The River Between* (1965). These early writings were partly inspired by the optimism spawned by global socio-cultural and political changes in the 1950s and early 1960s. When I asked Ngũgĩ about the source of his courage to write a novel as an undergraduate, he located his response in global happenstances at the time: 'There was the Cuban revolution in 1954, the Caribbean Workers' Movement that brought about the independence of many Caribbean coun-tries, Mau Mau war in 1952, Ghana's independence in 1957, Algerian war in 1960, Tanzania's independence in 1962; country after country was becoming independent. There was a lot of hope and energy that we could transform our societies. There was a lot of optimism that the future was going to bring funda-mental changes' (2010 interview).

His first novel, *Weep Not, Child*, captures the hopes and the possibilities of a new beginning, a new dawn. But it is a beginning that is defined by pain-ful anxieties that midwifed post-colonial Kenya and its post-colonial subjects. These anxieties are interspersed with a mixture of dreams of opportunities offered by decolonization and disillusionment of unfulfilled promises of political independence. Let us remember that Ngũgĩ started writing at a time of change and transformation when no one seemed to know the meaning of that change. The importance of Ngũgĩ's early work lies in its ability to invite readers to think about literary careers from their beginnings and to inter-rogate the circumstances that informed those beginnings. 'He demonstrated that black people could write about themselves', James Currey said about the importance of Ngũgĩ's early work when I interviewed him in 2014.

Equally important is the role of institutions in the construction of Ngũgĩ's career. The generation of readers that emerged at the cusp of colonialism and post-colonialism encountered *Weep Not, Child* as a set book in schools at a time when the dominant literary texts were on alien experiences such as daf-fodils in the English countryside. *Weep Not, Child* introduced readers to char-acters they could identify with, to recognizable landscapes, to familiar sounds, and localized cultures. 'When I read *Weep Not, Child*, I saw myself in Mwihaki. I am Mwihaki in *Weep Not, Child*', said Wangui wa Goro in my interview in 2014. 'Everything in the novel is so familiar that I didn't feel like I was reading it in English. I read it in Gĩkũyũ.'

In 1965, Ngũgĩ joined the University of Leeds for graduate work. According to Martin Banham, who was teaching at the University of Leeds when Ngũgĩ joined the college, 'this was a period when the school of English at Leeds was developing strong interests in the study of cultures, writings and the arts of the Anglophone African countries. What Ngũgĩ found when he got to Leeds was the opportunity to develop his creative side, which took precedent for him over the mere acquisition of more qualifications ... [The] qualifications he wanted were those of a writer' (personal interview, 2010). At Leeds, Ngũgĩ interacted with, and was influenced by, socialist thinkers such as Arnold Kettle. During this time, Grant Kamenju introduced Frantz Fanon's *The Wretched of the Earth* to Ngũgĩ. This encounter with *The Wretched of the Earth* was transformative, especially because 'we did not have tools to theorize or think about independ-ence and the contradictions that accompanied it. It is Fanon who made us look at post-colonial Africa differently' (interview with Ngũgĩ, 2010).

The influence of his experience at Leeds is reflected in his borrowing from Fanon and socialist thinkers to represent the crushing edifice of the post-colony. Illustrative of this influence are his two novels, *A Grain of Wheat* and *Petals of Blood*. Set in contemporary times in Kenya, these two novels are driven by radical ideas that are centered around unending predicaments of peasants and workers who are perpetually ensnared in an oppressive neo-colonial society long after political independence. Ngũgĩ ends the 1960s disenchanted. Like his own novel, *Weep Not, Child*, which opens with an extrapolative sense of sanguinity but metamorphoses into a narrative of melancholy and disappoint-ment, Ngũgĩ entered the 1960s with hopes and dreams and ended the decade cynical and disillusioned by the unfulfilled promises of independence.

By the end of 1960s and the beginning of the 1970s, Ngũgĩ had already emerged as part of the first generation of African writers who were solidly educated in the Western tradition. As a product of colonial cultural and education institutions, he understood Europe very well, enabling him to play the role of a translator of Africa to Europe in ways that powerfully challenged European ideas and images of Africa. He belongs to a cluster of writers who emerged at the age of decolonization, and who were influential in shaping debates and offering counterpoints to European perspective at a time when only Europeans were running the existing institutions of cultural production. When Ngũgĩ started writing, there existed a long and established tradition that Africa had neither a history nor narratives and traditions of self-understanding. Ngũgĩ challenged that tradition in very influential and imaginative ways, using essays that were also crucial in transforming and displacing what he called 'European centers' in African scholarship.

Ngũgĩ's other significant influence in the 1960s was the revolution he helped midwife, along with Taban lo Liyong and Henry Owuor Anyumba, which led to the abolition of the English Department at the University of Nairobi in 1968 and its replacement with the Department of Literature. This revolution produced a model for re-thinking institutions of literary education not just in Anglophone East Africa but also in Anglophone West Africa and later in the Anglophone Caribbean. The premise of this revolution was that to study literature even in European languages is not to assume there was a natural relationship between Africa and Europe. Ngũgĩ was trying to create ways of thinking about Africa sometimes in relationship to Europe and also sometimes in opposition to European structures of knowledge and understanding. He was offering ways of challenging dominant ideas while suggesting other ways of thinking about Africa outside the established paradigms.

Phase III—Ngũgĩ: The Revolutionary (1970s)

Ngũgĩ entered the 1970s disillusioned but also as a revolutionary. He had just returned from Northwestern University, Evanston, USA as a visiting Associate Professor. Just before he left for Nairobi, Ngũgĩ spent an evening with the late South African poet Keorapetse Kgositsile, who pleaded with Ngũgĩ not to return. 'I told him: The system will either kill or detain you', Kgositsile said in my interview in 2014. Defiantly, Ngũgĩ responded, 'Kenya is for all Kenyans. Kenya is not Jomo Kenyatta's plantation.'

He started the decade of the 1970s at the University of Nairobi, playing a critical role as a teacher, writer, critic, and as a public intellectual. He was at the center of key debates about Kenya's history, culture, creative writing, literary expression, and theatre. But Ngũgĩ started the 1970s also struggling to do what he had failed to do in the 1960s: to go beyond mere explanations of

the contradictions that haunted the post-colony in pursuit of a future without
them. In this pursuit, Ngũgĩ goes through metamorphosis; from disillusionment to a revolutionist: a creative thinker who left the seminar room to work
with peasants at the Kamĩrĩĩthũ Community Education and Cultural Centre.
It is the revolutionary Ngũgĩ who, alongside Ngũgĩ wa Mĩriĩ, participated in
a literary project by co-authoring *Ngaahika Ndeenda* (I will Marry When I
Want), for the Kamĩrĩĩthũ Community Education and Cultural Centre.

Although the staging of the play of that name would lead to Ngũgĩ's detention in 1977, at a personal level, his involvement with the community theatre
was clearly redemptive. He was to later write in *Detained* (98): 'My involvement with the people of Kamĩrĩĩthũ had given me the sense of a new being and
it had made me transcend the alienation to which I had been condemned by
years of colonial education.' It seems, however, that the seed that germinated
to become the Kamĩrĩĩthũ project was sowed after the successful production
of *The Trial of Dedan Kimathi*, which Ngũgĩ co-authored with Mĩcere Gĩthae
Mũgo in 1976.

After the production of *The Trial of Dedan Kimathi*, Ngũgĩ started to have
doubts about the influence of his work on his audience. While *The Trial of
Dedan Kimathi*, one of Ngũgĩ's most radical works, was performed at the Kenya
National Theatre before an elite audience, if the idea was to use literature to
change the world, didn't one have to speak directly to the audiences and, in
his case, peasants? The Kamĩrĩĩthũ project was Ngũgĩ's answer. For the first
time we see Ngũgĩ leaving the seminar room and spaces occupied by the elite
and start working with peasants: the subjects in his books but who had never
read them because they were in English. The Kamĩrĩĩthũ project was very successful, and there are images of busloads of people flocking to Kamĩrĩĩthũ to
watch these open-air performances. For the first time, Ngũgĩ became aware of
the existence of another kind of an audience that he had never thought about
before.

If some critics have argued that Ngũgĩ was detained because of the radical nature of *Ngahiika Ndeenda*, it is precisely the setting of the play rather
than the grievances it raised that flung open the detention doors on Ngũgĩ.
The subjects and grievances in *Ngahiika Ndeenda* are not different from those
in his other work, including the most radical, *Petals of Blood*, which served
as a powerful intervention in the politics of Kenya, and ironically launched
at an event presided over by the then vice-president Mwai Kibaki. What was
transformative and dangerous about the Kamĩrĩĩthũ project is that Ngũgĩ was
now engaging an audience that understood the language. The space made all
the difference: he was operating at a village theatre built by peasants who also
served as actors and actresses.

Ngũgĩ started to see the difference that language made as well as the centrality of speaking to a particular kind of audience. Writing in Gĩkũyũ had a

tremendous impact but it is not the reason he was detained. It is the setting of the play, which allowed Ngũgĩ to develop relationships with the subaltern that began to worry the government. If *Ngahiika Ndeenda* had been performed at the Kenya National Theatre or at the University of Nairobi, it seems there could have been no crisis. The crisis was that Ngũgĩ had moved out of the university, reaching a larger public sphere, empowering a peasantry that could not make a distinction between facts and fiction. During the play, for instance, when peasants addressed certain injustices, they were no longer acting out theoretical or fictionalized grievances. When they mentioned home guards in the play, they would call out names of people in the village. For the peasants, the play was no longer an abstract, autonomous, aesthetic project. This is what made Ngũgĩ dangerous. As a writer, he wanted to produce work that 'would be consumed by peasants and workers. So the change is merely a reflection of my changing attitude towards my audience. In my later works I started moving towards a position where I was not only writing about peasants and workers, but I was writing for peasants and workers, especially in a language they could understand' (Sander and Lindfors 134). But in 1977, the theatre is destroyed. The play is stopped. Ngũgĩ is detained. Is he bitter?

> I don't carry the anger in me all the time. But it really hurts that a collective effort by ordinary men and women of the village, instead of being applauded by the power that be, the might of the state was deployed at the Centre. That hurts. There was so much promise that was broken. (Personal interview, 2012)

Ngũgĩ ends the decade of the 1970s in detention. For the first time, the intellectual Ngũgĩ is cut off from the institutions of knowledge and cultural production. By picking up the country's leading writer in the middle of the night and condemning him to detention without trial, it was clear that no one could be spared by the state. This act was symptomatic of that period. It marks the beginning of political disruption of the space occupied by intellectuals. Universities swiftly lost their moral authority. The sacred intellectual space of the university was violated and has never recovered.

It is while in detention he wrote his first novel in Gĩkũyũ, *Caaitani Mũtharabainĩ (Devil on the Cross)*, a novel produced under his struggle with 'language, with images, with prison, with bitter memories, with moments of despair, with all the mentally and emotionally adverse circumstances in which one is forced to operate while in custody' (*Detained* 164). In writing *Devil on the Cross* and *Detained*, Ngũgĩ 'took up deliberately and very sincerely a defiant position against the social classes that had been responsible for killing democracy in Kenya. The events that have occurred since my detention are proving me right' (Sander and Lindfors 168). But if detention was meant to teach Ngũgĩ 'a lesson in submission, silence, and obedience' (*Detained* xi), it also 'created its own opposite, a fierce determination to achieve something in a Kenyan language' (Sander and Lindfors 2006 170). While the consequences of the culture of silence gaining root in Kenya were numerous, most damaging was the loss of autonomy to ask questions in a protected academic zone.

Phase IV—Exile and Diaspora (1980s to present)

In the 1980s, Ngũgĩ is in exile. His early years in exile were spent in London where he joined other human rights advocates in pressuring the Kenyan government to release all political prisoners. Exile changes everything, especially because, before Ngũgĩ's exile, he had embarked on projects that could not survive elsewhere outside Kenya. They include the Kamĩrĩĩthũ theatre project, and the writing in Gĩkũyũ of two powerful novels, and he had already made his famous epistemological break from English and the world associated with it. In exile, we see Ngũgĩ the writer dislocated from Kenya in sometimes very productive ways, sometimes in very melancholic ways. Kofi Anyidoho captures the profundity of Ngũgĩ's dislocation:

> I once sat with Ngũgĩ at a National Theatre in Accra. I could see that he had become very pensive. He then took a deep sigh and said 'Kofi, you know, I may have been offered various opportunities in exile to continue my work as a novelist, as a scholar. But nowhere else in the world can I find a stage that I can claim to be my own. And yet, [theatre] was my life, earlier in Kenya. Theatre. I had access to a stage through which I could reach my people. Where in exile can I find a stage for the kind of work I was doing in Kenya? (Personal interview, 2014)

Produced in exile, Ngũgĩ's work reflects his self-awareness of the distance from his cultural resources, speakers and readers of his language, and his intended audience. His writing while in exile is fueled by a feeling of 'loss and longing'; a struggle to write 'stories of home' while located in the 'landscape of the other'; as he searches for 'what he both lacks and needs: a household' (Gikandi 229). The Kenya he is writing about is the one he can only remember because he has been uprooted from it.

His recent massive novel, *Wizard of the Crow*, is a quintessential work of exile; drawing a lot on Kenyan materials and sources and it is in many ways about the history of Kenya but it has to attach itself to international movements because it has to exist only in relation to those movements. If the Ngũgĩ of the 1970s was trying to make the local his habitat, exile forced him to occupy a more international space with all its contradictions. Globalization, which becomes one of his major themes, is the classic alternative to locality. The Ngũgĩ in exile must now write and attach his works to international movements because his dislocation from his cultural habitat and his residence in an international space require him to attach his works to international movements.

Ngũgĩ and the Politics of Language

In my conversation with Ali Mazrui in 2013, he stated that Ngũgĩ's main contribution is only partly realized and appreciated, and that is his defense of indigenous languages. 'He has carried it further than any westernized intellectual I know of', Mazrui said, adding that Ngũgĩ is willing to pay the price for that commitment. Considered as one of the leading advocates for the promotion and preservation of indigenous African languages, Ngũgĩ considers monolingualism to be dangerous for any society:

> If you know all the languages of the world and you do not know your mother tongue, that is enslavement. But if you know your mother tongue, then you add other languages, that is empowerment ... Every language is like a house full of treasure. Learning that language is like being given a key to that house of treasure. The more keys I have, the more houses of treasure I can open. (Personal interview, 2010)

Although Ngũgĩ has insisted that he has never been against the English language, he is clear that 'English is not an African language' (personal interview, 2012). This statement has drawn divergent responses. Let me share a few remarks from a number of scholars who are featured in my documentary and who have addressed the politics of language in relation to Ngũgĩ's work:

- Biodun Jeyifo (personal interview, 2015)
  I completely understand the theoretical, ideological and political reasons for [Ngũgĩ] to fight for African languages. But I think English has been on the continent for more than 600 years and has been massively Africanized. It [is]for our own good to use it but not to be dominated by it. I think we have reached that stage.

- Carole Boyce Davies (personal interview, 2014)
  I have heard debates where people say that English is an African language. But it is not. How can one say that English is an African language? It is English; English comes from a place called England, in which they created a language from their own realities.

- Austin Bukenya (personal interview, 2013)
  English is our language and we paid a very high price for it whether monetary or emotionally. We cannot deny ourselves the opportunity to use [it]. And by using it, we are also enriching it. It may have come from elsewhere; it may have come under negative circumstances by being imposed on us, but that is part of the price which we paid for it. If we have acquired it, I think it would be like throwing the baby with the bathwater if we say that we are not going to write in it.

- Grant Farred (personal interview, 2014)
  I understand the political point [Ngũgĩ] is making, but I would suggest that he has given the English language more than it has ever taken from him. He gave it a whole new set of linguistic possibilities.

- Wangui wa Goro (personal interview, 2014)
  It is an acquired language and we do not have roots to its heritage. We cannot claim it as English people can because it is their roots and their rights to an evolved heritage.

- Simon Gikandi (personal interview, 2015)
  We don't pay a lot of attention to the ways in which African writers took the English language and transformed it into something else. We could even start talking about West African English; East African English because the local conditions have changed the language. We have a task, actually to demand that English be seen as just another provincial language, which is picked by other people.

- Manthia Diawara (personal interview, 2015)
  People are not being honest. After they have labored to master English, French, Spanish; Ngũgĩ suddenly comes back and says: go back and learn your mother tongue. It is frightening!

Mũkoma wa Ngũgĩ has joined this debate in *The Rise of the African Novel* where he notes that we have been starting the African literary clock with the Achebe/ Makerere generation at the expense of a longer African tradition of writing in African languages, including Amharic and numerous South African writings in African languages. In my interview (2018), Mũkoma poses: 'What are the costs of starting the African literary clock in the wrong historical period?' The consequences are dire, and 'we end up in a crisis of periodization, the geography and languages of African literature'. For Mũkoma, whether English is an African language or not is a side issue.

Ngũgĩ at 80 and After

Ngũgĩ's long project has been a prophylactic one: to protect an environment that he so deeply cares about because the failure to do so would cause unspeakable suffering. After all, his lessons for more than half a century have revolved around the nonnegotiable duty to humanize ourselves and the other:

> If we can all feel that an African life is sacred; if the leadership in Africa feels that even a single African life is sacred and should be protected, I would see that as an important driving force. It is an expression of collective pride when I feel that I am diminished when the least among us is diminished. (Ngũgĩ, personal interview, 2010)

Part I

Serenades & Beginnings

1
Hyperbolic Praise Poetry for Ngũgĩ @80 … In Imitation of African Orature

Mĩcere Gĩthae Mũgo

Opening Cycle and Point of Entry

Hodi! Hodi!
Knock! Knock!

Gũkũ nĩkwaũ?
Gũkũ nĩkwaũ?
Gũkũ nĩkwaũ?
Menye nĩguo njarie cararũkũ
Wũĩ, wainaga!

Whose place (home) is this?
Whose place (home) is this?
Whose place (home) is this?
I want to know so that I can speak bluntly
Yes, singer/dancer that used to be!

Nĩkwa mũrata
nĩkwa mũrata
Nĩkwa mũrata
Aria, nakuo kwaria nĩkwendana
Wũĩ, wainaga!

It is a friend's (place) home
It is a friend's (place) home
It is a friend's (place) home
Speak, for to hold dialogue is to love
Yes, singer/dancer that used to be!

Mũrata ũrĩkũ?
Mũrata ũrĩkũ?
Mũrata ũrĩkũ?
Mũini wĩ ngumo nĩwa arata aingĩ
Wũĩ, wainaga

Which friend?
Which friend?
Which friend?
A famous singer/dancer has many friends
Yes, singer/dancer that used to be
Nĩkwa wa Thiong'o
Nĩkwa wa Thiong'o
Nĩkwa wakinĩ
Wĩgwaku mũciĩ; aria cararũkũ
Wũĩ, wainaga

It is wa Thiong'o's place (home)
It is wa Thiong'o's place (home)
It is an age-mate's place (home)
You are in your own home; speak bluntly
Yes, singer/dancer that used to be

With permission to enter the homestead, the poetess's imagination grows
    wings
Words trip over her tongue, impatient for the moment of utterance
Hyperbole seizes the license to decorate plain words with extra lacy
    language
Now only the feet drag with the weight of age as dancer after dancer enters
as if claiming territorial ownership of space: as if swearing to eclipse all
    competition

First Cycle (one score*): Entry into the Dance Arena

Wũi wakwa-ĩ! (Oh my!) I, dancer/singer that used to be!
Where shall I find the feet to enter this competition-bound dance arena
where younger, more nimble dancers are sworn to make a shadowy fool of
    me
stomping the yielding ground that readily surrenders to their aggressive
    youthful energy?
Oh, who will lend me youthful feet to enter the arena, I, dancer/singer that
    used to be,
to celebrate my age-mate, the son of Thiong'o, on this his eightieth
    birthday?
Of a truth, ancient proverbial wisdom did not lie: *wainaga nĩeroragĩra!*
(Sh/e who once danced/sang can turn into a spectator)!

---

* 'Score' is used in the sense of 'twenty years'.

But, refusing to turn into a spectator, I dancer/singer that used to be,
vow to call upon the spirit of rebellion to possess every inch of my body.
Yes, I, dancer/singer that used to be, will stand tall in celebration of old
    age
for, proverbial wisdom counsels that the strength of the elderly is
'in the ears and on the lips', not in the feet.
Of a truth, I, dancer/singer that used to be, will proudly enter the crowded
    arena
making music with my complaining bones; clearing an open path for the
    elders.
Of a truth, I will enter the forbidding arena and perform a praise song for
    my age-mate:
Ngũgĩ wa Wanjikũ; Wanjikũ daughter of Ngũgĩ
Ngũgĩ wa Thiong'o; Thiong'o son of Ndũcũ:
Ngũgĩ wa Wanjikũ na Thiong'o.

Yes, in the name of my age-mate being reborn this eightieth year of his life
I, singer and dancer that used to be, will enter the crowded arena boldly,
    stately
and perform an unheard-of praise-dance-song for my age-mate, Ngũgĩ wa
    Wanjikũ
in celebration of his rebirth as he clocks eighty years shy of a solid century.

Tell me, who says that I, dancer/singer that used to be, will not
perform a praise dance-song for the son of Wanjikũ *mwarĩ wa* Ngũgĩ?
Ngũgĩ, child of Wangarĩ, daughter of Ikĩgu
Ngũgĩ, child of Gacoki, daughter of Gĩthieya
Ngũgĩ, child of Njeri, daughter of Kĩbicũria.
Ngũgĩ, child of four different mothers?
Of a truth, I will perform a praise dance-song for Ngũgĩ wa Wanjikũ
    mwarĩ wa Ngũgĩ
in celebration of his rebirth as he clocks eighty years shy of a solid century.

Hayia-ĩ, the singer and dancer that used to be is intoxicated with
    hyperbole,
re-conjuring that special community-marked day of days on January 5,
    1938.
Her imagination has cut loose and now roams freely across the Central
    Kenya Highlands…
across Limuru, across Kwangũgĩ, also known as Ngamba Village: the sites
    of this birth.
The singer and dancer that used to be is all but dizzy with hyperbolic
    utterance.

Her imagination has meshed with memory and now stretches across
    eighty years
ready to recreate that day of days on January 5, 1938 when Ngũgĩ wa
    Wanjikũ was born.

Second Cycle (two scores): Celebrating Birth

On that day, all the surrounding
ridges danced in celebration
as whistling winds carried the happy news from valley to valley…
as in resounding ululation the valleys echoed back the happy news
till all the ridges throughout Limuru had heard the joyful story.
On that day, Manguo river flowed with unusual, unknown force
as it flooded the marshes and broke its banks reclaiming its river-hood…
as if to declare that the child's life-path would forever flow, unhindered.

On that day, mist cleared off the highlands and the eye traveled
    unhampered.
To the south sprawled the eye-catching, undulating Ngong Hills ridge
while still further, the spectacular mighty Kilimanjaro greeted the skies.
To the west, the Great Rift Valley seemed to have opened wider to
    welcome the day
even as the nearby Nyandarũa mountain range appeared to have grown
    much longer
in readiness to shield the new dawn and if need be, block the rising sun
    from setting.
Not to be overlooked, the lesser ridges jutted out announcing their
    dwarfed presence:
Longonot, Elgon, the Charangani, Satima, Suswa, Ol Donyo Sabuk and,
    name them all…

To the north-east, the three snow-capped peaks of legendary, sacred
    Kĩrĩnyaga
displayed unusual crispy icy jaggedness that captured the dullest of eyes:
Batian towered majestically
Nelion glowed in splendor and
Lenana simply sat in dignified solidity.

To the east, a brilliant sun lit the bottom of the skyline
welcoming the new day in Limuru township;
embracing the new birth in Ngamba village, also named Kwangũgĩ;
smiling upon the new day on the Kenya Central Highlands,
daring the 'White Highlands' to utter a word of vilification against

the birth of one more African child, who to the settlers was just another
'*kaffir*'
arriving to soil their bleach-whitened stolen soil, now settler-named
'White Highlands'
arriving to darken the bleach-whitened stolen land, now christened 'White
Man's Country'.

Unfettered by these living false colonial myths and imperial British-settler
lies;
propelled by the sweeping wind of resistant herstorical action-driven
change;
emboldened by the *Sankofa*-memory of the full weight of Kenya people's
history...
I, dancer and singer that used to be, now decide to fully occupy the
center-stage
my feet as artful as grace itself; my voice as clear as a crispy mountain
stream.
Yes, I, dancer and singer that used to be, now decide to fully occupy the
center-stage
joining mother nature to affirm the birth of Ngũgĩ wa Wanjikũ: Ngũgĩ, son
of Thiong'o
on this eightieth year of his re-birth and re-arrival in Ngamba village; to
wit, Kwangũgĩ.

I, dancer and singer that used to be, now call upon witnesses, for, the birth
of a child is
a collective endeavor and proverbial truth declares: it will take a village to
raise this child.
Oh, who was there to witness this famous birth that day of days on
January 5, 1938?

Scenematic Change

All the mothers of Limuru were there and in one voice
they approached the Thiong'o compound with such force
while dancing and singing that their voices could be heard
as far as Tigoni, Banana Hill, Nairobi City itself, and beyond.
Of a truth, all the mothers of Ngamba village, to wit Kwangũgĩ,
were there at Thiong'o wa Ndũcũ's compound
wildly ululating for the boy-child that had been born:

Aririririritiii.................................! One
Aririririritiii.................................! Two
Aririririritiii.................................! Three

Aririririitiii....................................! Four
Aririririitiii....................................! Five

Five *ngemi* for the boy-child that Wanjikũ, daughter of Ngũgĩ, has birthed.
Five *ngemi* for Ngũgĩ wa Wanjikũ, the boy-child who has been born.
Five *ngemi* for Ngũgĩ, son of Thiong'o, whose life journey has begun!

Third Cycle (three scores): 'Rememory-ing' (Oyee, Morrison!) and 'Sankofa-ing' (Oyee, Gerima!)

And now, eighty years, twenty score short of a century since that day of
   days,
I, dancer and singer that used to be, summon new teams of dancers and
   singers
from all corners of Kenya, commanding them to flood the dance arena
and welcome the eighty-year old child from Limuru, Ngamba, and yes,
   Kwangũgĩ.

Come all and witness this cultural feast overtake the feast of the stomach
as voices pierce the crisp air and feet test the firmness of the earth on
   which they stand...
Come all and witness this cultural feast confirming that Ngũgĩ was born
   before James was.

Witness colorfully dressed women elders, *Nyakĩnyua,* gracefully swaying
reluctant hip bones in rhythmic keeping with their circling movements
as they do the *gĩtiiro* dance and ululate to bless the new birth, singing:

Nĩngũmĩnyua, nĩngũmĩnyua-ĩ!
Nĩngũmĩnyua, na yarema ndĩthambe nayo!

I will drink it [sugarcane beer]; I will drink it-oh!
I will drink it and if I can't drink any more, I will bathe in it!...

Scenematic Change

And now enter brightly decorated young women, beaded from head to toe
doing variations of the *nduumo* dance in display of limitless creativity:
the Kĩambu version; the Mũrang'a beat; the Nyeri rhythm; the Kĩrĩnyaga
   step...

Scenematic Change

At this point agile Chuka drummers enter the arena, drumming their way
   to the stage

their light-feather feet decorated with ostrich feathers; their bodies poised
   like arrows;
their orchestrated movement swift, graceful and artful as they leap in the
   air with joy.

Competition has become the motif

As if determined to eclipse the Chuka drummers, a group of Ukambani
   wathi dancers
storm the stage, drumming even louder while also blowing whistles to
   demand full attention.
Leading the troop are acrobats performing mesmerizing eye-catching
   antics to steal the show…

Scenematic Change

Not to be outdone, *isukuti* dancers aggressively enter the scene, flouting
   well-built bodies
and shaking the ground like an earth-quake; dancing *kususuma* now in
   pairs, now in groups…
blowing an array of horns and beating *sukuti* drums, as if determined to
   scare off rivals…

Scenematic Change

No sooner do *isukuti dancers* take the stage than a dramatic entry captures
   the audience's eye
as *ohangla* dancers make their way through the arena, accompanied by
   Nyadundo himself
teaching them to turn the once-upon-a-time funeral dance into a festive
   beat celebrating birth.

Look! A variety of celebrants claim the hotly contested space

Giriama, Miji Kenda dancers ascend the stage, challenging the monopoly
   of this cultural space
as they ritually perform the indigenous Giriama birth-giving dance
   celebrated since *zamani* and
before Me Katilili wa Menza: now commemorating the eightieth birthday
   of Ngũgĩ wa Thiong'o.

Scenematic Change

Following on their heels come Maasai dancers performing the *adumu*,
   leaping high in the air,
lifting Ngũgĩ on his eighthieth birthday; reminding him that his maternal
   grandfather Ndũcũ,

'the child who always said *tūcū*', originated from Maasailand before
　　Mūrang'a adopted him.

Scenematic Change

To cap the vibrant show, dancers from Somalia proudly enter the arena on
　　galloping horses
performing the *dhantur*, variously known as the *dhaanto*, later
　　popularized by Aar Maanta and
other border-crossers who musically preach that song, poetry, music and
　　dance know no borders.

Scenematic Change

Teeming teams of dancers keep entering the arena till there is no more
　　room remaining.
Overcome by the sight I, dancer and singer who used to be, lose count and
　　simply surrender
to this human beauty, brilliance and wonderment, never before witnessed
　　in my celebrant's-life.

Closing the Third Cycle

On Ngūgī's eightieth birthday, limitless, potent artistic palm wine flows
　　like Manguo river
in full flood after the long rains, even as it did that day of days on January
　　5, 1938.
Four score years since Ngūgī's birth, artistic *njohi*, (sugar cane beer), still
　　flows unchecked.

Who but Ngūgī, the people's artist, would have swam in this *njohi* and
　　escaped intoxication?
Who but the child of Wanjikū, *mwarī wa* Ngūgī, a woman of few words
　　and sure, quiet action
would have taught her son the wisdom that 'when the cock is drunk, he
　　forgets about the hawk?'

African proverbial wisdom counsels that the heart of a wise person lies
　　quiet like limpid water
And yes, paradoxically, the same granary of wisdom yields the saying that
　　'wisdom is like fire!'
So, let us now say *Ashe! Afya! Moyo!* to this child of quietness, yet with
　　wisdom that is like fire.

Fourth Cycle (four scores): the journey

In the slave-resistance tradition of Amantine in *Sugar Cane Alley*,
Wanjikũ, *mwarĩ wa* Ngũgĩ,
who never went to school refuses to let her son be defined by settler
plantation slave labor
challenging him to dream beyond the confinement of White Highlands in
pursuit of education

Taking up the challenge, Ngũgĩ went to Kamandũra Primary School and
shone like a star; graduated from there and attended Mango Primary
School and here too shone like a star;
then moved to Kĩnyogori Intermediate School where his star rose too high
to contain locally.

Ngũgĩ became one of the chosen few to attend Alliance Boys' High School
where the 'cream' of Kenya youth underwent a four-year colonial
educational boot-camp that sought to militarize
their thinking and turn them into loyal native collaborators servicing the
colonial settler system.

But Ngũgĩ survived and went to Makerere, a surrogate of London
University, United Kingdom;
Makerere, where gown-wearers walked in the air, in the fashion of
anointed celestial beings.
But not him: he remained grounded on people's earth, rejecting token
colonial exceptionalism.

He went to Leeds, yet neither became an Achebean been-to, nor chose to
forget his language.
Instead he returned to his 'native land' in Aimé Césairean fashion, to
create liberated zones:
birthing, with others, the Department of Literature at Nairobi University –
decentering English.

For daring to create a university of peasants and workers at Kamĩrĩĩthũ,
with other rebels,
he became a political graduate of Kamĩtĩ Maximum Security Prison where
he learnt, à la Soyinka,
the secret art of composing a novel on toilet paper and smuggling it for
publication, uncaught

Closing Cycle and Point of Exit

Hurray to the author of three score books and more!
Salute to the de-colonizer of the mind, language and culture!
High fives, to the advocate of African and global indigenous languages!
Pongezi to the recipient of a score plus international honorary degrees!
Hongera to the annual winner of many Nobel Prizes of the heart!
Shangwe na vigelegele for a beloved Kenyan and African son of the soil!
Embraces to a champion of human rights and citizen of the world!
Five *ngemi* for Ngũgĩ, child of Wanjikũ: Ngũgĩ, son of Thiong'o!
Ululation for the 'beauty-full' one who was born four score years ago!
Ashe! Afya! Moyo!

2

A Song at Dawn (for Ngũgĩ wa Thiong'o)

Tsitsi Jaji

Grain-scatterer, we too have shed our apostolic alias
and followed you into the shade to hear our voices
bloom. Here *rapoko*, here *chibage*, here *zviyo*, here

nzungu, here *nhanga*, here sweet, sweet *nhope*.
Here a name we call ourselves.
Here a thing we will not do: thief.

Grain-distributor, we will trade words with you. We
give an *mbeu* here for a buried seed there. We
mark up the goods by candlelight, in blue or red

ink. We shrink with doubt from a place called
Nation. One thing we can say for sure: We will never be
a colony again. Need the obvious be stated this way?

Gainsayer, what would you ask us to ask now: What is dying
below the topsoil, that dusting of iron will, nitrous rage,
pot ash? What birthright is traded when a crow

takes cover in a rooster's nest? What will translate this
long century into a new election cycle, a conference
of women, men, young visionaries, old dreamers

debating under the Wangari's forest of green umbrellas?
We will plough your plot, furrow its surface, burrow in the
tunnels of language. Our dismay is our hope, present at

every meeting. In simpler times the answers might have
slipped off our tongues. Now family feuds erupt into wars.
It seems these devilish thorns and eroded rock are also our

inheritance: these lands, these languages, these mother tongues.
You have left us no choice, O stubborn prophet of Gĩkũyũ,
but to try our tongue, and listen as silence softly
breaks.

3
Ngũgĩ in Eritrea

Charles Cantalupo

'Farewell to English … for any of my writings. From now on
It is Gĩkũyũ and Kiswahili all the way', Ngũgĩ
Famously stated in 1986, and he became
African languages' greatest hero for literature,
Not knowing then 'all the way' would lead him to Eritrea,
Writing in African languages, in literature and
Orature, 'all the way' back, millennia; continual,
Written examples, unceasing, and where the colonial
Languages never became the norm in literature – thus
Different from most of Africa and still that way today.

Far more known then (and known more now, even after all this time)
Was the armed struggle of Eritrea for independence.
Nevertheless, Ngũgĩ wrote two decades after his 'farewell',
2006, after reading Eritreans translated:
'Four thousand years … from the ancient stele in Belew Kelew to
Twentieth-century battlefields … into the twenty-first…'
Poets from there never gave 'up writing in their … languages'.
Therefore, 'their poetry thrives'. He knew because he went there twice.

Early December in 1998 he visited
For the first time as an introduction yet in connection
With a big conference he agreed to lead, 'Against All Odds':
Focused on African languages and literatures, named
With the same phrase often used to brand the Eritrean war
For independence, an all but hopeless, protracted struggle.
Ngũgĩ, of course, was adverse to hype and thought the phrase too much
Without the 'languages' part. He even said, when I asked him,
'Heinemann's treated me rather well and has served African
Europhone writers well, too. But if the phrase applies to the
Struggle of African language writers it might not be an
Exaggeration'. In Eritrea, all the writers used
African languages – 'with our fathers, the Italians
As the exception', the joke said. Therefore, Ngũgĩ and 'Eritrea'
Seemed like a match made in heaven … or better, Africa itself.

Zemhret Yohannes, the Eritrean leader in culture
Hosted his travel, and Kassahun Checole, the publisher,
Made the trip happen and flew with Ngũgĩ from America.
On this first visit, again the war between Eritrean
And Ethiopian armies stalked the Horn, but '*che guerra?*'
Asked people in Eritrea's biggest city, Asmara.
Nor did the war appear elsewhere as he traveled the country:
Not, at least, this one. The pockmarked walls, abandoned armor, and
Regular rubble in piles evoked too many past battles.

All of the wars past and war now might have passed through Ngũgĩ's mind
On the Massawa beach where he sat enthralled by the Red Sea.
Other than war what else could have kept him staring out so long?
All of the people who knew him in Asmara on the street –
Saying hello as if he was also their greatest writer?
Meeting the president and, perhaps, the inescapably
Flickering visions of Kenya's president in the room, too?
Leaving Asmara, the drive down the escarpment through the clouds:
Almost two miles the descent through mountains terraced with peace and
Families meeting him there, embracing him as their own and
In their own languages, showing him the schools they have rebuilt
And the remains of their ancient farms: the orange trees, coffee,
Black pepper bushes, and even an old pool faintly turquoise?

When he beheld the Red Sea and couldn't move for a while,
Did he imagine, as he would later write, himself a bird
Flying among the divinities all over Africa:
Egypt, Zimbabwe, Meroe, and Aksum, before landing here?
Touching warm waters where Moses, Jesus, and Mohammed fled
Their persecution to save their faiths that later changed the world?
Nearby Adulis the ancient port of ships to the land of
Punt, camel caravans seeming endless, and monasteries
Where monks of Red Sea gods mastered arts of preserving the dead
Thousands of years without rotting? Also, when weren't there the wars?
Conquest, repression, and occupation; and the resistance;
Blood feuds among kin and kith? The bird he thought of as himself
Flew up a valley so steep and deep the ancient Sahos said
Time had begun there, and just a little further stood a stele –
Lonely, defiant – dark spike of respite in blinding sunlight.
Landing he pecked, that is, read, and locals buzzed in amazement,
Seeing the bird make itself at home deciphering the text.
What did it say? – part Sabean letters, older than Ge'ez.

'Wars ... the impossible ... maybe ... struggle ... always ... odds ...
    against...'
Then he flew north to a town called Segenyetti, where he found
Wordmongers gathered beneath the monumental sycamores.

Thirteen months later, to start the new millennium, Ngũgĩ
Came back a second time to Asmara. What would he say to
Hundreds of writers and scholars, students, activists, artists,
Civic groups, NGOs, educators, from throughout the world,
Joining the thousands of Eritrean citizens there, too,
Focused on African language art for seven days and nights?
'Both as an African and a writer, this is certainly
One of the happiest days of my life'. Ngũgĩ's opening
Words to the crowd sounded personal, continuing, 'Half my
Writing life was taken up by English, even though my books
Were about Kenya and Kenyan people'. But the second half,
'From 1977 to the present', Ngũgĩ said,
Changing his tone, 'I have written in Gĩkũyũ' – declaring
He was a part of yet totally amazed at how many
Writers in African language came together before him,
More overwhelmed by their presence and by where they all came from
Than by his suddenly seeing his ideas happen right there:
Doing for African languages what all intellectuals
Have done for theirs, which he slowly, surely spoke: 'The best
Written and thought in the world'. The spearhead of the conference
Had to be Ngũgĩ, but it was joining more than leading that,
He said years later, amazed him: 'We were ... in Eritrea ...
Writers ... primarily ... all there ... who wrote in their African
Languages, and it was beautiful to see. I was writing
Novels and published a journal in the Gĩkũyũ language'.

More of this kind of communion happened to him when the play,
Translated from the Gĩkũyũ, *Ngaahika Ndeenda*,
Translated into the English, *I Will Marry When I Want*,
Had its premiere in the Cinema Asmara, translated
Into Tigrinya. Enthralled, he could be seen saying the lines
In their Gĩkũyũ or English matching the new translation.
'Somehow he got it', said Alemseged Tesfai, translator
And Eritrea's most expert, eloquent historian.
At the conclusion, the theater's red walls blazing in stage lights,
Actors and audience rushed each other. Kenyan flags, Mau Mau
Songs in Tigrinya, and muses painted in the cupola
By a colonial artist who, of course, was Italian,

Freely got lost in each other, and it was total pleasure.
Later the play in Tigrinya toured all over the country.
Seen in the high schools and all the major towns, *I Will Marry
When I Want* has reinforced the drama of Eritrea.
Mes tabarhāni 'emer'o – Ngũgĩ loved the production.

Next day he met with the organizers of the conference,
Planning a statement on what it really meant and the outcome.
Berbere tagliatelle and a little wine sparked discussion.
Ngũgĩ began a preamble, writing on an envelope
He wouldn't show me when I peered over, hoping for a peek.
Later a plenary session gathered all the conferees,
Making suggestions for what we should say. Hundreds of people
Spoke from the floor and delivered it in writing one by one
Into the hands of the organizers sitting on the stage.
Three hours later they wearily retreated to compose –
What would become the Asmara Declaration – handwritten
Back in a storage room near the hotel auditorium
And the result of our egolessly following Ngũgĩ
Humbly compressing his twenty years of African language
Ideas and writing to improvise some basic principles
We could agree on – some edits and a few more also added.
Three hours later we came out with a declaration of
African languages independence. I recall Ngũgĩ
Saying this outcome now settled, once and for all, the language
Question in Africa. Later that night at a huge banquet
Spread in Asmara's art deco city hall, the conferees
Listened to all of the declaration read aloud and cheered.
Asked if they'd ratify what it said, they roared back one big 'Yes!'
Exhilaration and Eritrean music and dancers
Bursting on stage, the crowd joined them, leaving very little room.
Still Ngũgĩ joined, so I joined him, standing by Papa Susso
Playing his kora along with Sbrit, the Eritrean troupe.
Dancing we laughed when an Eritrean businessman, his tie
Flying behind him ran up and pasted one hundred nakfa
On Ngũgĩ's forehead and pasted bills on Papa and me, too.

As for the wordmongers gathered under huge sycamore trees,
I was there also when ancient Eritrean mothers saw
Ngũgĩ and gave him the special bread they baked for his coming;
And when they told him to break the loaves so everyone would eat.

If a term like 'the heroic' still has any use today,
It can describe Eritrea's revolution and struggle
For independence, but seeing Ngũgĩ in Eritrea,
I call it 'minor heroic', and write dactylic hexameters,
One of the oldest prosodic rhythms of my language kingdom.

4

Up From Makerere:
On the Publication of *Weep Not, Child*

Susan Nalugwa Kiguli

> Although I risk oversimplification, it is probably correct to say that it does not
> finally matter who wrote what, but rather how a work is written and how it is
> read. (Edward Said, 'The Politics of Knowledge' 385)

In reflecting on *Weep Not, Child,* I think it is important to first talk about
James Ngũgĩ who became James Thiong'o Ngũgĩ in 1960 then later Ngũgĩ wa
Thiong'o. I think it is also useful to build the context of the definition of key
literary concerns in the East African region that revolved around the publication of *Weep Not, Child,* including a summary appraisal of Ngũgĩ's time
at Makerere University College in the East Africa of the late 1950s and early
1960s. Ngũgĩ himself has said a lot about this time in his essays and memoirs.
In fact, because he takes this time as definitive for himself as an author, he has
now written a memoir, *Birth of a Dream Weaver*, specifically remembering his
time at Makerere. Ngũgĩ has made his attachment to Makerere a public matter,
and many of us know that whenever it is possible for him to come back to visit
Makerere, however briefly, he does so. He visited Makerere University again in
July 2013 to celebrate 50 years of the University of East Africa. My own impression is that while Ngũgĩ has traveled and his literary work has gone places, his
time at Makerere remains important to him as a writer. During Ngũgĩ's time,
as he humorously commented in his keynote address at Makerere University
in 2013, denying someone entry to Makerere was like denying him a wife. It
was that fundamental.

I have read some of the materials on Ngũgĩ's time at Makerere in the University
library's archive, and these reveal the vibrant spirit of the period and the power
of the sense of change in the 1960s. There is also an abundance of comments on
Ngũgĩ in this archive. In a letter of recommendation written on 13th November,
1963, a year before the publication of *Weep Not, Child*, Professor G. Walton, the
then Head of the English Department, describes Ngũgĩ as

> a man of considerable ability and real personal interest in literature. His written
> work is always of good quality and he achieves an A mark from time to time.
> He is a hard worker, although he neglects one or two authors who do not appeal

to him. This discrimination is of course in a student of literature a sign of intelligence and full involvement and is not likely to have an adverse effect on his
examination results.

This comment points to the fact that during his time as an undergraduate,
Ngũgĩ was already carefully selecting from the literary scene what was important to him as a writer and what he would ultimately present to his audiences.

In this letter, Ngũgĩ's forthcoming novel *Weep Not, Child* is also mentioned.
In fact, Ngũgĩ's time at Makerere is presented as a time of intense literary activity. He had already distinguished himself in November 1962 by producing his
play the *Black Hermit* at the National Theatre, Kampala, as part of the activities
marking Uganda's independence. The minister of Community Development
presented him with an award for the play from the East African Creative
Writing Competition Committee. From 13th to 19th November, 1962, adver-
tisements and commentary on the performance of the *Black Hermit* appeared
in the national paper *The Uganda Argus*. On the 17th November, 1962, a commentary in *The Uganda Argus* states that 'Mr. Ngũgĩ is the first African to write
a play of such a high standard'. Although this comment appears patronizing,
even presumptuous in our current context, it points to how Ngũgĩ's writing
was viewed in the region at the time. What Ngũgĩ's writing seems to have
meant to the region then is captured in an enthusiastic comment on the performance of *The Black Hermit* which appeared in *The Uganda Argus* of 14th
November, 1962:

> Plans to make Africans in Kampala feel that the National Theatre is theirs are
> being put into action by Makerere Dramatic Society, Mr. Ron Reddick its pub-
> licity secretary told The Uganda Argus … Said Mr. Reddick: 'We want to put
> African drama on the map so that we can raise the presentation of African
> drama in the world.' (4)

The spirit of the above quotation is echoed in various reviews of *Weep Not,
Child* when it made its debut in 1964. In his review of the novel in *Penpoint* 17
(September 1964), Tunde Aiyegbusi states:

> The appearance of a new work by an African author is something of a literary
> event. But the publication of Mr. Ngũgĩ's first novel 'Weep Not, Child' is a great
> event in its own right. It is a landmark in the literary history of East Africa. For
> the novel is the first one in English, yet to be published by an African on this
> side of the continent. (40)

If the performance of *The Black Hermit* and the publication of *Weep Not, Child*
raised the issues of visibility and the ownership of East Africa's written literary tradition, I would speculate it was because these works came from a
very active literature student. Before the publication of the novel, Ngũgĩ had

expressed his views on some of the existing African novels in essays such as 'Give Me My Black Dolls: The African Dilemma' published in the magazine *The Undergraduate* vol. 4 no. 1, March 1962 where he tackles what were key social and cultural concerns at the time, including colonization, displacement of the African's culture, and the contradictions in the life of the new African nationalist who, according to Ngũgĩ then, was very close to the Western way of life and yet longed for an idealized past.

Although Ngũgĩ would later come to question the Christian creed and its point of view and to interrogate the basis of Western culture and the West's relationship to the rest of the world, his early essays did not fully question what he termed the 'Western culture and its creed'. Still, the *undergraduate* essay expressed a keen awareness of the contradictions generated by the necessity to cope with two ways of life at the same time:

> I like and cherish the basis of Western culture. For its creed is Christianity which emphasizes the quality and dignity of each individual – that the one single lost sheep is as important as the rest of the 99 sheep. This is in the end, is the best challenge to Communism or any form of totalitarianism. Seen in this light, the Western culture ceases to be a wholly European creation. It has borrowed from all over the world. Hence it is not to be confused with European prejudices, mannerisms or fears. Even those Europeans who hold a Purist attitude to their culture, are being inward-looking and working against the ideals of 'their' culture. But none can deny the materialistic tendency of the present West. In this, the West can learn from our tribal way of life.

Ngũgĩ would also dismiss the use of the word tribe in his article 'The Myth of Tribe in African Politics' which appeared in *Transition* no. 101 (19–23).

Some of the concerns expressed in these early essays would become more evident in *Weep Not, Child*, the work that would set the trend of novel writing in East Africa. The novel integrates traditional mythology with the matter of nationalism and establishes the theme of the fractured nature of people's lives and identity. In this work, Ngũgĩ shows his deep-felt disquiet about what the colonial system was doing to people's sense of identity. He depicts nationalism as an assertion of what Edward Said has termed 'a sense of belonging in and to a place, a people, a heritage' ('Reflections' 176). Ngũgĩ presents the concern of education as an ideal even when he is so acutely aware that this ideal presents contradictions. In this novel, Ngũgĩ projects his nervousness about a system that does not seem to cater fully for his people. He shows that he feels the marginalization of his people deeply. And because of his deep sense of the susceptibility of the colonial subject to exploitation, Ngũgĩ makes the theme of memory and history central to his novel.

In *Weep Not, Child*, Ngũgĩ shows that writers do their work within specific contexts and settings, a quality that has made his first work significant in the development of the East African novel. In East Africa, then, *Weep Not, Child* is a work that speaks to issues that are still relevant today, including situations of displacement, violation of the body and mind, the relationship between land and nation, and the tension between oral testimony and the written text.

5
Encountering Ngũgĩ at Leeds:
An Interview with Peter Nazareth

Roland D. Nasasira

(Originally published in the *Daily Monitor*, Kampala, August 22, 2013. Reprinted with permission.)

What was it like being in the same class with Ngũgĩ?

Being in the same class as Ngũgĩ was not a problem but a joy. Once I had grad-uated, I wanted to learn things by myself. I did not want to continue studying formally but to learn. That is why I went to teach at St Mary's College, Kisubi. One of the best ways of learning is by teaching. I was the first Asian to teach at St Mary's, as far as I know.

When Ngũgĩ and I attended classes together [at Leeds], we attended what at the University of Iowa are called 'electives', namely, courses we wanted to take. We both attended lectures by Arnold Kettle and also attended a seminar on the novel. Both of us thought that Kettle's courses were the best of the best. Kettle's two-volume book on the novel [*An Introduction to the English Novel*] was brilliant. Ngũgĩ was a very humble man and so knowledgeable. After the classes and the seminar, Ngũgĩ and I used to discuss what we had learned.

Did you know Ngũgĩ as a writer?

Ngũgĩ was a visionary, a political thinker, a person who keeps growing, who is persistent. It is not easy to be a novelist. And when everyone thinks you are done, you write a novel [*Wizard of the Crow*] of a thousand-plus pages (edited to seven hundred and sixty-eight pages), a novel which is funny and deep and readable. I taught the novel in my African literature class this Spring and students loved Ngũgĩ's novel. They did not find it difficult to read. The essay published on this novel, *Wizard of the Crow*, [in *Approaches to Teaching the Works of Ngũgĩ wa Thiong'o*] edited by Oliver Lovesey is by my former student, Steve Ellerhoff.

Ngũgĩ taught us how to pursue our visions without staying at one point. This is both strategy and growth. I said to Ngũgĩ when we met some years ago that ninety per cent of what I teach my students is what I taught myself. 'That is the best way', said Ngũgĩ.

How distinctive did you find Professor Ngũgĩ?

I never found Ngũgĩ to be arrogant. But he has faith in his vision and pursues it. In this sense, he is like a prophet. He has always wanted to tell the story and to change society and the world.

He never gives in to pessimism, he does create characters, juxtaposes them with characters who do not give up but who learn, and if they do not, he does not 'sell out' as a writer. I think he knows he has a gift as a writer and he does not exploit it. I don't think he seeks any public honors and because of this, they come to him. We can learn from this, in our own way.

Ngũgĩ produced his first play *The Black Hermit*, for Uganda's Independence Celebrations and I wrote a review of the play. He was still a student at Makerere and I was teaching at St Mary's, Kisubi. I think a good reviewer/critic can learn from the text and contribute to the growth of the writer.

Was much of your education in Uganda?

I started studying at Makerere University College (as it was known then) in 1957. I had studied at Kololo Secondary School. In those days, we studied at Makerere for the Preliminary Arts [degree] for two years [instead of the High School Certificate]. After those two years, studying three subjects, we were accepted to study for a degree if we did well enough in the final exams.

Ngũgĩ and I lived in two different halls of residence. I was in Mitchell Hall [the old Mitchell, which was closed in 1962] on one side of the hill, not very far from Mary Stuart Hall, and Ngũgĩ was in Northcote Hall [current-day Nsibirwa Hall], on the other side of the hill. Ngũgĩ soon acquired a reputation as a writer. His first one-act play was performed at the English Department Inter Hall Competition in early 1962. My play *Brave New Cosmos* was performed at the same competition. It was my third one-act play and was later produced by the BBC African Theatre.

Did he inspire you with his works?

Ngũgĩ struck me (and many other students) as a visionary who was therefore dedicated as a writer. We were both editors of *Penpoint*, the English Department magazine: I was on the first editorial board and he was on the board in 1961 when I left it to prepare for my final exams.

After I took my exams, I had a special meeting with Ngũgĩ, sitting on the lawn outside the canteen. I told him of the strategies I had discovered on how to do well in the final exams on which our degree was based. He told me about all the African writers he had read and that was my deep initiation into African literature.

I taught at St Mary's Kisubi (with Pio Zirimu, who became a good friend at Makerere) and continued to go to Makerere to meet Ngũgĩ. I read the manuscript of his first novel, published later as *The River Between*, when it was called *The Black Messiah,* and gave him suggestions for improving it.

After a year of teaching (at St Mary's and then my alma mater, Kololo Secondary School,) I went to Leeds to do postgraduate work. Pio Zirimu was also there with me, as was his wife Elvania (doing her first degree) and Grant Kamenju (also a friend from my Makerere days). Ngũgĩ joined us as a postgraduate student the following year. It was during that time that we all (including Ime Ikiddeh from Nigeria) became very close friends and discussed writing and politics.

It was at that time too that I read and was inspired by Ngũgĩ's essays on [Joseph] Conrad, which he wrote for his special project in his last year at Makerere. I was very inspired by his essay on Conrad's *Nostromo*. I drew a lot from this essay in my dissertation at Leeds, for which I continue to give him credit.

In fact, I only began reading and re-reading Conrad because of Ngũgĩ. I felt that if Ngũgĩ loved the work of Conrad, then I should read and re-read it until I understood it. So, it is fitting that *Critical Approaches to Teaching the Works of Ngũgĩ wa Thiong'o*, edited by Oliver Lovesey and published by the Modern Language Association, contains my essay on *A Grain of Wheat* in dialogue with Conrad.

What do you currently do?

I am the professor of English and African-American studies at the University of Iowa in Iowa City where I and my wife work for the International Writers Workshop, which brings in writers from all over the world in the fall for ten weeks.

6

The Book that Made Me: On *Weep Not, Child*

Simon Gikandi

(From *Weep Not, Child@50*, ed. Nairobi: East African Educational Publishers, 2004. Reprinted with permission.)

On the surface, *Weep Not, Child*, Ngũgĩ wa Thiong'o's first published novel, would seem to have come slightly late in history of African literature. It was completed at Northcote Hall, Makerere University College in 1962, ten years after the publication of Amos Tutuola's *The Palm Wine Drinkard* and it was published in 1964, six years after the publication of Chinua Achebe's *Things Fall Apart*. Within this historical timeline, Ngũgĩ's novel appears to be a work suspended between two distinct moments of literary history. On the one hand, the work appears to belong not to the first generation of African writers, but to a second "postcolonial" generation. Unlike his predecessors, Ngũgĩ can claim to have drawn his works on models of African writing, a library that was available to him as he set out to write his novel. As he told Dennis Duerden in a 1964 interview, he had read Achebe and Ekwensi who, together with a group of Caribbean writers, set his imagination flying. Moreover, by the time Ngũgĩ started writing, the idea of Africa literature had firmly been established. The historical conference of African writers held at Makerere University in 1962, which Ngũgĩ attended, was evidence of the coming into being of African writing. At this conference, Ngũgĩ, an apprentice novelist, would rub shoulders with the makers of the new canon of letters. Given the existence of this canon, it could be said that Ngũgĩ didn't suffer the anxiety of dealing with a radical starting point or what Edward Said would call an "intransitive beginning" (*Beginnings* 73). *Weep Not, Child* was born into an ever-expanding family of African scribes and critics.

On the other hand, however, *Weep Not, Child* carries within its language and structure a deep anxiety about the possibility or impossibility of writing. Ngũgĩ has written about this anxiety in considerable detail in *Dreams in a Time of War* where he looks back on in his own childhood desire to become a writer without the authorization of the institutions of colonial power. In retrospect, we can read Njoroge's struggle to be educated and his striving to acquire a proper sense of himself as part of the crisis of writing. Ngũgĩ's project in *Weep Not, Child* was to write a narrative in which Njoroge, his alter ego, would be able to produce a *Bildung*—a completed picture of himself—against the violence of colonial control and violence. The tragic tone of the novel, the source of most of its power, results from the tension between what Njoroge imagines himself to be and the historical forces that work against this imagined, ideal self. The tragic tone is in turn enhanced by the moments of melancholy attendant to Njoroge's education—the loss of the land, the father's ineffectualness, and of the spiritual homelessness that makes the young protagonist perpetually estranged. But perhaps the major source of melancholy in the novel is Njoroge's relationship with his mother, the woman who gives him unconditional love, sends him to school, but cannot protect him from the violence of the times.

Melancholy in literature is, of course, an aesthetic effect that depends on an individual reader's relationship to a text and its shifting contexts of reading. For me, rereading *Weep, Not Child* returns me to a site of memory.

My encounter with *Weep Not, Child* will not take place until 1968, four years after the publication of the novel. I'm in standard six at Tumutumu Intermediate School, and being a voracious reader, I have exhausted the two bookcases that constitute the school's library. I have turned to bribing girls at the neighboring high school to borrow the novels they are reading for their examinations. It is from one of the girls that I borrow that now rare orange and white paperback with the nativity scene cover drawn by Eli Kyeyune. Oh, holding that text in my hands feels magical. It will be the first work of fiction that will speak to me, in English, of a world so close to me that I feel as if I'm reading the life back into the fiction. *Weep Not, Child* brings a new dimension to the already known world—the landscape, the school, the social classes, and the violence of history—but it does so in the authorized language of the institution of literature. At the same time, the novel relives lingering anxieties about the fragility of the new order of things. Like Njoroge, I have embraced school as the path to social mobility, but all around me there are signs of the postcolonial crisis and the possibility of catastrophe. *Weep, Not Child* instructs me about the unfinished business of decolonization and replays the terror and fear that we have been taught to forget so that we can move on with our lives.

For a young person with literary aspirations, *Weep Not, Child* authorizes the project of writing and of literary scholarship. For 1968 is not a good year for aspiring artists. With the landing of two Americans on the moon, our teachers remind us that we have entered the age of science. At Tumutumu Intermediate School, the prominent writers the school had produced, including Gakara wa Wanjau and Jonathan Kariara, are being forgotten. In 1968, Tumutumu families travel to Nairobi in buses to witness the "crowning" of two former pupils of the school, Francis Gichaga and James Kamwere, with degrees in Civil Engineering and Surveying, respectively. In my six-grade class, no one wants to be a writer when they grow up. Everyone wants to be either a civil engineer (like Gichaga), or a land surveyor (like Kamwere). Unable to declare loudly that I would like to be a writer when I grow up, I read the borrowed copy of *Weep Not, Child* silently, under the table, waiting and hoping that the science fad will soon die.

If I seem to identify wholly with Njoroge, it is because I can't imagine him as the product of another person's imagination. He exists for me as an expression of a reality I have lived and a life I have known. Indeed, up until I arrive at the University of Nairobi at the end of 1976, I never associate the novel with a living person; the work is the product of a vague institution that goes by the name of James Ngũgĩ, the name on the cover. Even at the university, my encounter with the author is from a distance—I sneak into the seminar room to hear him discuss the novels of Chinua Achebe in their social context, but I'm too shy to accost him in the corridors, a common practice among students at the university. The closest I come to him is at the National Theatre during the rehearsal of the *Trial of Dedan Kimathi*, where I'm one of many students playing "Mau Mau" and other extras. Occasionally I sneak into the lecture room and listen to him teach West African Literature. And then, in the year I'm supposed to formally take his class, he is arrested and detained.

But fate has to do its work. In 1980, twelve years after I first read *Weep Not, Child*, the author and I will share an office at Heinemann East Africa, on the ninth floor of International House in Nairobi, thanks to the foresight of Henry Chakava. How I relish what appears to be my moment of arrival! There he is, one of the most prominent writers in Africa, sitting across the desk from me, a recent graduate of the department where he is now barred from teaching. Although I am very young at the time, I have been entrusted with the task of editing *Ngaahika Ndeenda* and *Caitaani Mũtharabainĩ*.

As if that is not enough to boost my ego, I seem to have crossed the line that divides the writer and reader. Between going through galley and page proofs, we discuss the politics of orthography and of African literature. Occasionally he takes me to lunch at Kariakor market in his old pickup truck. As we wait for the *nyama choma*, we talk about the events and places that inspired his novels; but rarely do we discuss the emotions that went into the making of *Weep Not, Child*. I sense that these are too deep and personal to be rehearsed in everyday conversation. As we drive through the city streets, no doubt followed by the agents of the state who trail him everywhere, I think of Njoroge, the child forbidden to weep.

7
Note from a Literary Son

Peter Kimani

A waiter at a popular café in Irvine, California, narrated his encounters with an elderly customer. He came in regularly, the waiter recalled, usually on his own, and sat in a corner, under a heap of paper. Page after page, he ploughed through, reading out in a language the waiter did not understand, pausing to scribble before reading some more. The old man, the waiter concluded, was a refugee from some African country, and was learning English to enhance his chances of securing residency in America. So, in solidarity with a fellow African, the waiter ensured the old man's coffee bills were heavily discounted, always excluded gratuity.

One can imagine the waiter's chagrin when, months later, he came across a feature in a major American newspaper profiling his hermitic customer. The article said the elderly man was one of Africa's greatest living writers, and a distinguished professor of English at the University of California, Irvine. The waiter had merely encountered Ngũgĩ wa Thiong'o at work, probably polishing up novels that he usually writes in his first language, Gĩkũyũ.

Ngũgĩ means many things to different people. Like his fictional character, *Matigari*, whom Kenyan authorities sought to apprehend in the early 1980s, apparently because everyone was talking about him, he has been able to morph into larger-than-life forms. He was deified in Moi's Kenya, whispered about because his memory inspired suspicion from the authorities, who claimed he wanted to overthrow the government. Since writers bear pens, not guns, this vista of a revolutionary camouflaged as a writer inspired awe and dread.

Our first encounter was in 1986, when I joined high school. Our point of contact, his seminal novel, *Weep Not, Child*. The family feud re-enacted in the novel had Shakespearean echoes, for sure, but this was *my* story, talking about what elderly folks in my village called *Mbara ya Imageneti*. The Emergency War. And the characters in the novel bore names like mine and my classmates. For the next two decades, what sustained and buoyed my interest in the written word was the conviction that a Kenyan writer had written such a compelling story about his time. So, there was no reason for me not to make a similar attempt. By the time I left high school, I had read virtually all his published works, which all bore the portrait of the artist as a young man on the book's blurb. Ngũgĩ's mug-shot in a polo-neck sweater inspired me to declare at the end of my schooling that I wanted to be a writer.

When that came to pass, when my first novel, *Before the Rooster Crows*, was published in 2002, I mailed a copy to Ngũgĩ, then still in exile, thanking him for his mentorship! Over the years, we would correspond on email until December 2003, when I toured California.

Finally, the man that I had known as a polo-necked young man, morphed into a short, stocky elderly man who stood by the door to his office. The only thing that hadn't changed was the mat of unkept hair and eyes that pierced with intensity! We sat for lunch—he had shrimp on the rocks—washed down with espresso. As for the revolutionary writer I had created in my imagination, I looked for signs but found none! What was supposed to be a one-hour lunch date unfurled into two, three, four hours, ending with a brief detour through his home, and the beginning of a lifelong friendship.

Since that first encounter, I have been with Ngũgĩ in different capacities, and in different parts of the world. I was the journalist assigned by the *Daily Nation* to cover his homecoming in July 2004. I watched as the roiling swirl of humanity danced with joy at the return of the native son, after 22 years in exile. I accompanied him on his tour of East Africa, through Uganda and Tanzania, through the villages of central Kenya as he reconnected with relatives. In all these instances, Ngũgĩ's ability to connect with ordinary folks, dignitaries in posh places, students or teachers, was genuinely touching.

Ngũgĩ has remained a comforting presence in my life. He was on my doctoral committee at the University of Houston in 2014. The following year, he was among my first friends who arrived at our home to 'greet' my youngest son, Samora, when he was born. And when my other 'baby', *Dance of the Jakaranda*, was unveiled in New York's Brooklyn Public Library, Ngũgĩ was there to join in the celebration in a joint reading. He regaled the audience with his memories of Makerere and the trauma of learning to dance without crushing the toes of trainee nurses from Mulago and Mengo hospitals in Uganda, as captured in his memoir, *Birth of a Dream Weaver: A Writer's Awakening*.

It's hard to imagine how my dream as a writer would have panned out without Ngũgĩ's writing and, in subsequent years, his steady guidance and support. Indeed, when we met by chance at the African Studies Association's annual conference in Washington DC in 2016, he proudly introduced me as his 'literary son'. I couldn't think of a better compliment from Africa's greatest living writer, who paved the path that I now tread with confidence. Many, many, happy returns to my friend, mentor, teacher, and literary father!

8
What is in a Name?

Ime Ikiddeh

(Originally published as 'Preface' to Ngũgĩ, *Homecoming*. Reprinted with permission.)

'I am not a man of the Church. I am not even a Christian.' Those were the stunning words with which James Ngũgĩ opened his talk to the Fifth General Assembly of the Presbyterian Church of East Africa in Nairobi in March 1970, reproduced in this collection [i.e. in *Homecoming*] as 'Church, Culture and Politics'. He had hardly ended his address when a wiry old man visibly choking with anger leapt to the floor, and, shaking his walking-stick menacingly towards the front, warned the speaker to seek immediate repentance in prayer. The old man did not forget to add as a reminder that in spite of his shameless denial and all his blasphemy, the speaker was a Christian, and the evidence was his first name. Ngũgĩ had never given serious thought to this contradiction. Now it struck him that perhaps the old man had a point, and the name James, an unfortunate anomaly, had to go. This volume of essays is James Ngũgĩ's first major publication under his new name. Those who might retort with 'What's in a name?' should ask themselves why several African countries have changed their names during the last fifteen years, and why in the Republic of Zaire (itself a recent adoption) a name-changing revolution has swept through an entire Cabinet. The change in Ngũgĩ's name is in itself perhaps of little consequence. What lends it some importance for our purpose is its significance in the wider context of the writer's beliefs, particularly as the heresy which shocked the Presbyterian congregation in Nairobi forms an essential part of those beliefs. This foreword cannot attempt a detailed evaluation of Ngũgĩ's thought. What it seeks to do is merely to direct the reader's attention to some of its major features as revealed by these essays, and offer a few background comments in addition towards a richer appreciation not only of the essays themselves but also of the writer's creative work.

It will be seen that although the essays are grouped under three separate sections, they are vitally linked up by their dominant concerns, which are, put rather imperfectly and with particular reference to Africa: the confusion in values that has resulted from a drastic historical change in the political, economic and cultural ethos; the effect of such confusion on both society and the individual psyche; and the need to retain what is ours and recreate from it a new set of living values. The point of departure is the beginning of colonial rule and Christian missionary activity, with a reaching back to the slave trade seen as the earlier and more barbaric form of colonialism. In short, Ngũgĩ is concerned here with the very subjects that have dominated African writing and the utterances of our more sensitive nationalist leaders for about half a century. Colonialism and capitalism are identified here as twin brothers whose mission is to exploit the material wealth of subject peoples, and who, in order to gain acceptability and perpetuation, enlist the services of their more sly but attractive first cousins, Christianity and Christian-oriented education, whose duty it is to capture the soul and the mind as well. Thus, history and values are distorted and reversed, and social order, disrupted beyond recognition, is replaced by another that is both foreign and unjust. With local variations, the African story is the same for Asia, the Caribbean and Latin America. It then becomes in these places a betrayal of trust by an indigenous elite, that has taken over power with the active support of the people, to continue the same inequitable system as the colonial oppressors. Two essays, 'Church, Culture and Politics' and 'The Novelist and his Past' carry the burden of this argument.

These essays are packed with an interest that goes beyond the writer's repetition of old themes. Here, freed from the limitations of fiction – for there are limits to what a writer can create and to what he can meaningfully communicate through fiction – Ngũgĩ can make explicit statements informed and carried through by a passion and intellect which are only in circumscribed evidence in his best creative work. Most of the essays are dialectical in approach, and yet their messages remain at all times unambiguous and direct. They are often erudite without meaning to be so, and differ from the novels in dimension, in tone, and in the clarity of commitment. The fire that so often blazes within them is lit by indignation whose burning base is total conviction. Whatever critics might think of the preoccupations of these essays, it remains true that there can be no end to the discussion of the African encounter with Europe, because the wounds inflicted touched the very springs of life and have remained unhealed because they are constantly being gashed open again with more subtle, more lethal weapons. In any case, as an African who grew up in Kenya during the most turbulent days of that country's colonial history and who is now living through its aftermath, Ngũgĩ's sentiments should surprise no one.

In order to clear up any doubts that may arise, two points of a background nature may be helpful here. The first has to do with Ngũgĩ's Marxist thinking. One cannot go very far in these essays without being assailed by well-known phrases like 'the ruling classes' and 'the exploited peasant masses and urban workers', but if anyone regards these as empty traditional slogans then he cannot have known much of the history of Kenya. The irony is that it was the experience of social and economic relations in Britain, more than in Kenya, that actually settled Ngũgĩ's socialist conviction. Starting from a commonsense appraisal of the situation in his country at independence, in particular, the need for a redistribution of land in the interests of a deprived peasantry. Ngũgĩ arrived in England in 1964 and settled into the revolutionary atmosphere of Leeds University where he studied for the next few years. Extensive travels around Britain and Europe, acquaintance with some eminent British socialist scholars, including his supervisor, Dr. Arnold Kettle, and discussions with the radical student group led by Alan Hunt – these revealed that the root cause of incessant industrial strife in Britain was no more than the old inter-class hostility inherent in the capitalist system. Thus Leeds provided an ideological framework for opinions that he already vaguely held. It was at this time too that we both read two books which became major influences: Frantz Fanon's *The Wretched of the Earth*, that classic analysis of the psychology of colonialism; and Robert Tressell's *The Ragged Trousered Philanthropists*, one of the most moving stories ever told of the plight of the working class in Britain. Echoes of Fanon are to be heard in some of these essays.

But although Ngũgĩ sympathizes with the Marxist idea of the 'workers of the world', it is important to point out that he sees the experience of the black man as being unique in the world and as having a certain basic unity. He has re-emphasized this in a recent letter to me dated 4 September 1971 in which he writes:

> for I believe that we as blacks have suffered doubly under colonialism and capitalism, first, as part of all the working masses, and then as blacks. By which I mean that a white worker by the very nature of his position was a beneficiary of the colonialist and racist exploitation of Africa and of black people everywhere.

This forms part of what he has described as the 'black dimension' to his beliefs, and a year's stay in the United States between 1970 and 1971 more than confirmed his views.

The origins of the 'black dimension' are to be seen in Ngũgĩ's early interest in the Caribbean which he mentions in the essay 'A Kind of Homecoming'. That interest led him between 1965 and 1967 into an intensive research into the literature of the West Indies, an exercise which yielded the essays on the Caribbean in this volume. If the Caribbean essays exhibit a certain learned quality which many of the others do not, it is because they are the product of what was a scholarly research. The writer in fact would place little value on that quality. What was of greater importance to him was his discovery, through the novels he studied, of Africa's dominant presence in the West Indian consciousness, of the writers' agonizing sense of exile and persistent groping for some form of cultural identity. Ngũgĩ's study does not stop with writers of African descent; it includes, for example, V. S. Naipaul whose attitude to the cultural problem in the Caribbean is cynical, often condescending and contemptuous.

I think Ngũgĩ interprets Naipaul with more seriousness than he deserves. But this by no means invalidates the kinship of the experience avowed by writers like Lamming, Braithwaite and Patterson.

It should be clear that Ngũgĩ's conception of society is of a complex in which politics, economics and culture are inextricably tied up, and nowhere on that spectrum can he see capitalism offering any hope of progress and social justice that can be said to be accessible to all. In a post-colonial society and in a setting which in doctrine and practice runs counter to traditional communal values and works against the total involvement of the people in what is theirs, capitalism has nothing to recommend it. In that short talk to Makerere students, 'The Writer in a Changing Society', which incidentally brings together all the major themes of his novels, play and short stories, he is in fact recommending a socialist program as the ideal means of harnessing all African aspirations when he says: 'For we must strive for a form of social organization which will free the manacled spirit and energy of our people so we can build a new country, and sing a new song.'

It is in this light, although he is not offering a new philosophy, that Ngũgĩ must be seen as a writer who is also a thinker, and whose depth of thought and degree of commitment are yet to be attained by many African writers. These essays reveal a militancy not commonly associated with his creative work. It is of interest that his appreciation of other African writers in this volume is from the point of view of their apprehension of the African problem and what serious hope they can offer for the well-being of their society. Ngũgĩ's great strength lies in his realization that in the search for social well-being, questions arising from the experience of yesterday must lead to a consideration of the here-and-now as a basis of hope for the yet to-come. Not only 'where the rain began to beat us' and how severely, but also how to save ourselves from perpetual exposure, and our house from flood.

9

In Exile: Between Britain & Kenya

Odhiambo Levin Opiyo

(Originally published as 'Exiled Ngugi wa Thiong'o Was Subject of Talks'. *Sunday Nation*, 23 April 2017. www.nation.co.ke/oped/opinion/Exiled-Ngugi-wa-Thiong-o-was-subject-of-talks/440808–3900242-0e825wz/index.html)

On January 11, 1985, Kenya's President Daniel arap Moi held a two-hour meeting with Sir Geoffrey Howe, the British Secretary of State for Foreign and Commonwealth Affairs who had called on him in Nairobi. Several issues were discussed during the meeting, among them trade and diplomatic relations. But it was the President's concern over the activities of Kenyan academic and writer Ngũgĩ wa Thiong'o, who was living in exile in London, that dominated the meeting.

Declassified British government documents show that Moi accused Ngũgĩ—now a professor based in the United States—of conducting propaganda among Kenyan students in the UK and planning to start a communist party. President Moi also wondered why Britain had allowed Ngũgĩ to live and work freely yet when the President's son Gideon—now Baringo senator and KANU chairman—visited London he needed a visa to stay even for a day. The President's demand was clear: Britain should reject any visa extension application by the Kenyan academic and force him to relocate to another country. But, according to the declassified documents, the Secretary of State told Moi that it was impossible for the British government to take any action against Ngũgĩ unless he committed a criminal offence. The British official also suggested that ignoring Ngũgĩ was a better strategy to avoid giving him publicity.

The renowned author had been detained for a year in 1977 by the Jomo Kenyatta government after his Gikuyu play *Ngaahika Ndeenda* ('I will Marry When I Want'), written with Ngũgĩ wa Mĩriĩ, was performed in an open-air theatre in Limuru. After his release, Moi, who took over in 1978, blacklisted him and no university wanted to employ him. In 1982, after the launch of his book, *Devil on the Cross*, in Britain, Ngũgĩ feared for his life and did not return to Kenya. He would remain in exile in the UK until 1989 when he moved to the USA.

Moi's meeting was not the first time Kenya was expressing concern about Ngũgĩ's stay in Britain. Another declassified document marked 'confidential' shows the matter had been raised on November 12, 1984 by the Kenyan High

Commissioner to London Benjamin Kipkulei when he called on the British Secretary of State. Kipkulei reportedly said Ngũgĩ was receiving more attention than he deserved.

The British High Commission in Nairobi was not spared either. In one meeting to discuss Moi's planned tour of Britain, Foreign Affairs Permanent Secretary Bethuel Kiplagat told High Commissioner Leonard Allinson that Kenya was aware Ngũgĩ had been employed by the Islington Council in London and was not happy about it. This is captured in a letter Sir Leonard wrote to J. R. Johnson, a senior official at the Foreign and Commonwealth Office in London. He said in the letter: 'Kiplagat told me the only thing on the President's mind that hurts our image is the presence and activities of Ngũgĩ. Kenyans think he is now being employed by Islington Council or the GLC (Greater London Council). If the Secretary of State comes out here he will need to say a mollifying word on this subject.' Johnson responded with a letter dated December 31, 1984. 'There is no truth in Kiplagat's allegations that Ngũgĩ is now being employed by the GLC or Islington Council. This probably arises from a confusion over the sponsorship of his play by these two bodies.'

Johnson would later visit Kenya in August 1986 for an official engagement and Moi summoned him to State House, Nakuru, where the issue of Ngũgĩ was again given prominence. It was his first substantive meeting with Moi, according to a confidential letter he sent to London after the meeting. Also on the agenda was the President's deep suspicion of the relationship between Britain and the Central Kenya political elite among them one-time powerful Attorney General and former Cabinet minister Charles Njonjo and 'lies' propagated by the British press, particularly the BBC, about Moi's wealth. The President also expressed suspicions about his Vice-President Mwai Kibaki.

In the meeting, Moi narrated his political contributions to Kenya since the 1950s, including how the British Secretary of State for Colonies and Commonwealth Relations Lord Duncan Sandys convinced him to work with Jomo Kenyatta ahead of Independence to help hold the country together 'through difficult times'. The two then talked about aid to Kenya with Moi expressing his dissatisfaction with the way the British government was dragging its feet on some construction projects. Johnson responded by pinpointing the projects his government had undertaken. The further they delved into the discussions, the more Moi appeared to reveal his discomfort and fear of the Central Kenya elite at that stage of his presidency, according to the declassified documents. In his report, Johnson alleged that Moi blamed the group for being behind the instability in the Rift Valley, particularly on land issues. Moi, however, expressed confidence that the younger generation in Central Kenya and the 'common man' largely supported him.

The discussion then turned to Ngũgĩ. Since Kenya had no grounds to ask for extradition, Moi wanted the British to make life so uncomfortable for the author that he would have to relocate to another country. But the British official repeated the line that Ngũgĩ had not committed any crime hence there was no ground to extradite him. Ngũgĩ lived in Britain until 1989 when he moved to the USA.

Part II

Memories, Recollections & Tributes

10

Remembering Early Conversations with Ngũgĩ

Bernth Lindfors

James Ngũgĩ (Ngũgĩ wa Thiong'o) was the first African writer I ever met. This happened some time in 1962, while he was still an undergraduate at Makerere University College but was already contributing a fairly regular weekly or fortnightly column for Nairobi's *Sunday Nation* entitled 'As I See It', which was meant to represent an African point of view of Kenyan affairs, just as a parallel column under the same title by N. S. Toofan was intended to provide a voice for Kenya's Asians. Ngũgĩ had earlier published a few short stories in *Penpoint*, a campus literary magazine, as well as in the *Kenya Weekly News*, and he had completed the first draft of a longer story he called 'The Black Hermit', which he entered in a novel-writing competition sponsored by the East African Literature Bureau, but at the time I met him he was known primarily as a journalist.

I was then teaching English and History at a boys' boarding school in Kisii, Western Kenya in a program called *Teachers for East Africa*, which had been set up by the U.S. Government to supply American teachers to East African secondary schools in need of qualified instructors. Those of us in the first wave of this program had had a six-week orientation at Makerere before going out to our schools, but I did not chance to meet Ngũgĩ at the university. It was only after some months of reading his newspaper commentary that I decided to seek him out on one of my trips to Nairobi. I found him at the *Nation* office, and we went off to have a chat at a hotel bar nearby.

I cannot recall everything we talked about, but much of it may have concerned local topics he had written about in the paper: education, politics, history, language (especially the importance of Kiswahili), women's issues, etc. We also discussed some of the new writing that was emerging in parts of Western and Southern Africa. I had started reading African novels, plays, and poetry while at Makerere, and I was curious to learn about his own literary education and the opinions he had formed of Western and African authors whose works he had read and studied.

Eventually we were joined at the bar by one of his friends, Hilary Ng'weno, another journalist at the *Nation* who subsequently went on to found and edit such influential publications as *The Weekly Review*, *The Nairobi Times*, and *Joe Magazine*. At that point our conversation turned to more contemporary political and social issues. It was an engaging and entertaining afternoon of talk, and I continued to follow Ngũgĩ's contributions to the press thereafter until he left for the University of Leeds in 1964.

It wasn't until twelve years later that I had an opportunity to return to Nairobi for a summer, this time to interview a number of East African writers, publishers, editors, and scholars who were contributing to the creation of a lively local popular literature. James Ngũgĩ, who had changed his name to Ngũgĩ wa Thiong'o, was by then East Africa's most famous author, having published significant novels, plays, and short stories, as well as literary and cultural criticism. He was teaching at the University of Nairobi's Department of Literature, having helped to transform it from a conventional English Department, and he was also beginning to serve as Chairman of the Kamĩrĩĩthũ Community Education and Cultural Centre in Limuru, where he directed a play he had co-authored in English with Mĩcere Mũgo, *The Trial of Dedan Kimathi*. He was very busy so I seldom saw him during this brief visit, except one afternoon when our paths crossed and he spontaneously invited me to join him and a few of his friends at a local restaurant that served roasted meat on long skewers and plenty of beer. As before, the conversation there was spirited, robust, and very enjoyable. The topics ranged from food to football, from literature to theatre, from parliamentary shenanigans to academic politics.

I returned to Nairobi in the summer and fall of 1978 to continue my research on East African literature. Ngũgĩ in the meantime had been detained at Kamiti Security Prison on December 31, 1977, apparently for his role at the Kamĩrĩĩthũ Centre in co-authoring and co-directing with Ngũgĩ wa Mĩriĩ a political play in Gĩkũyũ, *Ngaahika Ndeenda* ('I Will Marry When I Want'), even though he was never formally charged in court with having committed a crime by doing so. However, Ngũgĩ was not released from detention until December 12th, so I just missed seeing him on that visit.

When I came back to Nairobi in the summer of 1980, Ngũgĩ was still trying to get reinstated in his job at the university, and he was using the Heinemann office downtown as his postal address. I remember meeting him there when one of the sub-editors was examining an annual stockholder's report of the large multinational corporation abroad that owned Heinemann and about ten other publishing companies. But of their total portfolio this was only a small part, represented by a narrow band on the colorful chart illustrating the full spectrum of their worldwide investments. They had much larger holdings in mining, manufacturing, energy, and a range of other industries. Ngũgĩ took a long look at this chart which revealed the extent of one giant corporation's capitalist exploitation not only of Africa but of other parts of the world as well. It was a vivid lesson in postcolonial economics. Ngũgĩ was aware that every author in Heinemann's African Writers Series would have been contributing in some small measure to the bottom line of this alien behemoth, and this didn't make him happy. A long discussion followed on the politics of international finance and foreign publishing. It was interesting to hear him cogently express his views on these matters.

Ngũgĩ, throughout his career, has always sided with the poor and dispossessed, the struggling masses in society who too often are victimized by the rich and powerful. He has been an articulate advocate of their interests, exposing the economic injustices they have suffered. His work at Kamĩrĩĩthũ was an example of the kind of commitment he felt in drawing attention to the vulnerabilities of such people. He once explained why he thought speaking out on their behalf was productive:

> I believe that the play, *Ngaahika Ndeenda*, was very popular because it talked about the extreme poverty of the people. I believe the play was popular because it talked about landlessness in our country. I believe the play was popular because it talked about the betrayal of the peasants and workers by the political 'big-wigs'. I believe the play was popular because it talked about the arrogance and the greed of the powerful and the wealthy. I believe the play was popular because it depicted the true conditions of the rural people in the rural villages. (wa Gacheru 95)

It was his success in addressing his own people in their mother tongue that persuaded Ngũgĩ in mid-career to publish his future novels and children's books in Gĩkũyũ before releasing them translated into English. His decision to write in an indigenous language and to encourage other African writers to make an effort to do so made him exceptional among his literary peers and reflected his determination to adhere to a principle that would serve the masses, not just elites fluent in English or other European languages.

My early informal encounters with Ngũgĩ back then led me to continue to follow with great interest his progress in later years when he was solidifying his reputation as one of Africa's most profound thinkers and most talented writers. Over time I have had additional opportunities to interact with him at conferences and social gatherings, and I can confirm that he has remained an engaging conversationalist with wide-ranging interests, strong opinions, and a good sense of humor. Today the friendly young man I met fifty-five years ago has become an iconic world-class intellectual, but he is still at heart an accessible man of the people, and I continue to find his words and actions fascinating and inspiring.

11

Ngũgĩ wa Thiong'o at 80: *Pongezi* (Congratulations!)

Eddah Gachukia

Looking back over a period of five decades, I believe that my decision to resume school as a mature age student was a turning point, with Ngũgĩ wa Thiong'o unknowingly playing a critical role in my studies and future orientation. Although I had studied English Literature at secondary school and at Makerere College, I was oblivious of the fact that Africa had a body of literature worth studying. I proceeded to teach English Literature at secondary school level for nearly four years before going to Leeds University to study for a certificate in 'The Teaching of English as a Second Language' for a year. By coincidence, the topic I picked for my main paper at Leeds was entitled 'The Teaching of English Literature in Kenyan Secondary Schools'.

Although I recorded the challenges of culture and background in understanding such literature, it never occurred to me that there was any other alternative. My training as a teacher at Makerere had taught me that in the teaching of any subject, you started from the known to the unknown as a mandatory cognitive principle. How then was I supposed to relate Jane Austen's *Emma* to the 'known' in my introduction? How were my students and I expected to relate to the 'drawing room' in the novel? For us the drawing room was the room where Emma retreated whenever she wanted to draw!

Mercifully, my entry into the first-year degree program at the University of Nairobi coincided with the great debate generated by the trio—Ngũgĩ wa Thiong'o (James Ngũgĩ at the time), Owuor Anyumba, and Taban lo Liyong. In a 1968 paper entitled 'On the abolition of the English Department', they sought to adopt the 'Literature Department' as the preferred title of the program, and went further to employ the cognitive principle of beginning from the known to the unknown. But their proposal was not simply a title change; they were calling for the total overhaul of the curriculum of the then English Department.

The proposed curriculum recognized the importance of African Literature as a critical, central core of the study of literature in Africa. East African Literature was to become the most logical introduction to African Literature in English. The curriculum also identified a cluster of related literatures that

were to become central to the identity of the department, including Black/
African American Literature, Caribbean Literature, and literature from other
formerly colonized populations. Ngũgĩ and his colleagues had expressed their
shock at the lack of recognition of orature as a literary genre worthy of study.
Behind this lack was the colonial assumption that, whether we were dealing
with history or literature, what was not written did not exist. A key assumption in the overhaul of the curriculum was that the response to the colonial
experience had similarities and challenges for creative writers in former colonies. The proposed curriculum hence recognized the need to view the colonial
experience as one common phenomenon that would engage creative writers
in all former colonies.

My concern in this contribution has to do with my spontaneous response
and that of my colleagues—undergraduates at the University of Nairobi—to
this overhaul of the literature syllabus. Not only did we begin to feel grounded
in our literary education, but also were guided to produce more original work
in our review and study of literature. We continued to enjoy Shakespeare,
Dickens, Lawrence and other English writers, but our center of interest was
now works by African writers such as Ngũgĩ and Okot p'Bitek, oral literature,
and biographical works that provided the political and cultural backdrops to
our understanding of literature. When our teacher, Taban lo Liyong wrote his
provocative essay on the 'Barrenness of East African Writing', we challenged
him with evidence of all the written works in existence in the region.

It is hard here to capture the keenness with which undergraduate and post-
graduate students undertook research into African writing, the oral literatures
of different Kenyan groups, popular culture, and every genre of which we were
aware. Significantly, the overhaul of the literature syllabus in the Department
of Literature at the University of Nairobi would be extended to the secondary schools' literature curriculum. Now that the universities were producing teachers primed to the need to decolonize the mind through the study
of national and African Literatures, works by African writers such as Ngũgĩ,
p'Bitek, Margaret Ogolla, Marjorie Oludhe Macgoye, Francis Imbuga, Chinua
Achebe, and Sembene Ousmane would, over the years, become set books for
Kenyan schools. Oral literature would also become an important feature of
study and examination at the high school level.

Ngũgĩ was for me a passionate teacher. He appreciated student dynamism
and encouraged views contrary to his own. At post-graduate level, when some
of us wanted to focus on writers we had studied since high school—Dickens,
Shakespeare, and Lawrence, for example—Ngũgĩ would ask a simple question: 'Don't you think those writers have been studied adequately in their own
countries? Why not focus on your own as a priority so that others can also
learn from you?' We were not coerced but convinced. Criticism of African
Literature was scanty and mostly by critics from other traditions; we felt that

it was our turn to bring a truly African perspective to our literature. Ngũgĩ directed us to less-studied authors where our work could be original, and over the years, our libraries became enriched with bound volumes of theses by newly-developed writers and critics. In revisiting my BA thesis entitled 'The Mau Mau War and East African Creating Writing' (1971), and my PhD Thesis 'Cultural Conflicts in East African Literature' (1981), I'm struck by how prominently Ngũgĩ featured in my literary and scholarly development. In addition to being one of the central writers discussed in my two theses, he was also a guide and mentor.

12
Ngũgĩ wa Thiong'o at 80:
Inspiring Encounters

Willy Mutunga

Ngũgĩ has been my brother, mentor, comrade. As one of the leading African
Marxist intellectuals and revolutionaries, a Pan-Africanist, and a Kenyan
patriot, he has been one of my role models and teachers. Since I met him
through his novel *Weep Not, Child* in the 1960s, and later as a colleague at the
University of Nairobi in the 1970s, he has inspired and guided me in my intellectual, ideological, political, cultural and overall revolutionary development.
He has taught me, and many others, what it means to be an organic intellectual
in our country, region, continent, and the world. In celebrating Ngũgĩ's 80th
birthday I want to share some of these inspiring encounters.

Encountering Ngũgĩ's Works

I first met Ngũgĩ through his novel *Weep Not, Child* when I was a student
at Kitui Secondary School in Eastern Kenya. My English Literature teacher,
Michael Drury, had spent some time at Makerere College (later to become
Makerere University), where he had met Ngũgĩ. He talked to us a lot about
Ngũgĩ as he taught us English Literature through our set books, which included
Shakespeare's *Macbeth*, George Eliot's *The Mill on the Floss*, Gerald Durrell's *My
Family and Other Animals*, and Robert Bolt's *A Man for All Seasons*. Mr. Drury
was particularly able to relate Ngũgĩ to the last title, but his greatest influence
was to simply ask us to read Ngũgĩ's works. He prophesied that Ngũgĩ would
one day become a great and world-famous writer.

I did not get to read Ngũgĩ comprehensively until I joined the Faculty of
Law at the University of Nairobi in 1974. The Department of Literature was
then the leading radical and revolutionary department at the University of
Nairobi. Among famous lecturers in the department were Ngũgĩ, Mĩcere
Gĩthae Mũgo, Kimani Gecau, Gacheche Waruingi, and two great Ugandans,
John Ruganda and Okot p'Bitek. The Department of Literature inspired me
immediately. After deciding to teach my law courses within historical, socio-
economic, cultural, and political contexts of Kenya I valued the activism and
works coming out of this department. Soon Ngũgĩ's *Petals of Blood*, *The Devil*

on the Cross, Ngaahika Ndeenda ('I Will Marry When I Want') found their way
into my reading lists at the Faculty of Law. One of my brilliant law students,
Professor Kivutha Kibwana, now Governor of Makueni, was active in the projects of the Department of Literature, particularly the Free Travelling Theatre.
It was during this period that I came to know Ngũgĩ very well. I attended many
of his talks at the University. When the play *Ngaahika Ndeenda* was staged
at Kamĩrĩĩthũ Community Centre in Limuru in 1977, I attended many of the
performances. I also widely distributed the script of the play to many of my
Kikuyu friends and students. The script had been nicely bound for effective
distribution. One of the songs in the play that I have not forgotten was called
Mwikũ? Mwikũ? (Where are you? Where are you?). In a play whose great theme
was the class struggle between workers and peasants on one side and capital on
the other, the song asked members of the audience which side they were on.

The December 12th Movement (DTM) and the University Staff Union

Ngũgĩ was one the leading intellectual ideologues of the December 12th
Movement (DTM), an underground movement in Kenya. He was the leader
of one of the DTM's cells. I came to know this after the movement's leadership
was detained and exiled in 1982. Ngũgĩ, who had been detained for a year from
1978 to 1979, eventually fled the country in 1982. While in exile in London he
formed, with other Kenyan patriots, the Release Political Prisoners Committee.

I was recruited to the DTM a year after I joined the University of Nairobi,
in October 1974. The DTM brought together intellectuals who wanted to think
through the liberation of Kenya. Under the brutal and repressive KANU-
Kenyatta-Moi dictatorship, the University of Nairobi had become the main
base of resistance to this dictatorship and the DTM was one of the main centers of opposition. As a member of this movement, and through its publication,
Pambana (Struggle), I was able to put into practice the radical knowledge that
I had acquired at the University of Dar es Salaam.

It was through the work and initiative of the DTM that the then-defunct
University Academic Staff Union (UASU) was resurrected in a special conference held on February 28, 1979. In 1976, officials of the Union had unconsti-
tutionally resigned under pressure from the University authorities. Ngũgĩ had
been a member of UASU. The special conference accepted the resignations of
the former officials and elected new ones. I was elected the Secretary General
of UASU, the name of which we quickly changed to the University Staff Union
(USU). I was part of the group that was involved in the mobilization of the
University Staff, Faculty, and students to join the DTM. We also mobilized
University Staff and Faculty to join USU.

On his detention in December 1978, the University of Nairobi had dis-
missed Ngũgĩ from his position as Associate Professor of Literature. One of

the campaigns USU undertook in 1979 was to agitate for Ngũgĩ's resumption of his position at the University of Nairobi. This struggle is documented in an appendix to the original edition of Ngũgĩ's book *Detained: A Writer's Prison Diary*. On May 1, 1980, I had compiled this appendix for inclusion in the book in my capacity as the Secretary General of USU.

Ngũgĩ's Legal Counsel

After Ngũgĩ came out of detention in 1979, he was closely watched by the state's security forces. This watch soon turned to blatant intimidation; shortly afterwards, Ngũgĩ would face trumped up criminal charges as part of this intimidation. He was charged in Kiambu Magistrate's Court with two counts of 'Behaving in a manner likely to cause a breach of peace' and 'Creating disturbance in a police station'. I joined Ngũgĩ's childhood friend and lawyer, Timan Ngũgĩ, to defend the author. In preparing for this case, I was inspired by Ngũgĩ's desire to have his prosecution politicized. He made us adopt a strategy that would make other issues, such as the violation of rights, intimidation, the dictatorship of the state, and his own refusal to be silenced, part of the case. So, this was not going to be a trial where only the prosecution witnesses would tell their stories; rather, we cross-examined them vigorously using legal-centric technicalities. Ngũgĩ urged us put the state on trial and use the trial to mobilize Kenyans against the KANU-Moi dictatorship. I believe we did the best we could, making sure we consulted Ngũgĩ continuously and consistently as the trial continued. He was eventually acquitted of the charges by Senior Resident Magistrate O'Kubasu, my former classmate at the law school at the University of Dar es Salaam and later my colleague at the Judiciary as a Judge of the Court of Appeal.

Lawyers call themselves 'learned friends', yet we are the most ignorant profession when it comes to the knowledge of other disciplines. We seem to readily accept the lie that law exists in a vacuum. We forget that trials conceal the deep-seated causes of the commission of crimes. The state and its machinery of violence is seen as the god of 'law and order', the protector of life and property of citizens. In these circumstances, it is very difficult to put the state on trial in criminal trials, and many lawyers are not taught how to do so. Defending Ngũgĩ provided me with a singular and effective education. I was familiar with studying, teaching, and analyzing law within its broad societal contexts, but I had not tried this framework in the actual practice of law. In addition, Ngũgĩ taught me that clients who are not lawyers can educate lawyers in matters of law. This lesson was to become resonant when I was fired from my job at the University of Nairobi after my detention in 1982, and I ended up defending bank robbers, tenants, and litigants against motor insurance companies.

Ngũgĩ's Homecoming

Ngũgĩ was in exile from 1982–2004. When he eventually came home to visit in 2004, I was involved in three encounters at his homecoming. First, the Ford Foundation funded Ngũgĩ to come back to East Africa as a distinguished lecturer, and, as a program officer for human rights and social justice at the Nairobi office of the Foundation, I accompanied him to Dar es Salaam University. He gave his second distinguished lecture there. It was fundamentally about his reflections on developments in the region while he had been away. It was a brilliant lecture. Ngũgĩ had never ceased to be my teacher and I found the lecture inspiring.

Back in Nairobi after giving his lecture at Makerere University, Ngũgĩ was attacked and his wife Njeeri wa Ngũgĩ was sexually assaulted while they were staying at Norfolk apartments in Nairobi. This was a painful and trying time for all of us. We faced a justice system that gave impunity and immunity to the 'untouchables' who commit crimes, including the state itself and its agents. But through Njeeri and Ngũgĩ I witnessed the true meaning of the revolutionary slogan *Aluta Continua Vitoria e Certa* (the struggle continues, victory is certain). They both knew who was behind the assault, intimidation, and oppression, but they did not give up the struggle to expose the real culprits of the assault. They taught us that when the oppressor hits us personally by attacking those we love, it takes a lot of mental and revolutionary strength to stay focused on the enemy. Both Njeeri and Ngũgĩ became my leaders in the struggle for justice.

My second involvement with Ngũgĩ's return revolved around the publication of *Wizard of the Crow*. He had confided in me that the book was his present to the Kenyan people on his return home after an absence of 22 years. After I finished reading the book on April 7, 2007, I decided that I would glorify my mentor's work by reviewing it. It so happened that between 2006 and 2011, I wrote a column for the Saturday edition of the *Daily Nation* newspaper in Kenya under the pen name of Cabral Pinto. I submitted this review to the paper. My goal was to glorify Ngũgĩ to the more-than two hundred thousand readers of the Saturday edition of the *Daily Nation*. But the editors of the newspaper turned the review down! I was not given the reasons for this rejection, a practice by newspaper editors that I find totally unacceptable. But as it turned out, I had the last laugh. I sent the review to Ngũgĩ who emailed me back singing praises for, and expressing appreciation of, the review. What else could I have hoped for? Ngũgĩ did not probably know that Cabral Pinto was my pen name. This review of the *Wizard of the Crow* (see Appendix A) reflects Ngũgĩ's influence on my thinking when I later served as the Chief Justice of the Supreme Court of Kenya.

My third involvement with Ngũgĩ after his exile took place on June 5, 2015 when, as Chief Justice of Kenya, I was honored to receive him and his family at the Supreme Court of Kenya when they paid me a courtesy call. After signing the Chief Justice's Visitor's book, Ngũgĩ and his family presented me with presents. Ngũgĩ gave me copies of *Weep Not, Child* and *Detained: A Writer's Prison Diary*. Later that day, in the evening, I found myself weeping. This is when I realized that Ngũgĩ had given me a copy of the novel that introduced me to him when I was a secondary school student. He had also given me a book that painfully reminded me of some of struggles in which he had been our intellectual ideologue and leader.

This visit was the culmination of all the inspiring encounters I had had with him over the years. In the first book he wrote this message: 'For CJ. *Haki iwe ngao yetu*/Justice be our shield and defender. Continue with the good work.' In the second book he wrote this message: 'For CJ. In great appreciation for all you have done and continue to do for Kenya.' His son, Ndũcũ wa Ngũgĩ, gave me a copy of his novel, *City Murders*, with the following message: 'For Chief Justice Willy Mutunga. Keep fighting for justice.' And his daughter, Wanjiku wa Ngũgĩ gave me a copy of her novel, *The Fall of Saints*, with the following inscription: 'For Chief Justice Willy Mutunga: With warmth.' It was a great honor to host Ngũgĩ and his children. It was comforting to observe the revolutionary spirit of my mentor residing in the works of his children.

Ngũgĩ and Progressive Jurisprudence

As the Chief Justice of Kenya and President of the Supreme Court I was able, over three years, to develop, in my concurring and dissenting judgments, a theory of interpreting the 2010 Kenyan Constitution. I based this theory on the historical, social, economic, and political contexts of the development and the promulgation of the Constitution and its ultimate text. I also invoked the text of the *Supreme Court Act 2011* which addressed the issue of interpreting the constitution in the context of Kenyan experiences. Through my judgments, I was able to make the case for a robust, decolonized, indigenous, progressive, patriotic, and transformative jurisprudence. I was convinced that judges could play their role in liberating their countries through judgments, extra-judicial writings, and speeches.

I saw the Judiciary as a political actor. I did not share the traditional and conservative view that judicial officers could not do politics. I made sure I seized on any opportunity I got in my work to perform this political role. I was able to convince my colleagues in the Supreme Court on the development of such a jurisprudence in a unanimous decision in the *Communications Commission of Kenya and 5 Others v Royal Media Services Limited and 5 Others [2014 eKLR]*. In this landmark case, the theory of the law in regard to constitutional values was mainstreamed in a decision that was binding on other superior and subordinate courts. In this case, as in other concurring judgments, I was able to demonstrate that our Constitution was not legal-centric. We needed a multi-disciplinary approach to fulfill the promise of the vision of the Constitution.

In a decision on electoral jurisprudence, *Gatirau Peter Munya v Dickson Mwenda Kithinji and 2 Others [2014 eKLR]*, I quoted Ngũgĩ's *The Wizard of the Crow* to call attention to this multi-disciplinary approach to the law, and to emphasize the importance of history in the development of our jurisprudence. In glorifying the right to vote in a democracy, I referred to '*the queuing demons*' of Eldares that Ngũgĩ uses in his book to condemn the subversion of democracy by rulers who express their will through the suppression of the rights of voters. The *Mlolongo* (queuing) election of 1988 was a blatant example of how the Moi-KANU dictatorship used the electoral system to subvert the people's resistance to its rule. The 2010 Constitution sought to put an end to such manipulated elections. Following the Preamble to the 2010 Constitution asking us to honor 'those who heroically struggled to bring freedom and justice to our land', I was convinced that our jurisprudence would also honor freedom fighters. In quoting Ngũgĩ, I wanted to emphasize the fact that our jurisprudence should not be confined to the law and lawyers, but should reach out to other disciplines as well, and, above all, to honor our freedom fighters.

Conclusion

Happy 80th birthday Ngũgĩ, my brother, mentor, role model. I will forever glorify and value your inspiration. You will always be my intellectual and revolutionary leader. I am glad I have been able to serve Kenya under your inspiration and leadership. I end by sharing with you the fighting words from Bertolt Brecht's play *The Mother*, which you immortalized in *Detained: A Writer's Prison Diary*.

A Worker's Voice

While you're alive, don't say never!
Security isn't certain
And things won't stay as they are.
When the ruling class has finished speaking
Those they ruled will have their answer.
Who dares to answer never?
On whom is the blame if their oppression stays? On us!
On whom does it fall to destroy it? On us!
So if you are beaten down, you just rise again!
If you think you've lost, fight on!
Once you have seen where you stand, there is nothing can hold you back
For those defeated today will be victors tomorrow...

13
Ngũgĩ in the 1970s at the University of Nairobi

Margaretta wa Gacheru

The day after I arrived in Kenya in 1974, I had my first encounter with Ngũgĩ wa Thiong'o. I had recently won a Rotary International 'Ambassadorial Fellowship' to study at the University of Nairobi for a year. So, I'd gone to new students' orientation at the Education Building Theatre 2 to hear the Chairman of the Literature Department speak to us newcomers. I stood way up in the back of the large room and listened to one of the most inspiring lectures I'd ever heard. The room was packed but I felt Ngũgĩ was speaking to me directly. He spoke passionately about the need for all of us to see ourselves as writers who would tell Kenyans' stories. He spoke as if he knew what he was saying and knew all of our potential to do the work required to create a body of literature that could equal or exceed that of canonical European writings.

Just a few years before, Ngũgĩ had spearheaded a cultural revolution at the University when he with others insisted on the transformation of the English Department into a Literature Department that was not Euro-centric, as the English Department had previously been, but Afro-centric. More precisely, the core course would be Oral Literature which would involve every student going out and interviewing elders who had oral traditions and stories about early Kenya to share. From there the curriculum would expand in concentric circles: it would go from oral to Kenyan literature, then to the study of South, West and North African and finally to literature of the Black Diaspora and the rest of the world.

Ngũgĩ's words that day lit a flame in my soul that has never died. His conviction about students' creative capacity made me hungry to listen to more of what he had to say and share. But when I went to his office and asked that I be admitted to his department, he refused my request. I discovered that Ngũgĩ could be hard core. In part his refusal might have been because I wasn't a Kenyan or even an African. Plus, I was a visiting student who might not be serious about literary studies. But those were not his grounds. As revolutionary as his approach to education seemed to be, he was still fixated on the British model which dictated that you couldn't enter a Master's program (which is what I'd wanted to do as I already had a Bachelor's in Sociology and

Comparative Religion plus a Master's in Education) unless you had done A levels in Literature and pursued the same course for the first university degree. So, his grounds for dismissing me were academic. As far as he was concerned, I did not qualify.

I didn't see Ngũgĩ for several months after that since University of Nairobi students went on strike for five months. They were up in arms over a lecturer that they claimed was a racist and had to be removed from the University. With the university closed and with time on my hands, I read a lot of African and Pan-African literature, met writers like Okot p'Bitek, and I got up my nerve to ask assistance from Ngũgĩ's good friend and fellow scholar, Dr. Mĩcere Gĩthae Mũgo who actually took pity on me. It was thanks to Mĩcere that Ngũgĩ relented and allowed me into the undergraduate program. That program was a three-year course, but as I was committed to getting an MA from the University of Nairobi, I took all the subjects and all the exams in one year. That was undoubtedly the most intense academic year of my life. If I wasn't reading, I was attending classes. And I made a point of attending every lecture, seminar and tutorial that Ngũgĩ gave. I was always seated either at his elbow or in the front row of lectures and involved in the more casual conversations that he had with his students. I tried to be inconspicuous, but at that time—the mid-1970s—it wasn't very easy since I was one of the few white students in the department.

What I found in Ngũgĩ was a person in love with literature, all literature. Whatever author he was teaching, be it Eldridge Cleaver or Ayi Kwei Armah, he was always encouraging us to read everything that particular author had written. He was so down to earth that he'd come to class dressed casually, like any other peasant or worker from his home area of Kamĩrĩĩthũ. The other thing about Ngũgĩ was his subtle sense of humor and irony that invariably showed through his lectures and more casual classes. He never came across as academically arrogant or proud. Instead, he struck me as one of the most humble, gentle persons that I'd ever met. However, I never forgot how curt he'd initially been with me, so I chose to keep my distance even though I wouldn't miss a single one of his lectures or sessions that he'd have in his office.

Ngũgĩ's political perspective was never far from his analysis of literature. As my background had been in sociology and the study of revolutionary social movements, I loved hearing his appraisal of how inherently political culture and literature were. Class consciousness was always understood by Ngũgĩ to be a component of every writer's point of view, however latent or subtle it might have seemed. When we got into discussions of African American literature with Ngũgĩ, his literary analysis included both class and race. In other words, he was talking about a post-colonial perspective before it was labeled as such.

It was during this period, when I was still taking classes with Ngũgĩ, that the play *Dedan Kimathi* by Kenneth Watene was staged. Ngũgĩ was clearly not impressed. He felt Watene had wholly swallowed the British perspective on the great leader of the Mau Mau, or Land and Freedom Army, and reproduced it on stage. That is how *The Trial of Dedan Kimathi* was born. Co-written by Ngũgĩ and Mĩcere, *The Trial* was first staged in 1976 at the National Theatre in Nairobi. By that time, I had been admitted to the Master's program at the University of Nairobi, but I was still stunned when Ngũgĩ asked me at the last minute to join the cast and play an 'ugly *mzungu*' (white colonial woman or *memsaab*) whose task was to scornfully sit through the trial of Kimathi. Needless to say, I was delighted to do it. *The Trial* had already been selected to go to FESTAC (the 2nd Pan-African Arts Festival) in Lagos in 1977, but I never intended to go as I knew there would be few tickets available and they were for Kenyans. But I had caught the theatre bug and took drama classes with John Ruganda who invited me to join the University's Free Travelling Theatre, which I did.

By this time, I was taking graduate classes with Ngũgĩ, who happened to love Russian literature. So, we got to read and talk about major Russian writers from Tolstoy, Dostoevsky and Turgenev to Gogol, Chekhov and others. I had the privilege of presenting the first paper in the class meant to contextualize Russian literature which Ngũgĩ understood as emerging out of conditions of 19th-century Russia where peasants (serfs) and workers were profoundly oppressed and the potential for revolution was ripening. Reading and discussing this literature in seminars with Ngũgĩ was life-transforming; for me, he embodied the best qualities of a true intellectual. Later in my life when I read the works of Antonio Gramsci, I came to realize that Ngũgĩ had prepared me to fully appreciate what an organic intellectual is.

After I had completed my course work, I got a job in journalism to help me pay for the completion of my master's thesis. It was during this period that Ngũgĩ was detained. He had recently published *Petals of Blood* in English, which I know was a big deal to him at the time since he'd occasionally bemoaned the fact that almost ten years had gone by since the publication of *A Grain of Wheat*. But after *Petals of Blood* was published in 1977, Ngũgĩ had started to formulate his perspective on writing in one's mother tongue. And undoubtedly, he was detained for writing and producing his overwhelmingly popular production of his first Gikuyu play, *Ngaahika Ndeenda*. The play represented a significant turn in Ngũgĩ's writing: It was attracting thousands of people to the village of Kamĩrĩĩthũ, an audience keen to see a play featuring a cast full of peasants and workers who'd been empowered by everything they'd learned from Ngũgĩ about social injustice and the theatre. The play was, however, considered subversive and the writer became the nemesis of the state during the last days of Jomo Kenyatta's presidency and the early days of Daniel arap Moi, his successor.

I had interviewed Ngũgĩ for the *Weekly Review* shortly after *Petals of Blood* came out, but my editor Hillary Ng'weno refused to publish the interview. I gather he wanted to stay on the right side of the government and Ngũgĩ had already been identified as a radical. But once Ngũgĩ was detained, Ng'weno apparently had a change of heart. He immediately published my interview with Ngũgĩ. What's more, when a year had passed and Ngũgĩ was unexpectedly released, it was Ng'weno who sent me to Kamĩrĩĩthũ to conduct another interview with the newly-freed writer. But my boss had given me an explicit set of questions to ask Ngũgĩ, questions like 'do you believe in peasant revolution?' Given the Kenyan government's fear of revolution, anything that smelt of 'peasant revolution' was anathema and it seemed as if Ngũgĩ was being set up. He refused to go with preset questions, so I asked him to fashion the questions that would elicit the answers he wanted to share with a world awaiting word from Kenya's number one writer and recent detainee.

But the interview did not go very well with my editor. When he saw the transcribed interview, Ng'weno was so livid that he was willing to sack me on the spot since it was obvious that I had disobeyed his instructions and reconstructed the conversation with Ngũgĩ. I had never seen Ng'weno so livid, but it was worth it, especially when that interview was published just as Ngũgĩ had presented it and I had the privilege of being the first journalist to interview Ngũgĩ before the international press corps arrived on the scene. But when my former lecturer alluded to me (namelessly) in the preface to his book *Detained*, he clearly didn't understand that I had risked my job to give him that open-ended platform.

I didn't see Ngũgĩ for quite some time after that, but I was delighted when he left the country and didn't come back in 1982 since the darkened days of Moi had already set in, and I was sure that my former professor wouldn't have survived if he had returned to Kenya.

14

'Professor, You are in Ngũgĩ's Book'

Rhonda Cobham-Sander with Reinhard Sander

Once or twice a year, an enthusiastic student will launch herself breathlessly through a door to inform one or other of us that she has discovered our names in the preface to Ngũgĩ's *Decolonising the Mind*. It's always amusing that such students seem to think they are telling us something we don't know, but also a pleasure to be reminded of how our lives became intertwined with Ngũgĩ's, especially between 1982, when the writer was forced into exile, and 1993, when he took up a permanent academic position at New York University. When a writer achieves the kind of status Ngũgĩ now enjoys, it's easy to forget how tenuous their intellectual and personal survival once may have seemed. Those struggles and the people and institutions that provided assistance, help shape a writer's work. As Ngũgĩ's generous acknowledgements in the preface to *Decolonising the Mind* remind us, 'any work, even a literary creative work, is not the result of individual genius but the result of collective effort. There are so many inputs in the actual formation of an image, an idea. The very words we use are a product of a collective history' (x–xi). In mapping the moments when our lives intersected with Ngũgĩ's during his years of exile, we hope to provide some insight into how those scattered encounters enriched us all.

Reinhard's friendship with Ngũgĩ dates back to the early 1970s, when Ngũgĩ spent a year at Northwestern University. Between 1967 and 1969, while Ngũgĩ was a lecturer in English at the University of Kenya at Nairobi, he had proposed the abolition of Nairobi's English Department, and in 1970 the University changed its name and scope from the Department of English to the Department of African Literature and Languages. By 1969, however, Ngũgĩ had resigned from the university in protest over violations of academic freedom (see Sander and Lindfors xix). At that point, he had published three novels – *Weep Not, Child* (1964), *The River Between* (1965) and *A Grain of Wheat* (1967) – and had established an international reputation in Africa, Britain and the British Commonwealth. A 1969–70 fellowship at Makerere and a 1970–71 visiting appointment at Northwestern University in Illinois provided him with funding and space to write at a moment of significant professional vulnerability.

Ngugi's welcome at Northwestern and Texas Southern was no accident, for as Martha Biondi has argued in *Black Revolution on Campus,* students at both these universities had been at the forefront of Black radical activism in the late

1960s. At Northwestern, Ngugi was one of a procession of Black intellectuals brought to campus between 1968 and 1982 in response to student demands for the creation of a Black Studies department. They included the Trinidadian intellectual C. L. R. James, the Guyanese novelist Jan Carew, and the African American journalist Lerone Bennett (Biondi 65–83). At Texas Southern, Biondi notes, student protests in 1967 culminated in a massive police assault and the arrest of nearly 500 students (29). The brutal response to radicalized students at this historically Black University (HBCU) had raised awareness of Pan-African cultural and political struggles around the world.

The Northwestern location also allowed Ngũgĩ to extend the audience for his work at a time when American readers were beginning to take note of African writing. In 1970, Reinhard, Ian Munro, and Richard Priebe signed on as the first three doctoral students to conduct research on African, African American and Caribbean literatures with Bernth Lindfors, then a freshly minted assistant professor at the University of Texas, Austin. When Robert Wren, who taught African Literature at the University of Houston, invited Ngũgĩ to lecture at Rice University in Houston, and Texas Southern University in 1971, Reinhard and Ian made the trip to Texas Southern to interview Ngũgĩ.

Ngũgĩ's 1973 interview with Sander and Munro provides one of the earliest comprehensive accounts of how Ngũgĩ's thinking about literature, language, and history was evolving. In the interview, Ngũgĩ explains how his views on the anti-colonial Mau Mau rebellion, which as late as the 1967 publication of *A Grain of Wheat* appear ambivalent, at best, had begun to shift. At the time, Ngũgĩ was working on the manuscript of *Petals of Blood,* the book many consider his most important work of fiction in English. Yet already in the 1971 interview he voices reservations about continuing to write in English, declaring that he felt he had 'reached a point of crisis' as an Anglophone African writer. The interviewers also provided Ngũgĩ with a platform to talk about Caribbean influences on his work. Ngũgĩ had begun graduate work in Caribbean and African writing under the supervision of Arthur Ravenscroft during an earlier stint at Leeds University, but he had abandoned that track to concentrate on completing *A Grain of Wheat*. However, this immersion in Caribbean literature informs several of the essays collected in *Homecoming*, which he worked on during his fellowship year at Makerere and George Lamming figures prominently in the 1971 interview as a source of political and aesthetic inspiration for what would eventually become *Petals of Blood*.

By the time he returned to Kenya in 1972, Ngũgĩ's political fortunes had once more shifted. He resumed work at the University of Nairobi, arriving in time to put the finishing touches to the newly revised literature curriculum. In 1973 he was promoted to chair of the new department and began work with Mĩcere Mũgo on the play *The Trial of Dedan Kimathi*. By 1976 he had founded Kamĩrĩĩthũ Community Education and Cultural Centre and begun working with the community on the script of *Ngaahika Ndeenda* ('I Will Marry When I Want'). *Petals of Blood,* which was to be his final novel in English, was published in Nairobi in 1977. With its many pop culture references and fierce critique of what Ngũgĩ, following Cabral, now referred to as the 'comprador class' it openly attacked the nationalist government. Yet it was hailed as a literary achievement by many educated Kenyans, including several in Kenyatta's party. By contrast, *Ngaahika Ndeenda*, with its less overtly political themes, threatened Kenyatta's government more directly because it was produced in collaboration with the Kamĩrĩĩthũ villagers and performed and published in Gĩkũyũ. It thus reached a much broader audience than Ngũgĩ's English plays or novels. By late 1977 Kenyatta's government had had enough and moved to detain Ngũgĩ at Kamiti maximum security prison.

Reinhard and I, both based in England by 1978, soon were caught up in the wave of international protests with which the Kenyan government's action was greeted. Reinhard's students at Sussex University mounted a production of Ngũgĩ's co-authored play, *The Trial of Dedan Kimathi,* which they took on the road to other universities to raise awareness about Ngũgĩ's detention. I was part of the London group associated with John La Rose's New Beacon bookshop and members of Amnesty International that demonstrated persistently outside the Kenyan embassy. Bowing to international pressure, Daniel arap Moi, who took over the Kenyan presidency after Kenyatta's death in 1978, made it one of his first items of business to release Kenya's best-known writer from detention. When Ngũgĩ was freed on my birthday, December 12th, the news felt like a special gift.

For Ngũgĩ, though, the difficult years were just beginning. By the early 1980s he had once more fallen out of favor with the Kenyan government. Despite run-ins with the government and death threats to his family, he continued work on an initiative to revise Kikuyu orthography, published his prison memoir, and completed work on *Caitaani Mũtharaba-inĩ* ('Devil on the Cross'). However, in 1982 he was denied permission to stage a new collaboratively produced play, *Maitũ Njugĩra* and the government shut down all theaters in the region around Kamĩrĩĩthũ. During a visit to Britain in 1982 to launch the English editions of *Devil on the Cross* and *I will Marry When I Want,* a failed coup against Moi heightened political tensions in Kenya, and Ngũgĩ chose to remain in exile in London. He left behind the comfortable home he had built following Kikuyu architectural principles, a well-paying job as Chair of the Department of Literature at the University of Nairobi, a wife, and seven children. Over the next fifteen years, as he was separated from his family, stripped of his Kenyan passport and deprived of a full-time job, Ngũgĩ became a peripatetic figure. It was during this period that he re-entered our lives.

In 1980, Reinhard and I moved to the University of Bayreuth in Southern Germany, which had been designated a center for African Studies by the

German Research Foundation (DFG). As Germany's newest university, Bayreuth sought to distinguish itself from the more established centers of African Studies, which emphasized African archaeology, philology and anthropology. Researchers at Bayreuth focused on modern African sociology, philosophy, art, music, urban studies, and postcolonial literature – fields so new within the German academy that most of the scholars brought in to staff the project had been trained outside of the country. With its rich international networks and generous funding, Bayreuth quickly became a major hub of African research, providing numerous opportunities for African scholars and artists to spend extended periods of time there, researching, writing and inter-acting with their hosts and the other guests.

In early 1984, Ngũgĩ accepted a semester-long position in Bayreuth, arranged by Reinhard. We found him a sabbatical rental across the street from our house in the village of St Johannis, on the outskirts of Bayreuth. We shared our meals with him, our cars, our friends, our nights on the town and the distractions provided by our two-year-old daughter, Petra. Once, when I apologized to Ngũgĩ for one such distraction he assured me that children's voices had been the constant backdrop for his writing in Kenya and the sounds he missed most while in solitary confinement. Those sounds, he claimed, now actually helped him to write. His words confronted me directly with one of the more painful costs of exile.

In his preface to *Decolonising the Mind*, Ngũgĩ has described how he reworked several of the essays in that collection during his time with us in St Johannis. The ideas that went into the essays had been percolating for many years – some dated back to that early interview with Reinhard in Texas – and earlier versions had circulated in previous collections and lectures. The Bayreuth sojourn provided a tranquil base from which to revise the essays and to try them out in various venues before publication. Ngũgĩ's acknowledge-ments provide a glimpse of the 'cosy and stimulating intellectual atmosphere' in which those revisions took place. Each day's writing brought to the fore some central idea with which he was grappling and each evening provided an opportunity for spirited discussion over dinner or drinks that unpacked them.

One particularly rambunctious debate took place at our local St Johannis watering hole. Ngũgĩ's housemate, the Senegalese philosopher Bachir Diagne, had put forward the proposition that there were such things as universal values, which made certain practices inherently abhorrent from any cultural vantage point. He took as his example the practice of female circumcision, which he considered an act of unrelieved barbarism. The author of *The River Between* begged to differ – not in order to defend clitoridectomy, but to challenge the premise on which Diagne based his claim of universality, especially when, as had happened in colonial Kenya, one culture's act of barbarism became the pretext for another culture's equally barbarous acts of domination. As the beer flowed, the debate raged for what seemed like hours and I've often wondered what the German villagers around us made of it all.

Ngũgĩ's willingness at this remove from the publication of *The River Between* to re-engage such a controversial topic dramatizes a familiar dilemma in postcolonial studies. As Spivak points out in her well-known essay 'Can the Subaltern Speak?', control over women's bodies has often been a way for male nationalists to thrash out their differences with their colonial oppressors. But that strategy leaves women unrepresented in the very discourse that names their bodies as sites of contestation. Ngũgĩ was not unaware of this paradox, which he highlights in *The River Between* when the Christianized character, Muthoni, chooses genital mutilation as a way to reaffirm her Kikuyu identity but dies as a result of having done so. In his critical writing, however, Ngũgĩ found it harder to balance those contradictions, and in *Decolonising the Mind* he reflects on imperialism's selective focus on African cultural practices that support its claim that Africans are barbarous primitives while ignoring all other aspect of the colonized people's culture – a strategy he labels a 'cultural bomb':

> The effect of a cultural bomb is to annihilate people's belief in their names, in their languages. In their capacities and ultimately in themselves … It makes them see their past as one wasteland of non-achievement and it makes them want to distance themselves from that wasteland. It makes them want to iden-tify with that which is furthest removed from themselves; for instance, with other people's languages rather than their own. (*Decolonising* 3)

The villages around Bayreuth provided Ngũgĩ with an unlikely connection to home. By this time, he was no longer composing literary works in English and his base outside an English-speaking environment may have helped advance that project. Nevertheless, he sorely missed being surrounded by the sound of the Gĩkũyũ language. To compensate, Ngũgĩ devoured the sounds of the languages around him. Although he understood neither German nor the Oberfranken dialect spoken in the villages around Bayreuth, he was intrigued by the stories about the local culture that we translated for him and he pounced upon any cultural convergences with Kamĩrĩĩthũ that he thought he divined. Not surprisingly, he also found ways to communicate directly with the locals over the flagons of beer so common in both Kenyan and German vil-lages. Many an early summer evening ended, with him swaying along, *krug* in hand, to the German folk songs at a nearby *biergarten*, serendipitously named Kamerun, after the West African state.

After Ngũgĩ left Bayreuth he arranged for us to host his eldest son, Thiong'o wa Ngũgĩ, who was just getting ready to start college. At the time, Ngũgĩ's books were banned in Kenya and his wife and children were subject to con-stant harassment. The prospects of Thiong'o being admitted to a University in Kenya seemed pretty slim and his father thought he might be better off attending university abroad. International campaigns in support of political detainees can transform them into saints or romantic heroes, but it was a source of persistent distress to Ngũgĩ that he had been unable to protect the son who carried his name from the inferno of hostility that his political stances had ignited in Kenya. During the six weeks in 1983 that Thiong'o spent living with us and attending German language classes, I got a glimpse into the grim realities of what detention and exile actually meant for children affected by their parents' political decisions. Thiong'o talked about what it had felt like at 14 years to suddenly lose access not just to his father, but also to the kinds of creature comforts most children of academics take for granted – food on the table; reliable transportation; unfettered access to the homes of other university children; visits from writers and intellectuals from around the world whose conversation sparked curiosity and enlightenment; cordial relations with adults in high places who valued a parent's scholarly or creative work.

Thiong'o eventually adopted the sobriquet Tee Ngũgĩ, to mitigate the hostility to which his infamous name exposed him, and he has since written about his early memories of his father in many of his journalistic articles, including one about a trip he made into the Kenyan countryside with Ngũgĩ and Chinua Achebe. When his father disappeared, many of these privileges disappeared as well and it was years before he managed to overcome his sense of loss. His experience made me wonder how my toddler daughter, who already took that world of writers and intellectual exchange for granted, would fare if the accidents of life ever placed her in a similar position. Germany, however, was not the respite for Thiong'o that it had been for his father. The only thing that connected their experiences was that he, too, seemed to feel most comfortable and safe while interacting with our daughter. Perhaps she reminded him of the siblings he missed. When we visited Kenya a year later, Petra's dogged insistence on visiting her 'big brother' brought a smile to Thiong'o's guarded face. I remember he gave her one of those little wire figures Kenyan children often make and use as toys and she kept it for many years.

The next time Ngũgĩ was our guest was in 1991, when he interrupted a 1990–92 visiting appointment at Yale to spend a semester as a Five College professor in Amherst, Massachusetts, where we now were based. Once again, he relied on us to arrange his housing and transport and, once again, his creative process was influenced by the circle of colleagues and friends into which we welcomed him. That semester, Reinhard, then based at Amherst College, Samba Gadjigo of Mount Holyoke College, and Ralph Faulkingham, of the University of Massachusetts at Amherst persuaded the Senegalese filmmaker Sembene Ousmane to come to the Five Colleges for a two-week residency. Sembene had turned down previous invitations to America, partly because he spoke no English, but also as a symbolic protest against American imperialism in Africa and elsewhere. His visit to the Five Colleges helped soften that position by introducing him to a circle of academics and political activists who shared his views. It also allowed Ngũgĩ to spend time with one of his political and aesthetic heroes. Ngũgĩ had tried his hand at film making in Sweden in the mid-1980s. His immersion in Sembene's work during the filmmaker's residency in Amherst encouraged him once more to explore film as a creative medium, an experiment that he ultimately abandoned.

Ngũgĩ also contributed to a Five College conference organized to coincide with Sembene's visit. The essay collection that came out of the conference brought together a range of Caribbean, African, and African American scholars including Toni Cade Bambara, Earl Lovelace, John Wideman, Caryl Phillips, Pearl Primus, and Michael Thelwell. Ngũgĩ's essay summarized the main ideas in *Decolonising the Mind* tracing the worsening image of Africans in Western Literature during the course of the colonial expansion that followed the 1884 Berlin conference, not letting the Africans speak, culminating with Conrad's *Heart of Darkness* – in which the African natives are allowed a total of four words, 'Mistah Kurtz, he dead' – and ending with novels by white south Africans.

One other high point of Ngũgĩ's time in Amherst was his public appearance with the South African writer Nadine Gordimer, who was also visiting the area that semester, on the invitation of Stephen Clingman at the University of Massachusetts. Both Ngũgĩ and Gordimer were being touted that year as possible Nobel Prize recipients and the day before their public conversation was scheduled to take place Gordimer learned that she had won. Overnight, what already had been planned as a major event turned into a security nightmare, as members of the public from beyond the College community as well as journalists from across North America thronged to the Amherst campus to witness the first public appearance of the new Nobel Laureate. Gordimer, for her part, though elated by the honor, seemed slightly embarrassed to have been the writer chosen, deferring to Ngũgĩ on many occasions during their public conversation in Johnson Chapel.

In 1993, Ngũgĩ accepted a tenured position at New York University and his peripatetic existence ended. By this time, he had remarried and started a second family. The political climate also was changing and, in 2004, Ngũgĩ's Kenyan passport was restored and he was invited to return to Kenya. Finally, Ngũgĩ was able to reconnect with all his children in the community of his birth. In 2016, on a visit to Amherst, Ngũgĩ also reconnected with our daughter, Petra, and was introduced to her daughter, Leona, then about the same age Petra had been when her constant interruptions had threatened to derail the production of *Decolonising the Mind*. Life, it seemed, had come full circle.

15
Mũraata, Mũrutani, na Mũthikĩrĩria (Friend, Teacher & Listener)

Ann Biersteker

Tareke ngũkũnyire mũraata	May we talk quietly, my friend
Kuuma aagu na aagu	Since long ago
Andũ nĩ maacookanagia nduundu	People have always gathered together
Makahehanĩrĩra	To talk quietly
Makoonania njĩra	To ask one another the way
Keenyũ na keenyũ cikoyanagĩra	Our individual works together
Nda.	Make a whole.

I have enjoyed being in the classroom again after more than six years. Seminars can be very stimulating although very demanding. The students with their passionate debates, quarrels, shoutings, and arguments make me feel at home, and I begin looking forward to every seminar. But, of course, I am daily struck by the absurdity of the situation. In my own country I was banned from teaching at the university, or in any school. (Ngũgĩ wa Thiong'o, 'Life, Literature and a Longing for Home' 5)

When Ngũgĩ wa Thiong'o and I became friends, he had recently arrived as a visiting professor at Yale University. A few weeks later at a time when I was traumatized and distraught, he helped me through a very difficult period by listening, by asking thoughtful questions, by providing sensible advice, and by making me laugh. An advisee and Kiswahili teaching assistant I had recruited to Yale had murdered his former fiancée and killed himself. Then a newspaper report claimed that this happened because of a violent African language cult at Yale where I was the Director of the Program in African Languages. The Dean of Yale College decided to investigate these absurd charges, although his secretary called it 'just a routine program review'. One afternoon, shortly after we first met, Ngũgĩ stopped by the Yale Program in African Languages office and overheard me on the phone talking with a reporter and telling him his questions were racist and ethnocentric. Ngũgĩ suggested that he answer the phone for me for a while and I listened while he calmly and patiently explained to the reporter that studying African languages was a worthwhile intellectual practice and not a bizarre or threatening activity. I relaxed and laughed for the first time in a while, and I began learning about Ngũgĩ's skills in effective listening, his kindness, and his generosity.

Later over dinner, and the first of what became over a quite a few excellent meals at a wide range of downtown New Haven restaurants, Ngũgĩ listened while I talked about what had happened. I'm not sure whether it was because he had not known the young people who died, or because he was temporarily at Yale and I could hence talk to him about things that I knew in confidence, or because of how he listened, but I immediately knew that I could trust and confide in Ngũgĩ and rely on his advice. I had a support community but there was so much that I could not tell them because of my concerns about confidentially and my commitment to supporting them through their trauma or my concern about how they would react. But I could tell Ngũgĩ everything about my grief, sorrow, anger, and confusion.

Although I had met Ngũgĩ only a few weeks earlier, I had, of course, known about him for all of my adult life and he had already had a significant impact on me. My English students in 1969 and 1970 at what was then Kenyatta College had persuaded me to read his novels and the changes that he made in the literature curriculum at the University of Nairobi turned me from a teacher of Shakespeare to a teacher of developing drama from oral narratives. When I heard that he was coming to Yale, I had written him a letter in Gĩkũyũ with the help of Kimani Njogu who was then a PhD student in linguistics at Yale.

Then the three of us (Athman Lali Omar, who was then an MA student at Yale, Kimani, and I) invited him for dinner at my apartment. Athman made chapati, we roasted goat meat, and I made *irio* and *kachumbari*. None of us had met him earlier and we were all anxious about meeting with him and concerned about what meeting him would mean for our lives in Kenya. But we so wanted to meet him and to welcome him to Yale and to New Haven. It was the first of many most enjoyable dinner parties.

At that time newspapers were not available online and it took two weeks for *The Nation* and *Standard* to arrive in Sterling Library from Kenya. One weekend Ngũgĩ came to a dinner party at my house from the library and told us that he had read in one of the papers that two weeks earlier he had been training rebels in Sudan with funding provided by Muammar Gaddafi! We all burst out laughing. Not just because of the ridiculousness of imagining our friend and colleague, the writer and scholar, as a military leader, but because we knew that two weeks earlier we had all been together in New Haven at a similar dinner at my house. Were we the rebels he had been training? Did he have a double or twin? The absurdity of the Moi government and the credulity of the Kenyan press were troubling, but the opportunities that the story provided for wild speculation were delightful!

During that semester Ngũgĩ also gave a talk at University of California-Berkeley where he mentioned that he did not himself have a copy of the Gĩkũyũ original of *Matigari ma Njirũũngi*, which at the time was banned in Kenya. After the talk, a Kenyan audience member approached him and told

him that he had a copy! Before he left Berkeley, Ngũgĩ had made his own copy
of the book and he came back to New Haven where we also made more copies.
Those copies were the basis for my work and that of Kimani Njogu and Gĩtahi
Gĩtĩtĩ on *Matigari ma Njirũũngi*. It would be years before any of us would be
able to purchase copies of the book.

Ngũgĩ's academic work with me at Yale also included serving as joint advi-
sors to Peggy King on her MA thesis in African studies. Peggy had served in the
Peace Corps in coastal Kenya. Her thesis was a study of Giriama resistance to
colonialism and was based upon her extensive archival and field research. She
was committed to writing a historical narrative that was based upon the narratives of ordinary people. She was also determined to write a work that could
be read by those she had interviewed in coastal Kenya. I remember Ngũgĩ's
detailed comments that helped Peggy draw together her narrative strands. It
was an impressive thesis and the first Yale thesis written in Kiswahili.

Ngũgĩ and I usually spoke in English, although when with Athman and
Kimani we often spoke in Kiswahili. My skills in Kiswahili have remained
high since 1983 when I first taught it in Kenya to groups of American students.
I began learning Gĩkũyũ when first in Kenya and then studied Gĩkũyũ and
Kĩembu for a year before beginning my dissertation work on tense and aspect
in Embu tales. During my field research and my dissertation work, my comprehension skills in Kĩembu became reasonable. My reading skill in Gĩkũyũ
improved as I wrote about and translated the novels of Gakaara wa Wanjaũ,
but my conversational skills remained weak.

When we began the initial work on the journal *Mũtiiri*, we agreed that we
(Ngũgĩ, Kimani, Gĩtahi Gĩtĩtĩ and I) would hold our discussions about the journal in Gĩkũyũ. It was a privilege for me to be working with these three most
brilliant scholars and wonderful teachers of Gĩkũyũ, but it was also sometimes
physically painful. My skills in the language improved greatly, but my struggle
to understand intellectual discussions far above my comprehension level often
resulted in headaches.

The article that I eventually published in *Mũtiiri*, a bibliography of publications in and about Gĩkũyũ, should have been listed as a joint publication as
Ngũgĩ wrote many of the headings and approved all of them. We discussed
the headings at length and I learned a great deal from these discussions. In a
few cases, I made preliminary suggestions but he generally rejected these and
kindly explained in detail why and how they needed to be revised. Some headings such as '*Ng'ano Nguhĩ*'/ 'Short Fiction' and '*Ng'ano Ndaaya*'/ 'Novels' were
easy but many others such as '*Ihumo na Makuhĩhia*'/ 'Bibliographic Sources'
and '*Afya na Maisha ma Mũngĩ*'/ 'Health and Home Economics' required
insights into the language that were far above my skill set. Our difficulties are
apparent in the difference between the title on the title page of the article,
'*Mũtaratara wa Mabuku marĩa Maandĩkĩĩtwo kana Gũtaũrwo na Gĩĩgĩkũyũ*'/

'A List of the Books That Were Written in or Translated into *Gĩgĩkũyũ*' and the title on the table of contents, '*Mbimbiriongirafia*'/ 'A Bibliography'.

A number of colleagues assumed that I had something to do with inviting Ngũgĩ to Yale. It was a reasonable assumption, but nothing could have been further from the truth. Michael Cooke of the Yale English Department invited him. My status at Yale, where I was then an untenured assistant professor in Linguistics and African American and African Studies, meant I could not have had a role in inviting a distinguished writer to Yale. Some years earlier, before I arrived at the University, Henry Louis Gates had invited Wole Soyinka to Yale where he staged the premiere of *A Play of Giants*. When I arrived at Yale, I was given an office in the basement of a College Street building, then the home of African-American Studies. It was a tiny room, perhaps eight by five feet, with a little grimy window that opened on to an outside staircase to the basement. It had a table, a chair, and a word processor but no bookcase, no filing cabinet and no heat. Still I was thrilled, but at the same time appalled, to have this workspace when I learned that it had been Wole Soyinka's office a few years earlier.

Ngũgĩ was much more fortunate in the office space with which he was provided than Soyinka had been. He taught in the center of a beautiful top floor library. There were comfortable chairs, appropriate lighting, and a beautiful carpet on the floor. His office was clean, well heated, and had tasteful and appropriate office furniture. The building had carpeting, drapes, and an elevator; all amenities lacking in the dingy and moldy spaces where I worked. With Ngũgĩ's arrival, I began to see the other Yale, that of prestigious departments such as Comparative Literature and English.

During his first year at Yale, I often sat in on Ngũgĩ's insightful lectures. I was most impressed by his skills as a lecturer and his insights as a teacher as well as by his patience with even the most trying of students. His discussion of his works, especially *Caitaani Mūtharaba-inĩ* and *Petals of Blood,* greatly informed my subsequent re-reading and discussions of his works in my own classes.

Ngũgĩ also honored me with introductions to his delightful wife, Njeeri, to two of his closest friends and to two of his children (Thiong'o, who completed the MA in African studies at Yale, and Wanjiku). As I recall, the first time that I met Ngũgĩ we talked about Abdilatif Abdalla and his poetry and the fact that they had both been held in Kamiti Prison. Ngũgĩ also mentioned their on-going political work in London. He later arranged for me to meet with Abdilatif in London in 1990 and he helped me arrange for the latter's subsequent visits to New Haven. He also shared their joint publications with me, including *Struggle for Democracy in Kenya* (published in 1988 by the United Movement for Democracy in Kenya – UMOJA). This collection of documents includes Abdilatif's poem, 'Peace, Love and Unity: For Whom?' a poem I then memorized so as to be able to recite it to friends in Kenya.

Subsequently, the late Ngũgĩ wa Mĩriĩ, who was living in exile in Zimbabwe, visited Ngũgĩ in New Haven while on a tour of the U.S.A. and Canada where he was organizing community theater projects to help communities deal with the crack cocaine epidemic. We tried to arrange for him to do a project in New Haven, but, unfortunately, we did not have enough time to do so. Those of us in African languages were thrilled and honored when Ngũgĩ wa Mĩriĩ and Ngũgĩ wa Thiong'o both visited the performances of our students' end of the year skits in African languages.

Shortly after I arrived at the January, 2000 conference, 'Against All Odds: African Languages and Literatures into the 21st Century' in Asmara (a conference co-organized by Ngũgĩ), I learned that the tribute to the late Mwalimu Julius Nyerere that I had suggested would take place and that my name was on the program between those of Ngũgĩ and Abdilatif. Despite jet lag, I remembered some lines from a poem that Mwalimu Nyerere wrote and I composed a tribute that I think was successful although, of course, not as impressive as those that preceded and followed.

With poetry readings every day and wonderful trips in and around Asmara, this was for me the most enjoyable conference I have ever attended. The highlight of the conference was the production in Tigrinya of *Ngaahika Ndeenda*. Although I had read the play in Gĩkũyũ, and in Kiswahili and English translations, and had taught the play in the Kiswahili and English translations, I had never had an opportunity to see a production. This was a superb production in the national theater before a large and enthusiastic audience. I do not understand any Tigrinya but I understood the performance completely. At the end of the play to thunderous applause, Ngũgĩ and Njeeri joined the cast on stage and danced with them. His sheer joy was evident in his movements and in his tremendous smile.

16
Fear & Trepidation in Asmara: Meeting Ngũgĩ

Jane Plastow

When I first met Ngũgĩ in January 2000, in Africa's most beautiful capital city of Asmara, Eritrea, he had long been for me a beneficent but slightly terrifying haunting. Given that the core of my academic research has been on East African theatre I could hardly avoid making Ngũgĩ's work in Kamĩrĩĩthũ a central point of reference. When I began working in the late 1980s for a PhD on political theatre in Africa – from a position of considerable ignorance – I remember Martin Banham, the then font of all wisdom on African theatre in England, most kindly telling me that I really should read Ngũgĩ's *Decolonising the Mind*. I can no longer recollect the order, but over the following years, I would read the novels, the plays and much of the polemic, and then begin to teach them; engaging with the restless intelligence that constantly sought new forms to express ever more accurately the history of the multiple on-going oppressions of the African everyman, by both black and white, of the capitalist, Christian establishment. I was also humbled by knowledge of the price Ngũgĩ had paid for his integrity, from the minor loss of western critical approbation when he turned his back on the well-made novel, to the major traumas of imprisonment without trial, enforced exile and the abuse of members of his family.

When I went to the University of Leeds in 1994 to teach in the Workshop Theatre of the School of English, I found Ngũgĩ had preceded me, having enrolled a couple of decades earlier on an MA he never completed because he had been preoccupied with finishing the novel *A Grain of Wheat*. He was beneficent because I agreed so strongly with much, though not all, of his political analysis, and because he wrote and engaged with life and people with such artistry and passion. He was slightly terrifying because of all the opprobrium he poured on white people working in Africa and on the comfortable middle-classes. I was undeniably a member of both groups.

What I could not have then known was that at the same time I was reading Ngũgĩ he was also becoming a favourite author of an Eritrean freedom fighter named Alemseged Tesfai, a *tegadalai* (freedom fighter) living in the northern mountains on little more than bread and lentils. Alemseged was a trained lawyer who had given up PhD studies in America in 1975 to spend sixteen years fighting for the freedom of his small nation from Ethiopian colonization. As one of a tiny number of highly educated Eritreans at the time, Alemseged was deployed first to help develop the revolutionary schools the Eritrean Peoples' Liberation Front (EPLF) ran in liberated areas of the country in the 1970s, and then, in the 1980s, to work on developing theatre among the network of Cultural Troupes. The extraordinary story of a decades' worth of intensive cultural work carried out at every level of the EPLF from platoon to central organization and from disabled fighters to prisoners of war, has been written about elsewhere (Plastow 1997, 1999, 2016, Matzke 2003, Warwick 1997). The troupes generally mounted variety style performances, and in the early days theatre was usually limited to short comic skits, but Alemseged wanted something much richer for his people. In the coming years he would write the first Eritrean guide to theatre, a mimeographed book for the guidance of would-be playmakers, simply entitled 'Drama' (1983); he would also write three plays of his own that went on tour for months to inspire the struggle and support women's emancipation. In preparation for this writing and instruction Alemseged read voraciously the work of whatever playwrights he could lay his hands on in the trenches of the northern Eritrean mountain fastness. Possibly the most influential was the work of Ngũgĩ wa Thiong'o with its clear socialist analysis, its peasant perspective, and its message of hope in face of great adversity. All these chimed with EPLF political views.

In 1991 Eritrea won its independence and Alemseged was influential in inviting international intellectuals and artists to visit his country to share their knowledge and skills with his people. We became friends and I was lucky enough to be one of those asked to visit. This led to a partnership that saw me spending much time in the country in the 1990s, running theatre training and making plays. I was, however, in Leeds when I got an email from Alemseged in 1999 asking if I would be interested in working on a play for the millennium, to be mounted in conjunction with a major international conference, 'Against All Odds: African Languages and Literatures into the 21st Century'. The play we were to put on was Alemseged's own Tigrinya translation of Ngũgĩ's *I Will Marry When I Want*. Was I interested? Of course, I was. Eritrea had become the country of my heart and Ngũgĩ was still the major socialist playwright of the region. There was a little hiccup while the government discussed whether I was African enough to be allowed to take on the director's mantle, but thanks, I think, primarily to having a half-African son, a decision was made in my favour. I and leading Eritrean director Mesgun Zerai, known universally as 'Wad Faradai', would co-direct, with Alemseged in the background as script consultant and advisor. I can't remember when I found out that Ngũgĩ was to be at the conference and would be at our premiere, but I do recall thinking that I would seek to keep a very low profile and if my white, middle-class presence was too offensive, I would make a quick exit after the show.

There was some discussion of just where we would stage *I Will Marry* and consideration was given to my suggestion that we might play it in an open, peoples' space, but that was never really going to happen. Cinema Asmara has, since it was built by Italian colonial architect Odoardo Cavagnari in 1918, been the de facto national theatre of Eritrea. In 2000 its renaissance nymphs still danced across the ceiling, its pink plush seating still rose in three curving tiered balcony levels and the heavy wooden foyer doors still sternly announced *Ingresso* and *Exgresso* – not that anyone paid any attention. There were a few drawbacks to working in this glorious, historic pile. The old-fashioned, high, narrow stage was not only antipathetic to the community-inclusiveness of Ngũgĩ's text, it was also crumbling at its front edge. The only way that actors could cross backstage was by physically leaving the building and running around outside as the backstage space was rammed with the decaying detritus of a thousand past performances. Then there was the matter of the toilets. By this time, I had been working in and around Cinema Asmara for nearly a decade and in all that time the toilets, situated either side of the main stage, had given out such a reek that I had never investigated their interior. So, I asked that if we were to make the play in Cinema Asmara please could the stage be repaired and access provided from the auditorium, the backstage cleared so that actors could traverse it, and those toilets be cleansed of their noisome smell. All was agreed, plus some extra titivations. I was particularly happy that our performance would be adding a new layer to the historical palimpsest represented by this building that had originally been open only to white people under the fascist rule of Italian colonization and was now finally free to put on theatre advocating the overthrow of both imperialism and capitalism.

Ngũgĩ's theatre has been marginalized, overlooked and by implication somewhat derided in the mass of critical literature on his writing. *I Will Marry* was of course not a single-authored piece but was co-created over six months with some 200 people in the community of Kamĩrĩĩthũ, and that creation process took place in Gĩkũyũ, so the English language text Alemseged worked from would necessarily have lost some of its linguistically situated piquancy and bite. It is not a piece of literary drama, which is where the literary critics have struggled in knowing how to discuss the play. It is undoubtedly polemical and some of the speeches of socialist analysis are long and tendentious. But I was interested to see how we could make it work as a performance piece. We did make a number of cuts. Some of those nomologic speeches were just too long and undramatic. We also had to have some very interesting conversations about how to deal with Ngũgĩ's persistent condemnation of Christianity. The problem was that while Ngũgĩ saw Christianity as part of the colonial-capitalist project of brainwashing Kenyans, in Eritrea the faith had a far longer indigenous history dating back to the 4th century. A strong Christian belief, channelled through the Eritrean Orthodox Church, is a deeply rooted aspect of the identity of nearly half of all Eritreans. We cut quite a chunk of the religious invective and for the rest came up with a solution that made me uneasy but worked for my collaborators. The Jehovah's' Witness movement has quite a strong minority foothold in major Eritrean towns, but their refusal to take part in obligatory national military service has made them an object of opprobrium for the Eritrean state and many have suffered significant persecution. In our version of *I Will Marry* the ridiculous, pompous, self-serving evangelists would be represented as believers in this church.

These were relatively minor problems. What was engaging me as a director was what would happen when we started to wake up the sleeping beauty of the text and put it on its feet. And this was when I found that, as for so many playwrights who work with performance and performers, and not in the isolation of the private study, a play that looked lumpy on the page began to work brilliantly when it was embodied. *I Will Marry* is half way to a musical – indeed the work that followed, *Mother, Sing for Me* was a full musical treatment. It comes to life in the imaginations of Kiguunda and Wangeci as they remember their personal and cultural past. This was a wonderful opportunity for us to profile the dance cultures of some of Eritrea's nine ethnic groups; a concept that could be 'read' easily by an audience used to performances by the EPLF Cultural Troupes that had invoked the song and dance of all the ethnicities in their variety shows in order to challenge colonial concepts of divide and rule with their central message of 'Unity in Diversity'.

I was also delighted to find considerable performance within the play. We staged the early confrontation between Kiguunda and the evangelicals by means of their parading, singing, down the central aisle of the theatre and disturbing the protagonist at his rest. The ensuing exchange led to the first of many bouts of hilarity. I think my favourite scene was the performance in Act Two of the central couples' Christian wedding day, where the absurdity of this long 'traditionally' married couple being coerced into an alien ceremony is beautifully undercut by the private comments between husband and wife on the hypocrisy of the guests imposed upon them by their rich, apparent patrons, the Kiois.

Inter-cultural translation is of course never simply linguistic. Besides our problems over interpretations of Christianity, our actors had considerable difficulty in understanding some of the behaviours of the Kiois. The cast were ex-*tegadelai* raised in the culture of sharing the very little that they had, nearly all of which had been distributed by the EPLF rather than earned in any capitalist sense. Very modest wages only appeared after independence for these performers who were still all employees of the liberation forces turned government. They therefore found it really difficult to understand why the rich Kiois should despise their neighbours simply on account of their poverty. We also had some problems in dressing the set. The houses of the opposing couples were merely suggested in the stage design, but for the dinner scene at the Kiois, we did need to evoke a relatively rich environment. To help us I asked the cast if they could bring items such as a water jug, glasses, table cloth, etc., to dress the stage. People were happy to help, and the next day I was offered bright plastic jugs and mugs and bowls. No-one in my cast of some 70 actors had any idea of what the home of a nouveau riche Kenyan capitalist might look like.

Our version of *I Will Marry When I Want* sought to envelop the audience in spectacle, music and dance, to bring them into the world of the play as Christians danced in the aisles, trumpeters played from the balconies and for the finale the cast filled the auditorium. But, as I and Wad Faradai were hauled on stage as the cast took their final bows, I wondered – where was Ngũgĩ? What did he think? Did I need to scuttle away? How fierce a critic was this fervent socialist Africanist champion going to be? It was a gala event, with an audience of the great and good in African literature. They'd been busy for some days with the conference while we'd been holed up in the theatre. But really, I was only worried about the one man. Then someone, maybe it was Alemseged, introduced me to this gently beaming, slightly stooped and quietly spoken man. He was saying nice things. He was smiling. Ngũgĩ thought we'd done fine. I think I only heard the words gradually.

As a champion of African language literatures, Ngũgĩ was likely to favour the idea of a Tigrinya version of his play. Though in Eritrea this was only to be expected. All plays are put on in local languages; no-one would dream of doing anything else. I remember that what struck me as I heard him talking was how he said he thought we must understand the mannerisms of Gĩkũyũ women because our actress who played Wangeci so incarnated what he thought of as typical gestures of the women with whom he first created the play. Nothing could have been further from the truth. Our version of *I Will Marry* was, apart from me, an exclusively Eritrean affair, the gestures being used were those of Eritrean peasant women. I have no idea whether this is some kind of pan-African embodiment, but it was a happy coincidence. Of course, Ngũgĩ could not understand the language of the production – neither could I – my Tigrinya is minimal and we had worked through a process of mixed showing rather than telling and by comparing of the English and Tigrinya scripts. He did, however, approve of the aesthetic of our show, and his praise was generous in the extreme.

So, it was that in the end I discovered that that fiery figure who had haunted me, had been a mere figment of an ignorant imagination; in person, Ngũgĩ the polemicist, was the most generous person. Since our meeting in Asmara, Ngũgĩ and I have met in England a couple of times – first, on the occasion of the University of Leeds honouring their alumni with an honorary doctorate in 2004, and then in 2012 When Ngũgĩ kindly agreed to come and give the annual lecture for the Leeds University Centre for African Studies, of which I was that time director. The latter was a visit I remember with special affection, for we had time to sit and chat, as our sons simultaneously made friends with each other. Ngũgĩ has a long-time affection for Leeds born of his time as an MA student, so it was lovely to sit and talk of his memories. But we also spoke of future plans. For some years now, we have been mulling over a desire to stage that other play – the one that never got a proper outing because of the draconian tyranny of the government of Daniel arap Moi. I am hoping that *Mother, Sing for Me* might soon, finally, get to be performed in the place where it belongs, the National Theatre of Kenya.

17
Ngũgĩ wa Thiong'o: A True Story

Grant Farred

This story, let us call it a 'story' only because I can think of no better term, has no proper beginning. Whether or not it has proper ending, well, that is a matter that has not yet been decided. Let us try for a beginning, then.

My colleague in the Program in Literature at Duke University, V. Y. Mudimbe, invited Ngũgĩ wa Thiong'o to present a series of lectures at our institution. On one of these afternoons, a couple of hours before he was scheduled to deliver his talk, I spotted Ngũgĩ on an East Campus bench, enjoying the warm Durham sunshine. I walked over to him, introduced myself, and proceeded to tell my story. He smiled, good naturedly; in his modesty, however, he scoffed at my account.

'I'll bring you a book tomorrow,' I said, 'to show you that it's true.' My promise of proof, in hindsight, is more like an ending – an ending of sorts, anyway – than a beginning.

So, let me try again.

It wasn't until I was in 'Standard Nine' (today it would be called 'Eleventh Grade' in South Africa, the equivalent of being a high school 'Junior' in the US) at Livingstone High School in Cape Town, a school designated for Coloureds only, that I first read any South African literature. Other, that is, than Alan Paton's *Cry, the Beloved Country*, which I'd picked off the shelves of my local library. Livingstone H.S., I should be clear, was a singular institutional animal in apartheid South Africa. The teachers, for the most part, were incredibly committed, no matter their race. Livingstone H.S. was a school that prided itself on educating its student body in two senses of the term: it taught the apartheid curriculum as rigorously as though us Coloured boys and girls were being instructed by Plato in Athens, no matter the discrepancy in resources, no matter the ideological strictures imposed by the apartheid regime's educational arm. (I should say, there were other schools such as Livingstone, Trafalgar and South Peninsula foremost among them. But Livingstone had one distinct advantage.) And, Livingstone's political and philosophical ethos was steeped in Marxist thought, most notably the work of Leon Trotsky. These two strains of thought emanated from the school's most esteemed graduate and its vice-principal, Richard Owen Dudley, a man possessed of a towering intellect, a man who read voluminously. His archive included the work of C. L. R. James, Raymond Williams, Marx, E. P. Thompson, and Trotsky, of course.

One of my Standard Nine colleagues recommended J. M. Coetzee's *The Life and Times of Michael K*. I read it, liked it (Coetzee has an eye and an ear for the outsider, for those who make a life on the far fringes of society, nowhere more so, of course, than *Waiting for the Barbarians*), but never followed up.

Not bad for a beginning, but now, having committed it to paper, it strikes me more as a bare alpha in need of a bridge to the omega. That is, a thread that connects Coetzee, Livingstone and Dudley to Ngũgĩ on an East Campus bench on a sunny spring afternoon.

Once more, into the breach.

Upon graduating from high school, I enrolled to read for a Bachelor's degree in law at the (again, segregated, for Coloureds only) University of the Western Cape (UWC), majoring in Private Law and English. In one of the modules in English II (second year English) we had to read African literature for the first time, as a concentrated course of study. The usual suspects, although they were anything but usual to us at that moment, composed the curriculum. The Nigerians Chinua Achebe (*Things Fall Apart*) and Wole Soyinka (*The Interpreters*) anchored the module but the novel that grabbed me was Ngũgĩ's *A Grain of Wheat*. (Spurred by these texts, I quickly read Tayeb Saleh – *A Season of Migration to the North*, Amos Tutuola – *The Palm Wine Drinkard*, and Sembene Ousmane – *God's Bits of Wood*.)

A Grain of Wheat is a novel marked by its anti-colonial subtlety. I won't rehearse the argument, suffice to say that betrayal among the colonized is rife. (Betrayal, as we know, is a recurring theme in Ngũgĩ's oeuvre.) Kihika is betrayed by the otherwise venerated Mugo; Kihika's sister Mumbi betrays her husband Gikonyo, a Mau Mau fighter, by having a child with Gikonyo's despised enemy, Karanja, who is a Home Guard; that is, a black Kenyan fighting on the side of the British colonial authorities. (Gikonyo, of course, commits his own betrayal by getting an early release from prison in order to be with Mumbi.)

English II met on Thursday, late-morning, in the D building on the UWC campus. When the lecturer, David Attwell, who has since gone on to become a key scholar of Coetzee's writing, presented his critique of Ngũgĩ's novel, I went home exhilarated. I'd been well, trained, like any half-decent Livingstone student, by very good – really good, in fact – English teachers at high school. Mr. Fiske and Mrs. MacArthur gave us an exceptional grounding in the canon of English literature. Shakespeare, Milton, the Romantic poets, Keats, Shelley, Wordsworth, John Donne, Robert Bolt, Gerald Durrell, D. H. Lawrence, Elizabeth Barrett Browning, Emily Dickenson, Dickens, T. S. Eliot – 'the morning comes to consciousness', 'the smell of steak in passageways'; 'Shall I wear my trousers turned, shall I eat a peach'; Hardy, both poems and novels, Gerard Manley Hopkins, how terse and regal a poet, how grammatically inventive and taut his lines – Mikki Flockemann, who taught poetry in English II, was just the kind of advocate Hopkin's poetry needed. Morgan MacArthur was my best teacher in high school. She instilled in me a deep and abiding love of English literature, a debt I hope never to be able to repay, so substantial it is.

Well trained, yes, all the building blocks in what we know – for good or ill, as the 'canon' – were made available to me. And I took them, eagerly, to heart. I treasure them, still. There are few authors, Jorge Luis Borges being the one who comes most readily to mind, who can match Shakespeare.

But, an anti-colonial novel textured by betrayal, refusing the politics of condemnation, favoring instead the democratic dispersal of complicity. Guilt, is everywhere; political innocence is nowhere on display. The anti-colonial, before the post-colonial (what a mess that is, as we all know), impure. Contaminated. By desire, ambition, the righteous slayed by those all others deem innocent. So overdeteminedly Christological in its iconography is *A Grain of Wheat*; appropriate, of course, given that 'James Ngũgĩ', as he was then (apostolically) known, derived the title from St. John's Gospel: 12.24: 'Very truly I tell you, unless a kernel of wheat falls to the ground and dies, it remains only a single seed. But if it dies, it produces many seeds.' The anti-colonial, rendered as the stuff of thinking, as the very stuff of life. The anti-colonial, rendered at once inimitable and eminently recognizable.

My mother got home from work and that evening I told her that I was done with a degree in law. I was going to concentrate on English, especially the kind of literature that Ngũgĩ wrote. My mother thought me mad. But she indulged me. I suspect that she knew, as I know only too well now, that I would have made a lousy lawyer.

After I attained my BA from UWC, I enrolled for a degree in English Honors (a year of specialized reading in just one subject). I was the only full-time student in the class. Five courses, three of them one-on-one with my teachers – this time David Attwell taught me Shakespeare, and Peter Kohler and David Bunn instructed me in African and South African literature. I was looking forward to Honors but I had no plans upon graduation.

The chair of the UWC English department, the wonderfully erudite and always verbally precise Stan Ridge, summoned me to his office one day.

'What do you intend to do once you graduate?' Stan asked, his beneficent smile hardly masking his incredulity when I murmured vague nothings in response.

Stan, a friend to this day, is possessed of an efficient and authoritative mind. He instructed me to speak to three people about a possible scholarship to the U.S. Two of them –David Attwell and David Bunn – were, or had been, my teachers, so no problem there. The two Davids had – or were in the process of completing – PhDs in the US, Texas (Austin) and Northwestern respectively. I duly approached them and had the conversations.

The other person, however, I'd heard of, he was a famous writer, but had never met.

His name was Richard Rive.

Nervously, I made an appointment with Richard. A Sunday morning in February, 1988, 11 a.m. I was punctual, Richard liked that.

We talked. Or, more precisely, it was the old story, he talked and I listened.

I was overwhelmed by Richard's library, which was impressively, and oh-so neatly, stocked with books. This was a thing to behold. But no section was so plentiful as his African literature one. What is more, as Richard proudly showed me, many, many of them were inscribed to Richard by other African writers. (Langston Hughes, and the Harlem Renaissance, took next in the order of pride of place.)

I relayed my Ngũgĩ moment to Richard.

'Here', he said, showing me a copy of his autobiography, *Writing Black*. 'There's a picture of Ngũgĩ.'

'I read several of his first stories when I visited Nairobi', Richard intoned in his well-rehearsed Oxbridge accent.

Thus, begun a friendship that would end, tragically, with Richard's murder on Tiananmen Square Day. Two tragedies, one global, the other of more modest import but a loss that stays with me to this day. The world that David Attwell's module opened up found substantiation of the most immanent variety in Richard's library, in a house which was but a stone's throw from where Richard Owen Dudley resided.

A few weeks later, I bought a copy of *Writing Black*. Richard, happily, inscribed it.

I followed Richard's trajectory to Columbia University in New York City, courtesy of a scholarship he, Stan, the two Davids and many of my UWC teachers were instrumental in me obtaining.

Everywhere I've gone, *Writing Black* has been in tow.

Imagine then the enormity of the moment when I introduced myself to Ngũgĩ wa Thiong'o on the Duke campus.

I had a story to tell, a gratitude to express.

And, I had an inscribed copy of a book written by a disenfranchised South African who had, decades ago, met and talked writing with 'James Ngũgĩ'.

This is the story that I told Ngũgĩ wa Thiong'o: 'I became an English major because of you.'

'I went to graduate school, in South Africa and the U.S., because of you.'

'You have much to answer for', I gently chided him.

He smiled, indulgently, as though I were a child to be humored. His work had set me on a path. *A Grain of Wheat* had made the world, the world of apartheid, different. From coming to South African literature late, and African literature still later (if only a matter of three years, but, still, as African living on the continent it took me long enough), here I was relating my story to the author, the author of my fate, in a way.

Ngũgĩ led me to Richard Rive, Ngũgĩ made thinkable the lessons of my Livingstone education. Ngũgĩ added, colonially educated as he too was, to what Peter Fiske and Morgan MacArthur taught me.

I met Ngũgĩ again the next day and showed him my copy of *Writing Black*, the page with his picture earmarked. I had no idea how Richard's book was supposed to lend veracity to my story. I still don't. I can only surmise that I wanted the tactile, the book, to stand as my unimpeachable evidence.

Such an understanding possesses no logic, not the kind that can stand scrutiny, anyway.

But, *Writing Black* was the cultural-political object that binds these three beginnings together. Or, the three beginnings culminate in *Writing Black*. Or, *Writing Black* is the only way to secure an end for all these beginnings. Or, both, perhaps, and even such a speculation leaves much to be desired.

It is, at any rate, the best I've got. And, however much Ngũgĩ brushed off my thanks, I knew this. Knew this, at the very least. Know this now, in the act of committing my Ngũgĩ moment to writing.

The story has the immense benefit of being true.

18
Ngũgĩ wa Thiong'o:
Tribute on His 80th Birthday

Chege Githiora

I have an early memory of meeting Professor Ngũgĩ wa Thiong'o briefly at the National Theatre in Nairobi in 1977. I was one of the lucky primary school kids who had been taken along on what was an exciting journey that night with my parents and relatives, to see an evening show of *The Trial of Dedan Kimathi*. The performance left in me a lasting memory of patriotic song, dance, and palpable emotions during a powerful show of theatre and audience participation. Above all, I actually had the chance to shake the hand of the great writer at some point during that evening. In all, it was an unforgettable event that inspired a feeling of having taken part in a momentous occasion, and it planted in me a fascination with language, theatre and culture. Ever since that day, Ngũgĩ's writing, and his ideas about language and discourse on colonialism, have loomed large in my intellectual and even personal life. Sixteen years later in 1993, I was once again an excited member of a group of students from Michigan State University, driving down to Ann Arbor, Michigan, to listen to a lecture by Ngũgĩ, who was accompanied by Kamau Braithwaite, the Caribbean writer and poet. At the end of the lecture, we crowded to get autographs, mingle and generally rub our shoulders with these two great writers. But I was on another mission: in my nervous hands, I held a manuscript I had written several years before and which I wanted to hand over to Ngũgĩ, to read in the hope that he would offer a few words of encouragement, if I had an opportunity. I was sure that I was not the only one in that group of eager students and budding writers trying to get the author's attention. To my surprise and relief, he received my manuscript with humility and respect, looked me in the eye, and promised to read it later. I was thrilled when he slipped it into the pocket of his jacket.

I held the manuscript dear in my heart, and in fact, up to that point I was the only one who had read it—several hundred times. I wrote it while living and studying in Mexico in my early twenties, lonely and far away from Africa, home and all things familiar. I felt particularly deprived of opportunities to speak or listen to Gĩkũyũ, a deep yearning I tried to fill by writing in the language. The manuscript was titled, *Marũa ma Maitũ* ('Letter to Mother'), and it was a lyrical narrative of some key historical, cultural and contemporary experiences of Mexico. In the letter, I used an African language to describe Mexico, while making analogies of language, culture, history, and colonialism. Unwittingly, I was engaged in what I came to know later as the 'South–South dialogue'—that conversation between the formerly colonized peoples of the southern hemisphere (the 'Global South'), without the linguistic and ideological mediation of the northern hemisphere (the 'West') and its hegemonic intellectual paradigms. I tried my best to capture the rhythm and rhyme of the Gĩkũyũ language in a narrative where sentences, phrases, words and idioms followed a natural rhythm and alliterations of the language. I wrote the sentences and truncated them wherever it sounded good to the ear and captured the rhythms of Gĩkũyũ—it was narrative prose, not poetry. I did not expect to hear much from Ngũgĩ, if at all. How many such manuscripts did he receive from other young writers the world over? I was happy enough to have received further inspiration about writing in Gĩkũyũ through his reaffirming lecture, and the fact that he had been receptive to my writing aspirations.

A few months later, I received a phone call in Mexico City where I was on a break during a year of PhD research among Afro-Mexican communities of the southern Pacific coast of Mexico. It was Ngũgĩ on the phone. I could hardly believe I had actually received a phone call from such an eminent person (this was before email and mobile phones) nor believe my ears when he told me how happy he had been with my manuscript, and that he had decided to publish it in series in *Mũtiiri*, a new journal in Gĩkũyũ that he was editing. Could he possibly have my permission to edit and publish it, he wanted to know? Of course, he could! I nearly shouted down the line. Although I had always written in my language since childhood, this was my first publication in Gĩkũyũ. I seemed to have spoken in a voice that appealed to Ngũgĩ, and in some ways, this re-connection with him was providential, for although I never was formally ever a student of his in Kenya or abroad, his influence upon my thinking and writing in and about African languages had followed me as surely as his books have found their way in every intellectual, cultural or linguistic space I had ever occupied in my life. My mother, to whom I dedicated the Gĩkũyũ manuscript, was a great lover of the Gĩkũyũ language in which she wrote extensively (letters, memoirs, notes, eulogies, community records, and more), and taught it throughout her long primary school teaching career. Like Ngũgĩ's own mother as described in his memoir, *Dreams in a Time of War*, my mother, too, was a great story teller.

Since those early encounters, I have been ever conscious of Ngũgĩ's cultural and intellectual activism, as a radical lecturer and, eventually, political prisoner and exile. He inspired admiration and emulation from writers like myself who agreed with his position on the centrality of African languages in the continent's present and future. Against that background, it was a sort of coming full circle when Ngũgĩ edited and published my manuscript, but it was just another beginning as our paths would cross again and again ever since. The journal *Mũtiiri*, which he founded in 1991, generated excitement among writers in Gĩkũyũ, for here was a chance to publish peer-reviewed, well edited material in all areas of knowledge, demonstrating the full potential of an African language. As I continued to publish in the journal, I had the opportunity to interact with Ngũgĩ many times over the next couple of decades. I was once again thrilled when he asked me to read a one-thousand-page manuscript in Gĩkũyũ, and to make comments about word coinage and orthography. I took the assignment with gusto, while enjoying a very early preview of what was to become the longest novel in an African language, published in 2006 as *Mũrogi wa Kagogo*, and translated by Ngũgĩ as *The Wizard of the Crow*. My engagement with this text, and its producer, was a wonderful learning experience which I continue to treasure to this day.

Following the success of a working group on Gĩkũyũ orthography along-side a conference on African languages and linguistics in Boston University in 1999, we carried the conversation forward during another workshop at SOAS in 2002. This was another great opportunity to interact intensively with Ngũgĩ, as for three days a group of us grappled and debated issues of orthography, creative writing, and publishing in Gĩkũyũ. At the end of those three days, Nigerian literary critic, Chinweizu, who was present throughout the meetings, quietly listening and observing, summed up the experience as 'the most beautiful workshop he had ever attended' in which a group of African writers and scholars seriously debated an African language in an African language!

Over the years, Ngũgĩ and I have seen our mutual interests gravitate from issues of orthography and writing in Gĩkũyũ to translation as a conversation among languages and cultures. We believe that as translations become part of the body of literature available in two or more languages, the boundaries of African literature will be expanded. During a translation conference in Ngũgĩ's home institution, the University of California Irvine in 2006, we shared the dream of establishing a translation center located in Africa, which would become a model to be replicated all over the continent. We followed it up with a string of funding proposals to international organizations and donors, only for our plans to be scuttled by the eruption of political violence, which had taken up an ethnic dimension in 2007. Overnight, donor funding priorities 'shifted', as the expression of linguistic diversity suddenly appeared incompatible with national peace and reconciliation in Kenya following politically instigated inter-ethnic violence.

I have, however, tried to keep in with Ngũgĩ's giant steps in the field of translation. In 2017, for example, I translated *Kaburi Bila Msalaba*, P. M. Kareithi's Kiswahili novel of the Mau Mau war, into English. The inspiration that Ngũgĩ has provided me has been of immense influence in my thinking about language and literature, and his position serves to reinforce what I have come to know and feel through my training as a linguist. This knowledge and feeling is expressed by the refrain of a famous poem by Tanzanian poet and writer, Shaaban bin Robert, in praise of Kiswahili and all mother tongues: *titi la mama litamu*—'a mother's breast is the sweetest'. I am humbled by the privilege of paying tribute to one of Africa's greatest writers and icon of the debate on the role of African languages and, as we celebrate his 80th birthday, I wish him many more.

Part III

Working with Ngũgĩ

19
Ngũgĩ & the Decolonization of Publishing

James Currey

The publication of Ngũgĩ's *Weep Not, Child* in 1964, two years after the foundation of the African Writers Series (AWS) with *Things Fall Apart* by Chinua Achebe in 1962, was the moment of take-off. The original plan was for the AWS to republish in paperback books first published by general literary publishers in hardback. However, Keith Sambrook and Chinua Achebe rapidly ran out of books by African authors to republish. At that point, Heinemann became the originating publisher in hardbacks for reviews and library sales, with their own paperback to follow.

All too often, writers of a successful first novel find it difficult to write the second. Not Ngũgĩ. *The River Between* (1965) had been written before *Weep Not, Child* and some of the reviews of *A Grain of Wheat* (1967) compared his writing confidence with that of Conrad. Along with Achebe, he was established internationally throughout the English-speaking world as evidence that exciting writing was coming out of Africa. Ngũgĩ was addressing an audience through English, the language of colonialism.

In 1962, at a meeting of teachers of English literature in African universities convened by Ezekiel (Zeke) Mphahlele and Eldred Jones at Fourah Bay College in Sierra Leone, it was decided that writing by contemporary writers from Africa should be used in teaching English literature at universities in Africa, and that the examination boards in West and East Africa should choose titles to prescribe as set texts. For example, in 1974, 50,000 copies of *Weep Not, Child* were sold in Nigeria in one month alone as it was the set book for the West African Examination Board for school certificate. Ngũgĩ was within sight of being able to survive from royalties on his writing.

Ngũgĩ may not have had trouble with his second novel but he certainly had trouble with the second stage of his career. He had become famous and the longer people waited for his next novel the greater was the level of public expectation. By the mid-1970s his philosophy had been transformed by pan-Africanism and the black power movements. The Caribbean writers he had studied at Leeds had influenced his work and thought. Ngũgĩ says of George Lamming in *Homecoming*:

He evoked through a child's growing awareness a tremendous picture of the awakening social consciousness of a small village. He evoked, for me, an unforgettable picture of a peasant revolt in a white-dominated world. And suddenly I knew that a novel could be made to speak to me, could, with a compelling urgency, touch cords deep down in me. (81)

In a letter to David Hill, Managing Director of Heinemann, dated 9 January 1973, Sambrook expressed the worries felt in in the company's editorial office when Ngũgĩ submitted his collection of short stories *Secret Lives*, which was to be published in 1975:

I am a bit puzzled by Ngũgĩ; he seems to have come to a full stop. The short stories are good but, in confidence, I don't think they show any advance on his previous, admittedly high, standard of writing. He is full of ideas, young, famous – what serious writing is he doing or planning?

Ballad for a Barmaid was the original title of the fourth novel, *Petals of Blood*, which Ngũgĩ was struggling to write during the early 1970s.

The launching of the novel in Nairobi City Hall in 1977 was a remarkable occasion. There were over 1,000 guests and all 500 airfreighted hardbacks sold immediately. (There were to be sales of some 20,000 paperbacks in Kenya alone in the next 18 months.) Ngũgĩ had managed to get Mwai Kibaki, future president but then the minister of Finance and Economic Affairs, to give the launching speech. Ngũgĩ had movingly started his own speech with:

I would like to start by introducing to this audience the woman who has all along inspired me. The woman who in fact made me go to school to learn how to read and write. I am referring to my mother, my peasant mother. (*Writers in Politics* 94)

Ngũgĩ said that his future work would be in Gĩkũyũ so that she could understand it.

This launch party marked another important step for Ngũgĩ in the decolonization of African publishing. His former student Henry Chakava had, at only the age of 30, now become the Managing Director of Heinemann Educational Books (East Africa). He, Keith Sambrook and I were already working out new editorial relationships between London and Nairobi. The African Writers Series had become renowned for novels. There had been much less demand for plays.

Although Ngũgĩ is internationally famous as a novelist, in Kenya it was his plays, especially in Gĩkũyũ, which were to lead to his detention and ultimate exile. For example, his play *The Black Hermit* (1968) was written at the same time, and with some of the same themes, as the novel *The River Between*, but it was the former that provoked political concern when it was performed in

Kampala. Similarly, *The Trial of Dedan Kimathi* (1976) was born out of intense controversy. When Ngũgĩ and Mĩcere Mũgo went to see a new play by Kenneth Watene about the freedom fighter Dedan Kimathi, they were shocked by what they saw and were stung into writing their own play to set the record straight. Heinemann (EA) rushed out the play and sold an initial 300 copies outside the theatre.

The publication of this play led to fresh thinking about the way the African Writers Series might expand outside its London base. On 3 August 1976, Henry Chakava, who had been offered scripts by Francis Imbuga and Joe de Graft, wrote a letter to James Currey proposing a new approach to the publication of plays:

> What would be your views if we proposed starting a single play series with a Heinemann (East Africa) imprint for which you would have the option to do an AWS edition for the rest of the world? Once started we would get all the local playwrights to publish with us since there is no active Drama series in East Africa at the moment.

The excited reaction to the Kimathi play reminded Ngũgĩ of the power of drama. In 1976 the University of Nairobi Free Travelling Theatre put on some plays including extracts from *The Trial of Dedan Kimathi* at the Kamĩrĩĩthũ Cultural Centre. At about the same time, Ngũgĩ joined the new management committee of the Centre and in December 1976 he and Ngũgĩ wa Mĩriĩ were commissioned to write what was to become *Ngaahika Ndeenda* (*I will Marry When I Want*). The performances were to begin on the symbolic twenty-fifth anniversary of the declaration of the State of the Emergency and the beginning of the armed struggle in Kenya. Ngũgĩ notes the effect of the Kamĩrĩĩthũ Centre on him in *Detained*:

> The six months between June and November 1977 were the most exciting in my life and the true beginning of my education. I learnt my language anew. I rediscovered the creative nature and power of collective work (76).

Ngũgĩ also emphasizes the totally transforming nature of the enterprise – it raised money for health projects and it reduced drunkenness:

> I saw with my own eyes peasants, some of whom had never once been inside a theatre in their lives, design and construct an open-air theatre complete with a raised stage, roofed dressing rooms and stores, and an auditorium with a seating capacity of more than two-thousand persons. (*Detained* 77)

But the District Commissioner, Kiambu, who had not even bothered to come to see the performance, saw the matter differently. On 16 December 1977 he withdrew the licence of performance and sent in *askaris* (police) to close the theatre. On the night of 30/31 December 1977, Ngũgĩ was taken in chains to Kamiti Maximum Security Prison.

Eleven months later he emerged clutching the manuscript of *Devil on the Cross* written in Gĩkũyũ on toilet-paper:

> Writing on toilet-paper? Now I know that paper is about the most precious article for a political prisoner, more so for one like me who was in detention because of his writing. At Kamiti, virtually all the detainees are writers or composers ... These prisoners have mostly written on toilet paper. Now the same good old toilet-paper – which has been useful to Kwame Nkrumah in James Fort Prison, to Dennis Brutus on Robben Island, to Abdilatif Abdalla in G Block, Kamiti, and to countless other persons with similar urges – has enabled me to defy daily the intended detention of my mind. (*Detained* 6)

In November 1981, Ngũgĩ and his associates planned to stage a musical play, *Maitũ Njugĩra (Mother, Sing for Me)*, at the National Theatre. The production had been conceived round their technical facilities. A cinematic technique was to be integrated to project scenes from colonial history, such as the burning of passbooks. The whole performance was packed with songs in Luhya, Kamba, Kisii and Kalenjin, as well as in Gĩkũyũ and Kiswahili. A licence was applied for in good time but the request was ignored by the authorities. In the meantime, rehearsals were being acted every night for three weeks before enthusiastic packed audiences in the theatre of the Education Department at the University of Nairobi. In an interview with Anne Walmsley, Ngũgĩ remarked on the perversity of the Kenyan authorities:

> The musical dealt with Kenya during the highly repressive colonial period. So, what is surprising is that the authorities should feel sufficiently strongly to suppress an anti-colonial play. It's very strange. But there is in Kenya a pattern where the authorities actively support, even financially, foreign, anti-Kenyan cultural offerings. This was in fact dramatised in our own case – at the same time that they were banning or refusing to grant us a licence for the musical, they were showing *The Flame Trees of Thika* by Elspeth Huxley. It is a novel which is basically racist, it isn't Kenyan, it isn't African. It was shown on Kenyan television as a seven-part serial. The government actually spent money on it. (*Index on Censorship*)

What Ngũgĩ does not point out is that at the beginning of the musical a black man drags onto the stage a cart with a white colonial administrator in a solar topee aboard. At the end the same cart is drawn on to the stage by the same black man. However, this time sitting on the cart, wearing the solar topee, is a black man.

When Ngũgĩ came out of jail he found the University would not renew his contract. Henry Chakava gave Ngũgĩ a desk in his office and between them they set out to decolonize publishing. The result was that East African Educational Publisher (EAEP) was to become the most outstanding publisher in Kenya and East Africa. Henry Chakava was to back all the publishing of his old teacher Ngũgĩ whatever dangers the books presented, whether political or commercial. Ngũgĩ was determined that the first publication of his books should be in Gĩkũyũ, although it had proved almost impossible to sell titles in Kenyan languages unless they were prescribed as set books for exams. Ngũgĩ was later to write children's books in Gĩkũyũ, which no publisher had tried before.

The political risks to the Kenyan company remained even after Ngũgĩ went into exile in the early 1980s. Alan Hill and Keith Sambrook gave Henry Chakava the right to decide what he should publish. We talked through the dangers with him. He and his staff were in the front line. It was their jobs which were at risk. I believe that the British directors of any other large educational company would have told Henry Chakava to stop publishing such politically sensitive material which would endanger their school textbook publishing and jeopardize their dividends. The dangers were worse than just financial. Henry suffered a *panga* (machete) attack outside his own gates; it was highly likely that it was one of the penalties of publishing Ngũgĩ.

In 1980, Heinemann in East Africa decided to publish both novel *Caitaani Mũthaaraba-inĩ* (*The Devil on the Cross*) and play *Ngaahika Ndeenda* (*I Will Marry When I Want*) at the same time. There were certainly political dangers in publishing Ngũgĩ in Kenya, but in addition there were commercial problems. If the Ngũgĩ books in Gĩkũyũ were banned by the government they would be unsaleable outside Kenya. At that time there was no record in Kenya of the banning of published books. To avoid that risk Johnson Mugweru, the company's Sales Director, planned that orders, which had discretely been gathered from across Gĩkũyũ country, would be invoiced out in advance and the books would be put by the printers straight into the boots of the sale's representative cars and be taken off to the shops to be sold to customers before they could be seized by the authorities.

There had been signs that the reception for these two books would be exceptional. Ngũgĩ, annoyed, had rushed into the office to see Henry Chakava because he had been told by a friend that he had bought a copy of the play. Why had the authors not seen a copy? Henry replied that no more had he. He rang up the printers who said they were still binding the book. So, somebody had slipped the very first copies out of the works and on to the streets of Nairobi. Ngũgĩ was hot enough to steal off the stack at the binders.

Ngũgĩ excitedly told Henry Chakava and me that new entertainments had entered the bar life of Kenya following the publication of the two books, the first to be written in his mother's own language. A man literate in Gĩkũyũ would read Ngũgĩ's novel aloud to the drinkers until his voice and his glass had run dry. He would then lay the novel page downwards on the bar until another drink was bought for him. Literacy paid. The script of *Ngaahika Ndeenda* which had been produced with such drama in 1978 at the Kamĩrĩĩthũ Cultural Centre, elicited similar reactions. Ngũgĩ told us about what happened when he had entered one bar: a person, previously unknown to him, introduced himself by the name of one of the characters in the play. Then other people in the bar cast clustered round him shouting out their own characters' names. Play-reading had broken out across Kenya.

Ngũgĩ has also told a fairy story of Kenya about his novel *Matigari*:

> Matigari ... goes around the country asking questions about truth and justice. People who had read the novel started talking about Matigari and the questions he was raising as if Matigari was a real person in life. When Dictator Moi heard that there was a Kenyan roaming around the country asking such questions, he issued an order for the man's arrest. But when the police found he was only a character in fiction, Moi was even more angry and he issued fresh orders for the arrest of the book itself. (*Moving the Centre* 175)

Heinemann in London gave Ngũgĩ an international start in English, and Ngũgĩ worked with Henry Chakava to decolonize publishing in Africa. However, he suffered in independent Kenya from authoritarian laws and procedures which mimicked those of the settler colony in which he had been born.

20

The Turning Point: Ngũgĩ wa Thiong'o & His Kenyan Publisher

Henry Chakava

The Beginning

The year is 1976. It is my first year as Managing Director at the Nairobi office of Heinemann Educational Books Ltd. Before me is a rather voluminous script which has come from James Currey of the London Head Office for a critical assessment. It is written by Ngũgĩ wa Thiong'o, an established Kenyan writer who, only four years ago, had been my literature teacher at the University of Nairobi. The previous year, I had made my first professional contact with him, and had played a pivotal role in the publishing of his play, *The Trial of Dedan Kimathi*, co-authored with Mĩcere Mũgo. London had rejected it for publication in the African Writers Series insisting that their policy was to publish collections rather than single plays. I had decided to publish it in Nairobi, the first of many other notable plays to be published by Heinemann Nairobi, now East African Educational Publishers Ltd (EAEP).

But I could have started this story in the late 1960s when Ngũgĩ was my lecturer in the Department of Literature at the University of Nairobi. I was a good student and had no problem socializing with him in and outside the classroom. I visited his rural home in Limuru a couple of times where, on one occasion, I had a brand-new experience—drinking *muratina* (traditional Gĩkũyũ beer) from a horn! In my third year I decided, for my dissertation, to write on the subject of 'guilt and betrayal' in Ngũgĩ's *A Grain of Wheat*. Ngũgĩ was not my supervisor but, through regular contact with him, I was able to gather important information and insights into the man and his works. I continued to visit and socialize with him even after I left the university. Indeed, Ngũgĩ was one of the conspirators, along with Prof Andrew Gurr, who landed me in a 'temporary' job at Heinemann Nairobi, and where I would shortly emerge as his publisher.

Petals of Blood: The Turning Point in Our Relationship

Back to the Ngũgĩ manuscript, which seemed then to go by a number of titles, including 'Wrestling with God'. I sent a detailed and comprehensive report to James Currey, who, upon reading it lifted the editorial veil, revealed my identity to Ngũgĩ and requested that both of us work closely together in the revision process. Ngũgĩ took my criticisms seriously, honored every appointment to discuss his progress in revising the novel, and addressed all my concerns comprehensively. Sembene Ousmane's novel *God's Bits of Wood* provided inspiration. Throughout this process, I was amazed at the simplicity and humility of this renowned author who displayed absolute faith and trust in me and accepted me as a key partner in this creative process. He was aware that he had not published a major work in ten years and wanted this novel to stand out from the rest. So, after several drafts and months of hard work, the novel that was to become *Petals of Blood* was now ready to go back to London for publication.

The book was published in 1977 to much critical acclaim. A launch was planned in London and Ngũgĩ was invited. I informed them that I also intended to launch the book in Nairobi since I felt very much part of its development. I ordered hundreds of copies and airlifted them to Nairobi for the purpose, much to London's surprise. I booked Charter Hall, the largest room in City Hall, in the center of Nairobi, and invited Ngũgĩ himself, Mwai Kibaki, Finance Minister and later President of the Republic of Kenya, as guest of honor, along with other dignitaries. Ngũgĩ brought his entire family, a privilege he had been denied at previous company functions, among them his wife Nyambura, brother Wallace, and his aging mother Wanjiku whose presence stole the show. Heinemann Nigeria sent their Sales Director, Joe Osadolor, and James Currey came from London, all in a show of support.

There were about one thousand people in that Hall that night, and all the copies of the book were quickly sold out. Okot p'Bitek and Taban lo Liyong, who had been the cause of some unease at previous company functions, were thoroughly relaxed and drank to their fill. The following day, I asked Heinemann to give me permission to quickly reprint the book to capitalize on the demand generated by the enormous publicity, and this was given. This is how *Petals of Blood* became the first novel in the African Writers Series to be reprinted locally. Many more were to follow in the 1980s, further enriching our fast-growing home-made fiction list.

Ngũgĩ's Influence on My Publishing Philosophy

The years 1976 to 1982 were to turn out to be the most crucial in my relationship with Ngũgĩ. Working together on *Petals of Blood* had deepened our friendship and built a strong mutual understanding and trust. It was now possible to speak freely and frankly to each other without fear of causing offence. We met regularly and discussed every possible subject under the sun, including colonialism and neo-colonialism, politics, philosophy, culture, language, literature, and religion. Then some of Ngũgĩ's ideas began to shape my publishing philosophy and priorities. I began to more appreciate local-language publishing, oral literature, and publishing for children. Listening to Ngũgĩ speak at the first conference on the teaching of Literature in Kenyan Secondary Schools at Nairobi School in 1973, I made up my mind to commission a textbook on Oral Literature. I first approached Henry Owuor Anyumba who was then the leading expert on the subject but he was unable to deliver in time. *Oral Literature: A Certificate Course* was eventually written by Asenath Odaga and S. Kichamu Akivaga and went on to sell thousands of copies, and is still in print today, having gone through more than twenty reprints. Encouraged by Ngũgĩ, I went on to launch The Oral Literatures of Kenya Series in which I issued individual volumes of the Oral Literatures of the major communities of Kenya. Ngũgĩ suggested a two-column layout which would give equal prominence to the original language and the English translation. It was not possible to adopt this format, but all the songs were rendered in the local languages with accompanying translations.

Another Ngũgĩ-inspired idea was the publishing of children's books in African languages. Once successful in the market, the plan was that those children's books would be translated into other African languages to facilitate what he described as conversation among African languages. In addition to Ngũgĩ, I proceeded to identify a number of key published writers from different parts of the country, including David Maillu, Grace Ogot, Asenath Odaga, Francis Imbuga, and commissioned them to write the books geared to a specific age level. Artists were hired to provide the best quality color illustrations as Ngũgĩ did not want our books to look inferior to imported ones on book shelves. All the books were published at once, to maximize on impact and reduce on the cost of publicity. Unfortunately, these books did not succeed, partly because the Kenya Curriculum did not recognize African languages, and hardly any books at that level could be sold as trade books. There were also, to some extent, quality issues arising from the use of the wrong type of paper, color separation and printing. In hindsight, if the current interest being shown in African languages and the positive change in the Kenya government policy towards local languages is anything to go by, this was an idea ahead of its time.

In 1977, when Ngũgĩ was in detention, I made another move which was consistent with the theme of promoting our local languages, a topic which had greatly engaged us in our earlier discussions—the strengthening of Kiswahili as our national language. I decided to publish a complete Primary School

Kiswahili course for Kenya schools, together with accompanying teachers' guides. At that time, commercial publishers were not allowed by the government to publish for primary schools and, in any case, Kiswahili was not on the curriculum. I went around the country and identified four leading Kiswahili experts and commissioned them to write the course. The project started well but dragged on for some time as three of the authors dropped out, leaving one, Zachariah Zani of Mombasa, to complete the project with his wife Tereza.

When the first three books of *Hatua Za Kiswahili: Masomo ya Msingi* came out in 1980, they were an instant success, reprinting in large quantities over a short period. The course was completed in 1982, the same year President Daniel arap Moi decreed that Kiswahili should be a compulsory subject in Kenyan primary schools. The Ministry of Education moved fast to prepare a curriculum modelled on our course with a view to producing their own books, but we were too far ahead of everyone else. The course books were now selling in hundreds of thousands of copies and, by 1985, it accounted for over 80 percent of our total company turnover. It was on the basis of this strong local performance that we petitioned Heinemann to sell part of the company to us in 1985, which they did the following year.

The Risk of Publishing Ngũgĩ

Ngũgĩ had been true in word and spirit in his commitment towards promoting local languages. He came out of Kamiti Maximum Security Prison at the end of 1978 with two manuscripts written on toilet paper in the Gĩkũyũ language. The first was *Ngaahika Ndeenda, (I Will Marry When I Want)*, the play that had attracted large audiences at Kamĩrĩĩthũ in his Limuru home town. It was later banned and was probably responsible for his detention. The second was *Caitaani Mũtharaba-inĩ (Devil on the Cross)*, a hard-hitting novel exposing the rot in our society. Ngũgĩ was not sure if I would have the courage to publish these books and told me not to take it as a test of our friendship. My bosses in London were even more cautious, discreetly suggesting that they wouldn't mind if I refused to publish the books. But after having the books assessed in the normal way, and after receiving positive reports to present at the Editorial Board Meeting, I signed publishing contracts with Ngũgĩ.

The editorial and production process was tedious, sometimes manual, because of the special nature of the Gĩkũyũ alphabet. This was the case with *Caitaani Mũtharaba-inĩ*, which was probably the first full-length novel to be published in Gĩkũyũ. But Ngũgĩ was in the office every day, correcting and re-correcting every page until he and his editors were satisfied. The book covers were given close attention, with several proposals being rejected until all the parties involved were happy with the result. Once more, Ngũgĩ was emphatic that a local-language product should not look inferior on the book shelves against imported equivalents. Finally, the books were now ready for press.

At this point, strange things started happening. I started receiving anonymous calls in the office and on my house phone number, mostly from a lady who seemed to be calling from a large hall, for her voice always had an echo. Then I noticed that I was being trailed by a turbaned person of Asian origin. I mentioned these things to Ngũgĩ and he told me that he too had been assaulted by people to whom he had given a lift in his car. Before the books came out of the printers, I was attacked at my Lavington home by a five-man gang wielding a gun and machetes. The aim was to take me away in my car but they had problems reversing it, after the gear lever snapped. They left me with bruises in the face and several deep cuts on my right hand. A few days later, they called to ask if I had learnt my lesson and I challenged them to come back. They never did. Surprisingly, the books were very well received in the market and sold mostly to individuals rather than institutional buyers, and reprinted three times in quick succession before the police caught up with us. This was 1982, the year of the attempted coup, and the year Ngũgĩ left the country not to return for 22 years.

The Long Exile and After

The years 1975 to 1982 were when I had the closest interaction with Ngũgĩ, both professionally and socially. When he came out of detention and his employers, the University of Nairobi, refused to give him back his job for fear of repercussions, it is to the Heinemann Nairobi office that he turned. I gave him a desk where he continued to do his work, use the telephone and receive his guests. It is while in our offices that he received foreign intelligence reports that his life was in danger, and it was from there that he planned his exit out of the country. After a few weeks, I met him in London at a UNESCO conference where he was a key speaker, and later that evening in my hotel room. The secretive manner in which he was behaving seemed to indicate that his enemies had pursued him to London. I knew that he would not be coming back home soon and I was right.

We continued to communicate while he was in London, courtesy of the Heinemann office. Sometimes he would request me to visit his family and give them some money out of his royalties for a specific need. Much later, I visited him in his tiny flat in Islington, London. He did not have a proper job and Heinemann were increasingly reluctant to give further advances. Frustration was gradually creeping in. This is the time when we were working on *Matigari*, another Gĩkũyũ language novel which was banned in Nairobi shortly after publication, and copies carted away by the police. It was at this point that Ngũgĩ decided to explore job opportunities in the U.S. For some years, we were out of touch, but we found each other again to work on that great tome *Mŭrogi wa Kagogo* (*Wizard of the Crow*), without a doubt Ngũgĩ's crowning literary achievement, the Gĩkũyũ edition of which was launched in Nairobi during his first homecoming in 2004.

In conclusion, I will make some general observations about Ngũgĩ the person, whom I have known well for all these years. Ngũgĩ is a prolific writer. Since his student days at Makerere University, he has published more books than any other African fiction writer known to me and is still writing. As a demonstration of his fidelity, he has stuck with us, EAEP, his publishers, throughout. He is a simple man who writes in simple accessible language for the ordinary reader. He is also a versatile writer comfortable in any genre: the novel, drama, poetry, essays, short stories, literary criticism, children's books, orature, translation, etc. He is a person committed to his cause, and has worked tirelessly, consistently, and fearlessly to highlight the plight of the downtrodden in all his writings, especially peasants, workers, women, and the poor in general. He has paid a price for this, of course, including detention and exile. All said and done, Ngũgĩ is a modest and hard-working family man, patient, determined, and slow to anger. As I have mentioned above, he will revise a script over and over again, until he and his editors agree, contrary to many other academics who would view this as a personal insult. Ngũgĩ is a patient and humble listener. Of late, when he has stayed at our home, my wife Rosalind, an ardent Christian, has engaged him in prolonged biblical debates, and I have been amazed by the knowledge and interest with which Ngũgĩ has responded. They have even given each other home work for their next meeting! In the past, in the days of writing letters, I can say Ngũgĩ was a poor communicator, but in these days of email, fast telephone and Skype, his communication has been excellent. May it stay that way as we celebrate 80 years and beyond.

21
Working with Ngũgĩ

Sultan Somjee

In 1977, I was invited by Ngũgĩ to join him in the production of *Ngaahika Ndeenda* at Kamĩrĩĩthũ, his home village. At that time I knew very little about the history of Kenya other than the text book school versions and even less about viewing the history from the point of the majority of Kenyans who are the peasants and workers. Fresh from Europe, I was a starry eyed young man eager to engage with 'African culture' and particularly the culture of the 'grass-roots' ethnicities of Kenya, my place of birth.

I was a junior researcher at the Institute of African Studies, University of Nairobi and out in the field a lot working on material culture. It was in the field that my eyes opened up to the atrocities of the Kenyatta regime and the gruesome poverty experienced by many Kenyans. I used to cross over to the Northern Frontier District (NFD) military zone where no journalist was allowed, and I saw places where there were Mau Mau type concentration camps. I witnessed humiliation of the rural citizens by the regime's forces and the administration. I saw that the pogroms against the intellectuals that followed both the performance of *Ngaahika Ndeenda* and *Maitũ Njugĩra* and the detentions and exiles were not different from those in the rural north of Kenya and later among the Pokot and Turkana peoples. In the city where I lived, I saw police brutality waged on students and passers-by. This was the reality of the non-elites in everyday Kenya. These sights made a tremendous impact on me and gradually I began to understand what Ngũgĩ was saying, why the regime needed to be confronted, and how he was doing it. Ngũgĩ addressed the peasant farmers, students and workers from around like those from the Bata shoe factory. He addressed them in their own language and music. Poverty was the context and dictatorship the reason for the risk of taking *Ngaahika Ndeenda* and later *Maitũ Njugĩra* to the public forum.

I began reading about the Mau Mau. I must have read every book on the subject available and started to understand the significance of Ngũgĩ's plays in creating an awareness of history for a better understanding of the politics of Kenya and the history that was concealed from the majority, the history that was barred from the school texts and from public discourse, the history that was even dangerous to talk about, let alone put on stage. Working with the villagers in Limuru, I realized the power of memory and the importance of keeping it alive. The stories of *Ngaahika Ndeenda* became alive to me.

Performance after performance was emotionally felt by us all – the actors, back-stage helpers and the viewers. The site of the infamous Lari massacre was not far from Kamīrīīthū and among the spectators were those who had spent time in the concentration camps or had some relatives and fellow villagers who were tortured or had died for the cause. That collective power of memory and personal stories was tangible at the evening rehearsals at the Kamīrīīthū Community Education and Cultural Centre where Ngũgĩ wa Mĩriĩ, the co-author of *Ngaahika Ndeenda* and a keen follower of the Brazilian educational-ist Paulo Freire at the time, was an adult education teacher. The vibrancy at the rehearsals in a hurricane-lamp-lit class room later flowed from across the stage to the seated audience when the play was performed. The word spread and the amphitheatre was full to the capacity with people travelling from as far away as Muranga and Nyeri to watch the play.

It was at such moments of creativity and connectedness like the commu-nal back stage meals at Kamīrīīthū that I realised what community-based and participatory arts meant and how they could be created and performed by the people to whom they were addressed. I witnessed what stories and memory meant for the people when the content and the style of storytelling were rooted in traditions. Though I did not understand Gĩkũyũ, I was moved by the emo-tions of the actors, the audience and other participants. I realized I was in a moment of decolonizing the theatre in Kenya. Something that was happening from the grassroots and by the people. The stage of the National Theatre in Nairobi where as a school boy I watched plays in English often set to texts of the colonial curriculum, was now becoming truly national by coming home. We designed the stage together with local carpenters using match sticks to make models. And then the costumes, using traditional dress patterns from the ethnic *muthuru* (leather skirt), and the soil color, *therega* – the color of the Kenyan earth that the Mau Mau used to take the oath. Immediately, the costumes and colors resonated with the audience as the men thumped their feet, the *mutumias* (women) with the *haangi* (loop earrings) swaying on their ears aspirated throat hums and the dresses whirled to the music of *mwomboko* (dance).

It was this liveliness and enthusiasm, the zeal of memory of local history that the drama at Kamiĩrĩĩthu brought to the fore as an expression of Kenyan culture. Dare I say, people's expression of a culture that gave hope – that they too can perform, speak out and change their lives? The evocative songs and music that spoke to the heart, the patriot in oneself, made *Ngaahika Ndeenda* immediate. This was different from what was imparted in foreign tongues and art forms divulging appreciation of unfamiliar aesthetics and values that we received as students of art and literature. It was this that I carried forward working with Ngũgĩ and applied it to my own work on the material culture of Kenya, indigenous education and public exhibitions. I began experimenting using ethnic aesthetics in art education in schools and community-based participatory exhibitions at rural sites among the people with whom I lived, worked, collected and documented artefacts. When in 1988, the Kenya Institute of Education included the material culture of Kenya in the new 8-4-4 art and craft syllabus, I felt as if I was speaking in my own languages of art and living in my own skin, which was different from speaking in English on the campus of the University of Nairobi.

I started experimenting on exhibiting material culture in regions where I made the collections. Thus began my process of self-education by learning from the community as Ngũgĩ had once asked me to do. There was so much excitement and so many conversations when these open air 'museums' were brought to the people in their villages. Often, they reminded me of the banned open-air theatre at Kamĩrĩĩthũ. I continued with this approach for the next twenty-five years and abandoned the one-man show as the sole curator of exhibitions in favor of community-staged displays. Later, I used this approach when starting the people-based village museums of peace. These museums became civil society spaces during conflicts outside the interference and control of the 'peaceful and benevolent', 'love, peace and unity' dictatorship. In a way, these museums were replicas of Ngũgĩ's rural theatre.

Like the theatre in Kamĩrĩĩthũ, the performers at the museums of peace sought ways to express themselves through the vibrancy of the arts and in that achieving pride in who they were and what was their history as known to their elders. Let me explain. The museums of peace became places where young men and women from various ethnicities in conflict zones created dialogues enhancing their arts and languages, and in that they connected with and learnt about each other's traditions. These were the traditions about sustaining communities and indigenous heritages of resolving conflicts independent of the central authorities, institutions and the brutal military on the mission to 'restore order.' Most importantly, the various ethnicities were able to speak about themselves to themselves as one Kenyan to another. These museums kept the collective and hitherto unrecorded memories of *utu* in mother tongues, and indigenous norms of social justice and reconciliation alive while also preserving the dignity of languages and cultures that I saw subverted by political propaganda, corruption, misinformation and humiliation.

In all, what I know from Ngũgĩ wa Thiong'o is that even under oppressive regimes, there are people who are courageous enough to take the risk and speak out, who believe in the freedom of expression, justice and preserving their heritage and history. But under dictatorships public space is denied to them. Ngũgĩ's writings and work on the ground defied that and showed that culture can be such a space to generate community awareness and togetherness. *Ngahika Ndenda* and *Maitũ Njugĩra* allowed the people to learn from history and dream to end dictatorship, corruption and police brutality. The end of the regime would bring communal wellness that is encompassed in the concept of *utu* or peace. The dictatorships of Kenyatta and Moi feared the people's dream and the plays were banned. The Kamĩĩrĩĩthu theatre that we built with such pride and hope was wrecked with vengeance lest the people dream again. The dictatorships feared the people's dream. There is a Turkana saying: *One who dreams is called a prophet.*

We know from history that artists of conscience who have shaped art to turn the culture of fear and silence into one of defiance for freedom of expression, have inspired future generations to dream of equality and justice. But such a dream would imply sharing of the national wealth. For this reason writers of some of the greatest works of literature have often been imprisoned or exiled. Nevertheless, their work continues to stir humanity and change society. This has been the world history of great literature. This is the history of Kenya's great literature and its writer, Ngũgĩ wa Thiong'o.

22
Recollections of *Mũtiiri*

Kĩmani Njogu

I was undertaking graduate studies in linguistics at Yale University when I learnt that Ngũgĩ wa Thiong'o would be a member of the faculty in the Comparative Literature department. I had read Ngũgĩ widely and his writings had inspired me tremendously. When he released *Petals of Blood*, I read a chapter every day to my high school class before embarking on other matters. In the evenings, I would engage in deep discussions on Ngũgĩ's writings with my room-mate (the late Kaara wa Macharia who, like Ngũgĩ, had to go into exile during the crackdown on dissident intellectuals in Kenya). Later I watched the performances *Ngaahika Ndeenda* (*I will Marry When I Want*) at Kamĩrĩĩthũ and the 'rehearsals' of *Maitũ Njugĩra* (*Mother, Sing for You*) at the University of Nairobi.

At the peak of those difficult days of Daniel arap Moi's rule, many students of literature, history, and political science were specifically targeted by the police because they were considered to be leftist and under the tutelage of radical scholars such as Ngũgĩ wa Thiong'o. But the students were reading on their own in study groups and drawing on the ideas of Nelson Mandela, Samora Machel, Che Guevara, Malcolm X, and Frantz Fanon. During a police search in our rural home in 1982, I was accused by three police officers, who had specifically come to arrest me, of hiding and distributing copies of the *Pambana* underground magazine, authored by radical academics. Three hours of searching for the seditious literature in every nook and cranny did not yield fruit and the officers left our home quite frustrated. For a fortnight, they assigned a plain clothes officer to follow me wherever I went. Soon after, several of my friends were arrested and others exiled. This was after the August 1, 1982 attempted coup d'état against the Moi regime.

Daniel arap Moi was particularly concerned about Ngũgĩ's continued stay in exile. In his *Daily Nation* article reproduced in this volume (Article 9), Levin Odhiambo Opiyo narrates how Moi constantly put pressure on the British Government to have Ngũgĩ repatriated, often accusing him of propaganda and planning to start a communist party in Kenya. From memos and related correspondence, Opiyo concludes: 'The President's demand was clear: Britain should reject any visa extension application by the Kenyan academic and force him to relocate to another country.'

The idea of going to Yale and the possibility of learning under the man who had written *Decolonising the Mind* and who had shaped most of my thinking on the role of language and literature in social change was overwhelming. It was equally so for Athman Lali Omar, my room-mate and friend. I had met Athman, an archaeologist from the beautiful Island of Lamu, on a boat to Pate Island in 1988. Within days, we were planning how we would share an apartment close to the Yale campus and split the utility bills.

Ngũgĩ's arrival in New Haven in 1989 gave the three of us an opportunity to not only discuss matters of language and literature, but also of resistance by coastal communities against Portuguese, Arab, and British colonialism. Ngũgĩ was particularly interested in the stories of resistance to colonial rule at the Kenyan coast as told by Athman in Kiswahili. Whereas Ngũgĩ appreciated my mastery of Kiswahili, he constantly urged me to speak with him in Gĩkũyũ when the two of us were alone together. It is quite likely that through me he sought to reconnect with his Gĩkũyũ identity and the experiences of the squatter communities from which I came. I shared my childhood experiences in the Rift Valley, the struggles over access to land and its resources, and the disillusionment of independence. We had deep conversations at the Tufts Apartments, where Ngũgĩ initially stayed before moving to a house near the Main Gymnasium the following year. It is in this latter residence where *Mũtiiri*, the Gĩkũyũ Journal of Culture, was born in 1994.

The initial conceptualization of *Mũtiiri* was driven by Ngũgĩ wa Thiong'o, Ann Biersteker, Gĩtahi Gĩtĩtĩ, and myself. In imagining the journal, we sought to create a platform for cultural sharing and linguistic engineering. We were interested in building the Gĩkũyũ lexicon and therefore most of our discussions were held in Gĩkũyũ. Ann Biersteker was extremely patient with us as we dug deep into the nuances of our language. After building consensus on the journal's title and agreeing that the term '*mũtiiri*', 'the supporter', represented what we sought to do with Gĩkũyũ language and culture, we grappled with the word for 'journal' in Gĩkũyũ. To resolve this issue, we coined the word '*njaranda*', conveniently borrowed from the Kiswahili term '*jarida*'. The Editorial Committee of the journal uniformly accepted borrowing from Kiswahili and other African languages as a strategy for lexical expansion.

The cover of the first issue of *Mũtiiri* was designed by Allan Stankiewicz, a high school art teacher and my Kiswahili student at the time. Discussions about the journal were deep albeit occasionally playful. At times, we had sumptuous dinners colored by powerful poetry readings. Gĩtahi Gĩtĩtĩ always lit up the evening with his rich use of language and symbolism. When he was not reading his own original poems, Gĩtahi would perform pieces translated directly from Spanish into Gĩkũyũ. I would occasionally read my Gĩkũyũ translations of Kiswahili poetry, especially from Abdilatif Abdalla's *Sauti ya Dhiki* (*Voice of Agony*) and Alamin Mazrui's *Chembe cha Moyo* (*Arrow in My*

Heart). For us, the coming into being of *Mūtiiri* was a journey of translation into, and across, languages and cultures. Ngũgĩ informed me that when New York University offered him a position, the funding of *Mūtiiri* was one of the conditions for his acceptance of the offer. NYU readily accepted to fund the journal. Later *Mūtiiri* became one of the main sponsors of, and the model for, the Asmara Conference that informed the 2000 Asmara Declaration on African Languages and Literatures.

Although I was a student of linguistics, there was no way I was going to be absent from Ngũgĩ's weekly seminar on African literatures. The seminar was popular not only because it was offered by one of Africa's politically committed writers, but also because of the significance of the issues it raised. I had studied literature and Kiswahili at the University of Nairobi and understood the postcolonial issues that Ngũgĩ's writings sought to unravel rather personally. Having been born on settler Hamilton's farm in Kipkelion and grown up in a multicultural peri-urban setting defiantly called 'Shauri Yako' ('It is Up to You'), I could relate to Ngũgĩ's characters well, and I easily saw the connection between literature and the historical experiences which Ngũgĩ often emphasized in his seminar. His regular invocation of Frantz Fanon and Amilcar Cabral was music to my eyes.

I will always be grateful to the then Head of the Linguistics Department, Professor Larry Horn, for understanding that in addition to taking linguistics classes, I needed to take courses from the departments of Comparative Literature and Anthropology. Those courses have served me well over the years. It is in the department of Comparative Literature that Michael Holquist introduced me to Mikhail Bakhtin and dialogism. My reading of dialogism took me directly to Ngũgĩ's writings and *gĩcandĩ* classical poetry. The riddle-like *gĩcandĩ* genre was the embodiment of creativity, performance, and criticism. Ngũgĩ became for me the *gĩcandĩ* poet, constantly challenging African intellectuals to a duel on our role in society. Like the roving community griot, Ngũgĩ was not constrained by time and space in his creative explorations. When I started thinking about my PhD dissertation on dialogic poetry, I turned to Ngũgĩ wa Thiong'o, Ann Biersteker, Michael Holquist, and Larry Horn for guidance. The dissertation research took me back to Lamu, Kiambu, and Zanzibar as I tried to understand how dialogism works.

As fate would have it, after Athman Lali Omar left to join the University of Florida, I was lucky to have Ngũgĩ's son Thiong'o as my room-mate. Thiong'o had joined Yale as an MA student in African Studies and soon became part of the team of Kiswahili teaching assistants that I would work with. While Athman had given me Kiamu (the Swahili of Lamu), Thiong'o gave me German and literary theory. For months, our evenings would be defined by discussions around philosophy and literature, with occasional excursions into Kenyan politics and our role in social change. Occasionally, I would be an observer of the father–son intellectual duel, and I would relish every moment as Thiong'o took contrarian positions in order to engage his father in debate.

I remember a call in the spring of 1990 from Professor Sara Suleri asking if I could read through a Gĩkũyũ article that Ngũgĩ had written for the *Yale Journal of Criticism*. I was thrilled! Apparently, Suleri had invited Ngũgĩ to contribute to the journal. Ngũgĩ, having only recently bid 'farewell' to English with the publication of *Decolonising the Mind*, retorted 'I write nowadays in Gĩkũyũ!' But Suleri urged him on. The article 'Kĩĩngeretha Rũthiomi Rwa Thĩ Yoothe? Kaba Gĩthwaĩri' ('English as the Language of the World? I would Rather Kiswahili') was the first African-language article to be published by *Yale Journal of Criticism*. Ngũgĩ would later tell me how he had come to write the article:

> It happened that in London, I had given a presentation in a BBC seminar organized by the English Union whose patron was the Duke of Edinburgh. The conference was on English as a language for the world. I wrote my paper in Gĩkũyũ, read the first paragraph in Gĩkũyũ, but read the rest of the presentation in English; that is the translation. My paper argued for Kiswahili (not English) as the language of the world. What I did not know was that The Duke himself as the Patron of the English Union was in the audience but at the back behind the curtain. At the reception he came straight to me, and we chatted for a few minutes. He said he understood my position very well. He was Greek after all, so came to English from Greek; very diplomatic. I thought. This was the paper that I gave to Suleri, on condition that the Gĩkũyũ version and the English translation be published as two separate papers and not on opposite pages. So ironically my first major scholarly paper in Gĩkũyũ was first published in the *Yale Journal of Criticism*. (Personal communication)

When I returned to Kenya after my studies, I helped form CHAKITA (The Kenya National Kiswahili Committee) and became its founding chair. Soon after, I linked up with Ngũgĩ's friend, the late Gakaara wa Wanjaũ and, together with other language activists, we formed the UUGI Language Association to support the growth of Gĩkũyũ terminology. I also joined the national constitutional reform movement to advocate for linguistic and cultural rights. Ngũgĩ's thinking on language required a policy and legislative framework and we were going to provide the anchor.

When Ngũgĩ returned to Kenya in August 2004 after many years in exile, I was privileged to moderate his public lecture on 'Languages in World Politics' delivered at the Kenyatta International Conference Centre to an overflowing audience. The lecture took place at a difficult time because the memories of the attack on Ngũgĩ and his wife Njeeri at the Norfolk Towers were still quite fresh in most people's mind. Since then we have built the requisite national framework for the advancement of Ngũgĩ's thinking through policy formulation and legal instruments. At the continental level, the activities of the African Academy of Languages (ACALAN) will contribute to the realization of Ngũgĩ's dream of moving the center so that many voices can be heard.

Part IV

The Writer, the Critic & the World

23
Bricklayer & Architect of a World to Come

Emilia Ilieva

'The patience of the bricklayer/ is assumed in the dream of the architect', Gael Turnbull has written (in Owens 'Gael Turnbull: The Bricklayer Reconsidered'). In the all-important project of building Kenya into our imagination, Ngũgĩ has worked as both the bricklayer and the architect. Plunging in the early years of his career into history, he has cleared the ground of colonial and neo-colonial narrative falsehoods, of chaotic, narrow and superficial representations of Kenya, and carefully, brick by brick, he has imagined a Kenya whose past was an unbroken chain of resistance to conquest and oppression, and in which the agents of every creative endeavor were the common people. Turning later to the post-colonial present, he has peeled the camouflaging tarpaulin spread over the body of the nation and exposed the 'petals of blood' feeding on its flesh. His pathos of rejection has only been equaled by his pathos of analysis as he strived to 'suggest a future' – a Kenya free of the all-consuming greed of a powerful minority in which the principle of humanity triumphs. This architectural dream of a world to come constitutes the most sacred aspiration of the Kenyan people and nurtures their indomitable spirit.

Ngũgĩ's concern, however, has been not only with Kenya, but with Africa as a whole. *Re-membering Africa* (also published as *Something Torn and New*), in particular, is dedicated to this other project – the transformation of Africa from a repeatedly dismembered, torn apart plaything, into a complete being with a limitless capacity for re-generation and growth. Ngũgĩ is inspired by the idea of making the twenty-first century a century of genuine re-birth for Africa, its peoples and their cultures. The depth of this idea and the hope that permeates it turn his essays into significant interventionist strategies.

The African experience, because of slavery and colonization, has been fraught with notions of fragmented histories and cultures. Colonial inscriptions and skewed knowledge production on and of Africa have arrested the development of the continent on many fronts. The Empire also made deliberate attempts to either erase or deny the African and other colonized peoples' history altogether. But as Edward Said has argued in *Orientalism*, 'history cannot be swept clean like a blackboard, clean so that "we" might inscribe our own future there and impose our own forms of life for these lesser people to follow' (xiii).

With special insight Ngũgĩ has outlined the pernicious process through which colonialism shattered the memory of the people of Africa: 'The ambitious colonial scheme of reconstructing an African whose historical, physical, and metaphysical geography begins with European memory was almost realized with the production of ... a native class dismembered from its social memory' (*Re-membering* 21–2). Such 'invented' people, obviously, are rootless, and their identities are problematic. The memory of their past consists in seeing only what the forces behind the dismembering wanted them to see. The process of 're-membering' then is an arduous one. Yet there is no way out rather than the endeavor to reconnect the past to the present as a basis for the future through the use of the expressive media of art, dance, literature and cinema. The vastness of the exercise calls for guidance from 'the great re-membering vision of Pan-Africanism' (49).

As an intellectual and thinker, steadfast and confident in his belief, Ngũgĩ stresses the necessity to foreground African languages in this broad movement of revival. At the same time, he guards against the isolation of African languages from the tradition of progressive human thought expressed in a diversity of languages and cultures. The memory of others in the globe is bound to be enriching. But most important is the realization of the conjoined nature of power/knowledge, so that in being active creators of knowledge, the African people can lay greater claim to world/global power order and relations.

Ultimately, Ngũgĩ's ideas speak also to the world at large. They are ideas about the role of culture at a time when the numerous ills that afflict our planet diminish our faith in ourselves. The Kenyan writer believes that to overcome this crisis culture must assume the function of a world outlook. Indeed, this is how it used to be in the glorious moments of our collective past. Today we stand in awe of Egypt's wondrous pyramids and cities of the dead, of Europe's gigantic Gothic cathedrals. The full meanings of their creation elude us. What we do not doubt is that it is these meanings that held millennial kingdoms together.

But for culture to be restored to the pedestal where it belongs, it must have its priests and knights. Kenya – and Africa – are fortunate to have such a priest and knight – builder and architect – in the person of Ngũgĩ wa Thiong'o.

24
Revisioning Goethe's Idea of 'World Literature'

[Commendation Address On the Awarding of the Dr. Phil. h.c. (Honorary Doctor of Letters) to Ngũgĩ wa Thiong'o, University of Bayreuth, Germany, April 2014]

Anne Adams

In *Globalectics,* a book from 2012 on postcolonial literature, Ngũgĩ wa Thiong'o invokes Johan Wolfgang von Goethe to make the assertion that 'the postcolonial is at the heart of the constitution of Goethe's world literature' (55). He quotes Goethe's claim from the early nineteenth century that '"[T]he epoch of world literature is at hand, and everyone must strive to hasten its approach"' (44). Ngũgĩ himself comments further:

> One of the earliest to talk of a possible world literature, [Goethe] said that it could be fostered only by an untrammeled intercourse among all contemporaries … That was in 1801, in his journal *Propyläen* … For almost thirty years, between 1801 and 1831, in different fora, and in almost identical wording, he continued to restate that conviction. (*Globalectics* 44)

Ngũgĩ does acknowledge, of course, that Germany's most revered poet 'may have been thinking of Europe'. Indeed, if we regard Goethe's continued reiteration of the 'world-literature' concept up to the end of his life, we see that he clearly was equating 'world' with Europe: In the draft for one issue of his *Kunst und Alterthum* (1829), he wrote 'Erste Fassung: "Weltliteratur." Zweite Fassung: "Europäische, d.h. Welt-Literatur"' ('First version: "World Literature." Second version: "European, i.e. World Literature"').

Taking the liberty myself to extend the reflections of the twenty-first-century Kenyan being celebrated today on the ideas of the nineteenth-century celebrated German, I would add another Goethe statement on world literature, which adds a bit more substance to the concept, although this time, addressing journals (1828):

> Diese Zeitschriften, wie sie sich nach und nach ein größeres Publikum gewinnen, werden zu einer gehofften allgemeinen Weltliteratur auf das wirksamste beitragen; nur wiederholen wir, daß nicht die Rede sein könne, die Nationen sollen *überein denken, sondern sie sollten nur einander gewahr werden, sich*

begreifen, und wenn sie sich wechselseitig nicht lieben mögen, sich einander wenigstens dulden lernen.

[These magazines, as they gradually gain a larger audience, will contribute most effectively to a hoped-for general world literature; only we repeat that there can be no question that the nations should agree, but they should only become aware of each other, understand each other, and if they do not love each other mutually, at least learn to tolerate each other.]

In the course of the essay on postcolonial literature where those Goethe references appear, Ngũgĩ reconciles Goethe's nineteenth-century intent with his own twenty-first-century conception of world literature, and particularly with the place of postcolonial literature within it.

The place of Ngũgĩ wa Thiong'o himself in world literature can be appreciated through the accumulated strength of his writer-as-theorist-and-activist achievements in the sphere of African literary production. At the center of his work are questions of the relation between art and society, art and the state, the function of culture, power and knowledge. Ngũgĩ has grappled with these questions in his literary works themselves—a short-story anthology, seven novels, and four plays—in searching for aesthetic forms to engage the social issues. Likewise, he has addressed those questions through his essays, published in seven volumes, as well as in his two memoirs.

Those memoirs, which are among Ngũgĩ's most recent publications, provide a context for connecting the life to the work of the writer-activist. *Dreams in a Time of War: A Childhood Memoir*, published in 2010, was followed by *In the House of the Interpreter: A Memoir*, in 2012. The 'dreams' of the childhood memoir are those that accompanied his treasured opportunity to go to school, while the 'war' was the multi-faceted struggle for self-determination, not least of which was the resistance of the Mau Mau freedom fighters, of whom Ngũgĩ's older brother was a member. He relates the episode, when as a boy of eight or nine, he received, from his intrepidly resourceful mother, 'the offer of the impossible that deprived me of words' (*Dreams* 59) and eagerly assented to her only demand: 'Promise me that you'll not bring shame to me by one day refusing to go to school because of hunger or other hardships?' (*Dreams* 60). That would establish the context for his first published novel *Weep Not, Child*, from 1964. The second memoir, *In the House of the Interpreter*, chronicles his high school years at the prestigious Alliance High School, with its elite education at Alliance in the British liberal intellectual tradition, coinciding with the State of Emergency and independence struggle. That British liberal education, which continued through his undergraduate years at Makerere University College, eventually engendered the intellectual crisis that would underlie Ngũgĩ's early novels.

Following graduate studies at Leeds University he returned to Kenya to teach in the English Department at University College, in Nairobi. By now, critical of the centrality of European literature in the university's curriculum, the young lecturer, along with two other colleagues, spearheaded the move to ground literary studies in an African epistemology, based in Kenya's and East African traditional verbal arts and cultural epistemology, and subsequently expanding to literary and language study of the wider African continent and its diaspora, and ultimately to European and other world cultures. Their movement resulted in the abolition of the English Department at the University of Nairobi and its replacement with the Department of Literature.

Ngũgĩ's writing career had begun while a student at Makerere, in Kampala, Uganda, where his play *The Black Hermit* was performed, in 1962, as part of Uganda's Independence celebrations. This fact is all the more notable because this was the first performance at Uganda's National Theatre of a work by an African writer. From early on, his literary productivity was driven, in tandem with his activism, in the cause of social justice and cultural development in independent, neo-colonial Kenya. His first novels, starting with the bildungs-roman *Weep Not, Child* (1964), through *The River Between* (1965), and *A Grain of Wheat* (1967), which was set during the Emergency, focused on the Kenyan people's struggle against colonialism, including the role of Mau Mau freedom fighters, and simultaneously the relationship of the Western Christian humanist tradition of Shakespeare, Wordsworth, and the Bible—a source of language as well as philosophy—in which he had been steeped at Alliance High School and at Makerere. However, it is generally agreed among scholars of his work, that Ngũgĩ's novels that were written after his graduate education experience at Leeds University were greatly affected by his introduction there to Marxism and to the postcolonial theoretical writings of Frantz Fanon.

Hence, his focus, beginning with the post-independence epic *Petals of Blood* (1977), shifted to the neo-colonial state and its betrayal of the aspirations for which the Kenyan people had engaged in the independence struggle. In the words of the eminent Ngũgĩ scholar, Simon Gikandi (also, a former student of Ngũgĩ's), 'Ngũgĩ was now seeking ways of shifting his aesthetic ideology from morality and sensibility to history and epistemology' (*Ngũgĩ wa Thiong'o* 253) It is also significant that within this historical turn the evolving aesthetic ideology described by Gikandi has consistently given centrality to issues of gender in re-membering the nation's story. This is true not only from the early novel, *The River Between* (1965), where Gĩkũyũ cultural identity is problematized through the metaphor of female circumcision, but through to the most recent *Wizard of the Crow* (2006), with its female revolutionary activist on the ground anchoring the floating mythological wizard protagonist. For scholars of African feminism Ngũgĩ has long been included among African feminist writers.

His writings and social activism in the early decades of his career, particularly the production of plays in collaboration with a local peasant group in his home town of Limuru, most notably *I Will Marry When I Want* (1979), eventually led to his arrest and year-long detention without charge, which was ended because of a campaign by Amnesty International, recognizing him as a prisoner of conscience. The energized activity of common people, who had constructed their own theatre and performed in the plays in Gĩkũyũ, castigating the neo-colonial co-optation of the ruling classes, was suppressed by the government through the denial of performing rights and ultimately the razing of the community-built theatre. Subsequently, with his life under threat by the government, the writer was forced into exile, first in Britain, then in the U.S., where he held distinguished professorships at New York and Yale Universities, before taking up his present position at the University of California, Irvine. It would be twenty-two years, before Ngũgĩ could return to Kenya.

The novels, which had earlier been required readings in the Kenyan school and university curricula—giving, for the first time, the psychologically critical introduction of Kenyan literary faces and spaces for Kenyan school-children—were eventually all banned. This includes, most notably, the 'arrest' of one novel *Matigari*, when the President, hearing that someone called Matigari was going around the country asking questions about the betrayed expectations of independence, ordered to have this person arrested. Upon learning that Matigari was the protagonist of a novel, the President then ordered that the *novel* be arrested!

As of 1977 Ngũgĩ changed his name, dropping the Christian name 'James', and using instead his Gĩkũyũ patronymic 'wa Thiong'o'. Simultaneously, there emerged a shift in his subject matter from the anti-colonial struggle to the neo-colonial betrayal. That shift in focus was also accompanied by an evolution in the writing itself. In his style he was concerned with adapting the European bourgeois novel form to tell the Kenyan story and especially creating a vehicle for the orality of African story-telling. The principle that has driven Ngũgĩ's literary activism, certainly in the past three decades, is the conviction that a people's memory, i.e., the critical basis of their subjectivity, is preserved through their own language. Hence, his own practice of writing in Gĩkũyũ and his advocacy for the cultivation of other African languages for literary performance and for the promotion of translation work. During his detention, in 1978, he made the decision to write his works in the Gĩkũyũ language thenceforth, as the appropriate means of writing for and to, as well as about, the Kenyan people. And so, he wrote, while in detention, the fifth novel *Caitaani Mũtharaba-inĩ* in Gĩkũyũ, which he subsequently translated himself as *Devil on the Cross* (1980). *Matigari* (1986) and *Wizard of the Crow* (2006), the two novels published since then, were also written originally in Gĩkũyũ (*Matigari ma Njirũũngi* and *Mũrogi wa Kagogo*).

The significance of his creative writings notwithstanding, Ngũgĩ's international stature as a writer, critic, and theorist rests as much on his seven essay collections on cultural theory as on his seven novels and other creative writings. Indeed, his essays are the subject of critical studies in the social sciences as well as in the humanities. These essay volumes include several that are by now classics of literary theory, e.g., *Homecoming: Essays on African and Caribbean Literature Culture, and Politics* (1972); *Decolonising the Mind: The Politics of Language in African Literature* (1986); *Moving the Centre: The Struggle for Cultural Freedoms* (1993); as well as the more recent *Globalectics: Theory and the Politics of Knowing* (2012). Reflecting the trajectory of his thinking on various topics of cultural politics, all the essays interrogate, in one form or another, the matter of the role of literature in the articulation of African subjectivity, especially through education and language. In doing so, he engages not only other African and Diaspora writers and thinkers such as Achebe and Soyinka; Léopold Senghor, Aimé Césaire, W. E. B. Du Bois, and C. L. R. James, but also other iconic thinkers from Machiavelli and Hegel to Thomas Jefferson; from Edward Said, Fredric Jameson, and Gayatri Spivak to Michel Foucault; from Marx and Brecht and Tolstoy to Deleuze and Guattari; and, of course, Goethe, among numerous others. Pressing the urgency of producing and teaching literature that can re-form the subjectivity of African people, Ngũgĩ says, in his essay 'Literature and Society':

> A nation's literature which is a sum total of the products of many individuals in that society is then not only a reflection of that people's collective reality, collective experience, but also embodies that community's way of looking at the world and its place in the making of that world. It is partisan on the collective level, because the literature is trying to make us see how that community, class, race, group *has defined itself historically and how it defines the world in relationship to itself.* (In *Writers in Politics* 7, emphasis added)

The multitude of critical studies on Ngũgĩ elucidate his trajectory as a writer and the several artistic and philosophical stages of that trajectory, including the sometime contradictions in theoretical stance. Stages in the trajectory go from the earliest novels of the 1960s interrogating cultural nationalism, through his Marxism-based early theoretical writings of the 1970s, his imprisonment and prison writings in the late 1970s, followed by the decision to abandon English in his novels, and the subsequent debate over the role of national languages, for him particularly Gĩkũyũ; and the concomitant push to transform the nature of the African novel, 'the appropriation of the novel into the oral tradition' (in Gikandi 210). As Gikandi states, 'Ngũgĩ was using formal experimentation [orality] to rethink the politics of everyday life in contemporary Africa in terms other than the disintegration, decline, and failure' (Gikandi 215). His most recent novel, *Wizard of the Crow* (2006), virulently demonstrates that experimentation and the politics of everyday life in contemporary Kenya within a globalized community dominated by transnational institutions, such as the 'Global Bank', an obvious parody of the World Bank.

This time, with *Wizard*, combining parody, satire, the scatological, and the carnivalesque with Gĩkũyũ mythology, Ngũgĩ accommodates story-telling features of African oral narrative, providing numerous opportunities for the performative expression of the common people in their critique of dominant power. He depicts the nation, yoked to international capital, as a totally privatized 'corporony', offering itself as 'the first to be wholly managed by private capital, to become the first voluntary corporate colony, a corporony, the first in the new global order'. In that new global order in which Ngũgĩ satirically contextualizes the African nation, '[t]he world will no longer be composed of the outmoded twentieth-century divisions of East, West, and a directionless Third. The world will become one corporate globe divided into the incorporating and the incorporated' (*Wizard* 746). What is new in this latest novel—appearing twenty years after the previous one—is Ngũgĩ's extending of the formal narrative parameters to incorporate multiple registers, and his expanding of the geo-political boundaries of his focal African nation to incorporate the globalized community. But through it all, he continues his intrepid pursuit of what he has all along believed to be his engagement as a writer, as he states in his book *Writers in Politics*:

> The product of a writer's imaginative involvement—what Shakespeare called mirror unto nature—becomes a reflection of society: its economic structure, its class formation, its conflicts and contradictions; its class power political and cultural struggles; its structure of values—the conflict and tensions arising from the antagonism between those which are dying and those which are pointing to the future. (72)

With particular relevance to this latest novel, another statement from the same essay collection is germane here: 'the literature is trying to make us see how that community, class, race, group has defined itself historically and *how it defines the world in relationship to itself* (emphasis added; 7).

As I have stated, with *Wizard of the Crow*, Ngũgĩ brings a globalized perspective to the condition of the postcolonial African nation. This globalized perspective embraces many worldwide issues beyond the economic power relations and cultural renaissance, e.g., HIV/AIDS and forest ecology, a particularly controversial topic in Kenya at the time this novel was written, heightened by the 2004 awarding of the Nobel Peace prize to Kenyan eco-activist Wangari Maathai. So, this globalized perspective invites consideration of a theoretical bridge between the author's thinking with that 2006 novel *Wizard of the Crow* and the 2012 essay collection *Globalectics: Theory and Politics of Knowing*. His brief definition of the term *globalectics* is: 'the liberation of literature from the straightjacket of nationalism' (*Globalectics* 8). The essay that actually elucidates that theory is 'Globaletical Imagination: The World in the Post-Colonial'. Indeed, this is the essay in which Ngũgĩ invokes Goethe's concept of world literature, referencing also Karl Marx. Asserting the rightful place of African and other non-European, especially postcolonial, literatures within the concept of world literature, Ngũgĩ continues:

> No term can really substitute for the one coined by Goethe. World literature must include what's already formed in the world as well as what's now informed by the world, at once a coalition, a cohesion, and coalescence of literatures in world languages into global consciousness. It is a process.
>
> At present, the postcolonial is the closest to that Goethian [*sic*] and Marxian conception of world literature because it is a product of different streams and influences from different points of the globe, a diversity of sources, which it reflects in turn. The postcolonial is inherently outward looking, inherently international in its very constitution in terms of themes, language, and the intellectual formation of the writers. It would be quite productive to look at world literature, though not exclusively, through postcoloniality. (*Globalectics* 49)

Affirming Goethe's nineteenth-century insistence on a world-literature paradigm, the Kenyan writer up-dates it to the twenty-first century, as we learned from the opening quotation of this talk, by citing the cosmopolitanism that has been created through postcolonialism:

> In reality the postcolonial is not simply located in the third world. Literally rooted in the intertextuality of products from all the corners of the globe, its universalist tendency is inherent in its very relationship to historical colonialism and its globe for a theater. (*Globalectics* 55)

But, as Ngũgĩ's theoretical and creative writings demonstrate, the matter of the organizing of knowledge with regard to the vast 'sea' of literatures from the many 'streams' and 'rivers' from the world's peoples and cultures that produce it becomes an essential challenge. Obviously, as he says, 'it makes sense for any country, any nation, to prioritize its literature with the hope that the people would be able to see their own in other literatures and not study it in isolation' (*Globalectics* 56–7). In his own experience, the radical re-organizing, in the 1960s, of the teaching of literature at the University of Nairobi, of which Ngũgĩ was a prime mover, was a way of organizing that sphere of knowledge to embrace the world's literatures while prioritizing their own. But even then, 'their own' at the University of Nairobi was not only Kenyan but also African and pan-African.

Thus, in considering the organizing of literature departments and other knowledge-organizing structures, in pursuing Goethe's ideal of world literature, Ngũgĩ urges that new structures be considered, such as departments of world literature. And he is professionally supporting this approach to literature by means of his current position, as director of the International Center for Writing and Translation, at the University of California, Irvine. At issue for him is the fundamental question in overcoming 'aesthetic feudalism', which results from a hierarchy of literatures and cultures based on their language of composition. How do we read a text? Or, what baggage do we bring to the reading of a text? Ultimately, for Ngũgĩ, in pursuing world literature the act of reading becomes a process of self-examination (*Globalectics* 61). It is

> the mutual containment of hereness and thereness in time and space, where time and space are also in each other ... it is to read a text with the eyes of the world; it is to see the world with the eyes of the text. (*Globalectics* 60)

Professor Ngũgĩ's vision, which is rooted in a *re-visioning* of Goethe's concept of world literature, and whose object is the democratization of the organization of knowledge, offers an eloquent challenge for an engagement not only with literature, but also with theory, in any field, and with the over-arching politics of knowledge.

25

Globalectics: Beyond Postcoloniality, & Engaging the Caribbean

Carole Boyce Davies

(An earlier version of this article was published as 'Globalectics Beyond Postcoloniality'. The Global South Project, Cornell University. www. globalsouthproject.cornell.edu/globalectics-beyond-postcoloniality.html)

Today there is no longer a Department of English at the University of the West Indies (UWI). Instead within the Faculty of Humanities and Education there are departments of Literatures and Languages, specializing in the teaching of literature; departments of Language, Linguistics and Philosophy, devoted to the teaching of theories of language and a Department of Modern Language and Literature where one can get specialized training in foreign though largely European languages as they should be termed. At the Mona Campus, the website of the Department of Literatures in English proudly claims the following:

> Founded in 1950, as the then Department of English, we have produced distinguished alumni who have contributed immensely to Caribbean literary scholarship and creative writing … Although our strengths are primarily in Caribbean literary and cultural studies, the Department of Literatures in English at UWI, Mona offers a wide variety of courses ranging from Medieval and Renaissance Literature to Reggae Poetry. Students are exposed to British and American literature, the literature of postcolonial regions such as Africa, the Caribbean, South Asia, Australia and New Zealand, literary theory, film studies, and creative writing. (www.mona.uwi.edu)

While one cannot create a one-to-one correspondence with Ngũgĩ's landmark 'On the Abolition of the English Department', co-written with Henry Owuor-Anyumba and Taban lo Liyong in 1968, the fact that that essay appeared in his book *Homecoming* which included essays on Caribbean and African literature cannot be minimized. Such a discussion would surely have reached the faculty of the University of the West Indies campuses, engaged in similar decolonization tasks. So it is significant that the department at Mona identifies its strengths as Caribbean literary and cultural studies as it should be and thereby is realized one aspect of the 'Abolition' document which for African universities wanted a focus on African literatures and languages. The extent to which this has been achieved, or not achieved, at African universities is an issue worth studying in the context of some of the gains and failures of the postcolonial African state.

Still, it is true that, at the macro level, the University of the West Indies remains, as one of the senior UWI St. Augustine professors reminded me during my year there as a Visiting Professor 2007–08, one of two major institutions (the other being the cricket team) still carrying the name of the Columbian error (West Indies) and the subsequent British colonial fragmentation into a West Indian identity for the Anglophone Caribbean. But, more significantly, the fact that the Nairobi group had presented perhaps the most convincing argument for the decolonization of the study and teaching of literature would have impacted the internal re-structuring of an English department.

Indeed, students who read the 'Abolition of the English Department' essay are often surprised that such a construct as a Department of English exists, or existed, in universities in Africa and in other parts of the colonial world. Reading the essay makes students aware of the far reaches of colonialism in the academic context. Additionally, it is not much of a leap of imagination for students to come to understand that a Department of English in Africa, or in the United States, tends to do the same things – privileges the teaching of English literatures, creates a hierarchy of what is taught, and establishes the standards for good literature. Thus one can have still in the United States, several professors and therefore classes studying various periods, authors, genres of English literature, an ongoing struggle for American literatures and perhaps one professor and/or one class in African literature representing the entire continent or one professor teaching Caribbean literature, covering the entire Caribbean; and the extreme but not unusual one professor in some institutions assigned to teach all 'postcolonial' literatures.

Ngũgĩ wa Thiong'o's ongoing thinking on the nature of knowledge production in the academy worldwide is invaluable. His *Decolonising the Mind,* an essential text in the teaching of Black Literary and Cultural Theory in general, provides an extension of Fanonian decolonization, this time in the parallel area of language. It continues to provide the best arguments for how European languages served as a vehicle for colonialism and affected the nature of a writer's thinking and therefore his writing: 'The domination of a people's language by the languages of the colonising nations was crucial to the domination of the mental universe of the colonised' (*Decolonising the Mind* 16).

And so we arrive at an argument for the use of Jamaican patois such as the one provided in the various transgressive studies of language by UWI scholar Carolyn Cooper. The intellectual contributions of Cooper offer us some of the best extended discussion of the meaning of decoloniing language; here is a scholar who has experimented successfully with doing an entire theoretical paper in '*patwa*' (the way it is rendered locally rather than the French spelling *patois*) at an academic conference. Having been on the same panel with Carolyn Cooper as she engaged in that process of presenting a paper in *patwa*, I can testify to the communal reverberations of a scholar taking such a leap, and the affirmations she received from the community at large. This would lead to her subsequent writing of a column in the *Daily Gleaner* using *patwa* or 'nation language'. Additionally she became a defender of the importance of Jamaican-based language in various fora, such as electoral politics. Cooper's defense of Prime Minister Portia Simpson Miller during a campaign attack in which her opponents tried to present her as wild and irrational because she had voiced a condemnation of an attempt to reduce her to her class origins, was legendary. In her essay, 'Drawing Sister P's Tongue', Cooper articulated her defense of Simpson Miller in the following terms:

> In the 2007 election campaign, the Jamaica Labour Party (JLP) attempted to draw Portia Simpson Miller's tongue by provocatively distorting her battle cry. Her fierce words became the mouthpiece, so to speak, of the JLP advertising campaign. I suppose it was easier to knock down Portia Simpson Miller than to prop up Bruce Golding ... In 2011, the JLP has again resorted to drawing Sister P's tongue. G2K is desperately trying to revive that discredited commercial. Portia Simpson Miller's powerful words are misinterpreted as evidence that she needs 'anger management'.

Cooper is the author of a number of books on Jamaican orality, including *Noises in the Blood: Orality, Gender, and the 'Vulgar' Body of Jamaican Popular Culture* (1995), and *Sound Clash: Jamaican Dance Hall Culture at Large* (2004), and an edited collection, *Global Reggae* (2012). She is a faculty member of the Department of Literature at UWI, as indicated at the start of this essay, and through her work has ensured a place for the scholarly engagement with a range of Jamaican popular language and literary forms.

'Nation language' as defined by Kamau Brathwaite in *History of the Voice* was a similar attempt by the Caribbean historian and writer to account for the specificities of Caribbean language forms, as spoken and understood by the various local populations. He defines them not as 'broken English', but syntactically, lexically, and vocabularily combinations and reinterpretations of a variety of languages, including African, European, and native languages (5–6). In Jamaican poet and folklorist Louise Bennett's words, Jamaican language, is, as was English before it, 'derived' from earlier forms. One can see Ngũgĩ wa Thiong'o's 'decolonizing' discourse at work here, as these writers and thinkers from across the colonial world end up in conversation with each other, and as they attempt to examine, at the public level, some of the contradictions of working with inherited languages and creating decolonial space.

Similarly, this attempt to find decolonial space defined the new academic incarnation of African Diaspora Studies in the late 1990s. The version of

African Diaspora Studies that I worked with saw this field as challenging the general Eurocentric base of knowledge; hence the title of the collection that came out of a conference on this subject, *Decolonizing the Academy: African Diaspora Studies*. In the introductory essay to this collection, I asserted that the academy 'is a site for the production and re-production of a variety of discourses which keep in place certain colonial structures which have as their intent the maintenance of Euro-American hegemonies at the level of thinking and therefore in the larger material world' (ix). But the academy can also be a 'liberatory space, a site of transformation and knowledge production' (ix). Further, if we are able to accept a range of ideas from a variety of locations, we can continue the advancement of the epistemological assumptions of the institutions of higher learning.

One of the most poignant manifestations of this ongoing challenge to western epistemologies has been the production of a poetry which, following the publication of Kamau Brathwaite's *The Arrivants* (1967), applies the structures of nation language to provide both a theoretical and poetic basis for decoloniality. NourbeSe Philip's poem 'Discourse on the Logic of Language', with its extensive argument on language acquisition and use and with its famous conclusion that 'English is a foreign anguish', is a good example of a poetry of decoloniality. Also, in her essay, 'The Absence of Writing or How I Almost Became a Spy', NourbeSe Philip had tried to account for the ways in which what she calls the 'i-mage' was separated from the sense-making apparata that one has acquired from one's own culture and the images one creates and/or provides meaning to on an ongoing basis: 'Once the i-mage making power of the African had been removed or damaged by denial of language and speech, the African was then forced back upon the raw experience without the linguistic resources to integrate and eventually transcend it' (15). The only way the African artist could be in this New World, was to give voice to this split i-mage of voiced silence' (16).

In this context, the postcolonial has come as a mixed blessing for those formally colonized. At once a recognition of the afterness of colonialism, it nonetheless also has the potential of extending colonialism's effects beyond what was an assumed endpoint. Like other vexed formulations like 'post-raciality', it becomes prematurely celebratory when there are still actual colonial and racializing processes in place or at times recolonizing ones. The African postcolonial is in many ways a neo-colonial manifestation with a range of processes in place, including excessive militarization, corruption, and male dominance, without any possibilities for anti-postcolonial struggle, even after all the work done by scholars and activists to liberate these countries.

On balance, Ngũgĩ's critique of postcoloniality in *Globalectics* is handled in a sophisticated way. While recognizing the utility of postcoloniality as a theoretical framework in some academic contexts, he presents one of the best disclaimers available. For this reason, his discussion in my view should be part of the teaching of postcoloniality wherever it is deployed as a master discourse. This critique of postcoloniality by itself is not surprising since Ngũgĩ is one of the early definers of what has become the new language of the decolonial.

In more recent academic discourse, the decolonial has moved out of the state of 'arrest' that it was under and is fast becoming a framework used more readily by writers and critics alike. Junot Diaz talks about the search for 'decolonial love' in describing his creative project. Chicana women scholars have examined how gender works in the formation of the 'decolonial imagination'. Bringing much of this together theoretically, Walter Mignolo in 'Delinking: The Rhetoric of Modernity, the Logic of Coloniality and the Grammar of De-coloniality', argues that 'the grammar of de-coloniality (e.g., de-colonization of knowledge and of being and consequently of political theory and political economy) begins at the moment that languages and subjectivities that have denied the possibility of participating in the production, distribution, and organization of knowledge' are able to claim an epistemic space (452). Mignolo's argument is that

> A delinking that leads to de-colonial epistemic shift and brings to the foreground other epistemologies, other principles of knowledge and understanding and, consequently, other economy, other politics, other ethics. 'New inter-cultural communication' should be interpreted as new inter-epistemic communication (as we will see below, is the case of the concept of inter-culturality among Indigenous intellectuals in Ecuador). Furthermore, de-linking presupposes to move toward a geo- and body politics of knowledge that on the one hand denounces the pretended universality of a particular ethnicity (body politics), located in a specific part of the planet (geo-politics), that is, Europe where capitalism accumulated as a consequence of colonialism. De-linking then shall be understood as a de-colonial epistemic shift leading to other-universality, that is, to pluri-versality as a universal project. (452–3)

I see the return to the decolonial as both a valuable intellectual move and as a critique of the postcolonial. The 'coloniality of power', argues Peruvian scholar Annibal Quijano, created a framework for studying relationally a range of oppressive practices in an alliance of power and control. And if a decolonial practice is one which challenges coloniality's regimes of power in several axes, we can account anew for Ngũgĩ's 'decolonizing the mind', which Mignolo cites in his essay, as an example of how to find a way out of the 'grammar of decoloniality', which, in my estimation, still awaits fuller articulation.

Mignolo's argument is that while 'postcoloniality' wants transformation within the terms of the academy, decoloniality seeks a delinking of the two: 'the time has come, and the process is already in motion, for the re-writing of global history from the perspective and critical consciousness of coloniality and from within geo and body-political knowledge' (485). His claim is that when critical theory becomes de-colonial, critique itself will become critical border thinking, which will in turn lead to the decolonization of 'knowledge and of being' (485).

This is precisely where Ngũgĩ's *Globalectics* intervenes to offer a new theoretical model that takes us beyond the postcolonial to the global. One can also put 'globalectics' in conversation with Kamau Brathwaite's concept of 'tidalectics', which, though conceived with specific relation to the Caribbean, still imagines movement and fluidity. However, Ngũgĩ's concept of 'globalectics' imagines a much larger reach and is thereby able to provide 'world literatures' with a theoretical handle. It also advances beyond the logic of centricity which resided in Ngũgĩ's own formation of 'moving the center' and asserts a more engaged international model of thinking and studying literature and culture.

In 'Beyond Unicentricity: Transcultural Black Presences' I had critiqued the logic of simply moving centers, which I identified as crucial in one period of Ngũgĩ's work; I suggested the need for another model, one that that did not rely on any one 'centricity'. The idea of 'globalectics' provides precisely this refinement of Ngũgĩ's decolonial discourse and therefore has the potential to open another theoretical option for scholars who have struggled with the limitations of received European frameworks, from Hegel and Marx to Derrida. Thus, just as Marx built on Hegelian dialectics, subsequent scholars and artists can advance the idea of a 'globalectics', and see it as a scholarly basis for future theorizations. The importance of theorizing from other than Western standpoints is one of Ngũgĩ's major contributions to decolonial thinking.

Another dimension to this debate concerns what Cooper defines as 'low theory', a reference to the way subjects outside of academia theorize using the language that is used by the working-class masses and thus disrupting the hegemony that privileges knowledge production from 'the Eurocentric academy' (*ProudFlesh* interview). With a similar intent, Ngũgĩ uses the concept of 'poor theory' in *Globalectics* reminding us that 'the density of words is not the same thing as the complexity of thought; that such density, sometimes, can obscure clarity of thought' (3). A significant argument for sure, for the tendency in the academy at the turn of the twentieth century tended at times to confuse European-derived linguistic flourishes without substance with complex thought.

Ngũgĩ has been one of those writers who has advanced theoretical positions in the study of African and other world literatures, in the creative and theoretical arenas, and sometimes jointly in the 'creative/theoretical'. His discussion of language articulated in his *Decolonising the Mind* advanced decolonizing theory as it pertains to language and literature. *Globalectics* takes this discussion further, offering a way of moving beyond popular discourses of 'post-ness'. His articulation of a 'multi-logue', combining the global with the dialectical, offers a way of engaging a variety of cultural and theoretical positions (8). The influence of the theoretical mix of Fanon, Marx, and emerging literatures from the colonial world which he identifies in his chapters 'The English Master and the Colonial Bondsman' and 'The Education of the Colonial Bondsman' retraces the historical moves in literary and cultural decolonization as these related to the political decolonizations that were attempted in the periods he discusses. But Ngũgĩ moves beyond Marx. He recaptures the impact of the various colonizations which led to what he calls 'the decolonization of the cognitive process' (*Globalectics*, 42).

In many ways, the current demise of the 'postcolonial state' seems to mirror the nature of the postcolonial itself – an incomplete and therefore dangerous project. In the chapter 'The Globalectical Imagination: The World in the Postcolonial', Ngũgĩ recognizes the rupture that the postcolonial was supposed to represent, and the variety of international transformations of world literature that were intended. Offering a way of releasing literature from the 'strait jackets of nationalism' (8) by 'reading globalectically', Ngũgĩ enables us to work through the postcolonial, to make theory accessible in an interactive engagement with a variety of literatures worldwide. The spirit of his project is captured by the ending of Derek Walcott's poem, 'The Sea is History':

> and in the salt chuckle of rocks
> with their sea pools, there was the sound
> like a rumour without any echo
>
> of History, really beginning. (256)

26

Ngũgĩ & the Quest for a Linguistic Paradigm Shift: Some Reflections

Alamin Mazrui

If there is one issue in African literary studies that is most closely associated with Ngũgĩ wa Thiong'o it is likely to be the question of the language of African literature. Ngũgĩ has been the main and most persistent advocate for the 're-centering' of African languages in African creativity and in African societies more generally. One of the reasons for Ngũgĩ's seeming obsession with the language issue is the possibility that for long it has been an integral part of his journey as a writer to understand himself better, leading him back to Jean-Paul Sartre's fundamental question: 'For whom does one write?' For Ngũgĩ the answer came to be defined by his privileging of workers and peasants, and that answer ultimately influenced his decision to begin writing in Gĩkũyũ. Thus, the 'question of audience settled the problem of language choice; and the language choice settled the question of audience' (*Decolonising the Mind* 44).

I was among the critics of Ngũgĩ's position on the language in African writing, especially his specific argument that language somehow determines one's worldview in culturally specific ways. Over the years, I could not avoid seeing a line of relativist reasoning in Ngũgĩ most closely akin to the ideas of thinkers like Wilhelm von Humboldt, Edward Sapir, and Benjamin Lee Whorf. Like Ngũgĩ, Whorf had argued, for example, that languages influence, even determine, human perceptions of their world in a culturally circumscribed manner. I knew from my linguistic training that by the mid-1960s Whorf's claims had fallen into disrepute, having been discredited on empirical grounds. My own theoretical orientation, then, was to extend this 'discreditation' of Whorf to Ngũgĩ in the crucible of African linguistics.

However, more recent developments in linguistics demonstrate that the ideas of Whorf are being rehabilitated somewhat by a relatively new school of thought of Cognitive Linguistics (CL). This differs from most other branches of linguistics in the belief that the knowledge of language that speakers have also involves knowledge of their experiences of the world as mediated though language. In time, CL studies began to reveal in rather systematic ways that how we organize, categorize and classify experience in our real world is not only manifest in language but can also be influenced by language. In other words, Ngũgĩ's views on the interplay between language, culture and cognition are being vindicated, to some degree, by emerging developments in the study of language. It is perhaps for this reason that Ngũgĩ regarded writing in his native Gĩkũyũ also as an epistemological break.

As I am still struggling to understand Ngũgĩ better on the language-cultural-cognition hypothesis, however, the author has moved on to place emphasis on other dimensions of the language question. There is first the interplay between language and the construction of knowledge. 'I find it contradictory in Africa today and elsewhere in the academies of the world', remarked Ngũgĩ during a presentation at Cambridge University,

> to hear of scholars of African realities but who do not know a word of the languages of the environment of which they are experts. Do they think the Cambridge here would give me a job as a Professor of French Literature if I confessed that I did not know a word of French? ('Europhonism' 7–8)

Of course, this linguistic anomaly – that one can pursue knowledge on Africa in languages other than African – is itself a reflection of the degree of Africa's linguistic dependence on the West. It is virtually inconceivable for an academic to undertake research in China, Russia, the Middle East, Asia, or Latin America without some proficiency in the respective languages of those regions or, alternatively, without total submission to the mercy of an interpreter. In many parts of Africa, however, it is quite possible to carry out primary research on parliamentary proceedings or the structure of government administration, for example, with little familiarity with local languages.

At the level of research, however, the dependence on European languages results in a situation in which the knowledge that is generated about Africa is consequently 'assembled' in non-African languages. This assemblage, in Ngũgĩ's opinion, is part of the process by which Africa continues to be interpreted through a Western linguistic, and by implication, epistemological prism. The entire Europhonic project then is regarded as parasitic, content only on taking away and never giving 'anything back to the languages and peoples on whose behalf it makes its claims in the global community of scholarship in the arts, science and technology' ('Europhonism' 7). The epistemological cost for Africa of this pyramid of linguistic privilege, or what Ngũgĩ has called 'linguistic feudalism' (*Globalectics* 60) has been immense.

In addition to the cultural and epistemological dimensions of language, Ngũgĩ has also been concerned with the relationship between language and Africa's socio-economic well-being. He has argued that 'there can be no real economic growth and development where a whole people are denied access to the latest developments in science, health, medicine, business, finance, and other skills of survival because all these are stored in foreign languages' (1998: 90). One of the disturbing fallacies in the African experience, in fact, has been the association of European languages and the Western cultural legacy at large with modernity. There is thus a naïve assumption that European languages are a necessary force for modernization and indispensable instruments of economic transformation. Not enough attention has been paid to a range of Asian experiences where indigenous languages play a large role in economic transaction and educational policies (see Mazrui and Mazrui *The Power of Babel* 199).

The use of indigenous languages in pursuit of change in the academic, scientific, economic, legal and other important spheres of society should be seen as part of a wider design to make the process of modernization itself more organic to the African condition. Referring to this phenomenon as a case of 'indigenized modernization', Ali Mazrui has observed that:

> no country has ascended to a first class rank technological and economic power by excessive dependence on foreign languages. Japan rose to dazzling industrial heights by scientificating the Japanese language and making it the medium of its own industrialization … can Africa ever take off technologically if it remains so overwhelmingly dependent on European languages for discourse on advanced learning? Can Africa look to the future if it is not adequately sensitive to the cultural past? ('The African Renaissance' 36)

Both Ngũgĩ and Mazrui, then, came to see this lingo-cultural divergence as a serious impediment to the full maturation of Africa's own scientific genius.

But history has also demonstrated that the most successful attempts in the scientification of language are those built on literary foundations. In as much as African languages need to be scientificated, artists in African languages need to be made more naturally productive and engaged. After all, argues Ali Mazrui, 'languages rich in metaphors of poetry are languages which can also stimulate the scientific mind' ('The African Renaissance' 37). The imagination that innovates in science is also related to the imagination which has vision in poetry. And it is not accidental that Kiswahili poets like Ahmad Sheikh Nabhany of Mombasa, Kenya, for example, became very central in linguistic projects for the scientification of Kiswahili. Nor is it an accident that Ngũgĩ's Gĩkũyũ journalistic project, *Mũtiiri*, was inspired as much by literary explorations as by scientific concerns.

The question arises as to whether we are giving adequate attention to poets and imaginative writers in African languages. On February 17, 2002, the jury of 'Africa's 100 Best Books of the 20th century' competition released its list of winning titles, with special emphasis on the top twelve. The sub-category of the top twelve did not include a single title in an African language except, perhaps, Naguib Mahfouz's *The Cairo Trilogy*, a novel originally written in the Arabic language. Yet Mahfouz's was the only text in the list not mentioned by the title of its original language of composition: All the others were identified by their original Euro-linguistic names, in English, French, and Portuguese. It is not unlikely, therefore, that the one text which came closest to having been composed originally in an African language was, in fact, assessed for its merits on the basis of its translation in a European language, English (see Alamin Mazrui 'The English Language in the Post-Cold War Era' 181–2).

When, in 1998, the Modern Library Board of the USA released a list of 100 novels deemed the best in English published in the twentieth century, some of us had occasion to comment that the judges probably had an Anglo-Saxon bias in their selection. Are we now confronted with the possibility that the all-African jury for the 100 best African books was itself too Europhonic in their terms of reference? If not – if the results indicate relatively poor African language submissions in quantity and quality – then the mission of marrying scientific creativity and artistic vision in the development of African languages clearly requires much greater effort in promoting African poets and writers in African languages than is currently the situation. Africa must not underestimate the extent to which the scientific imagination may need creative vision for its ultimate maturation in language, the kind of vision that inspired the *Mũtiiri* project with the goal of enriching both the artistic and scientific limbs of Gĩkũyũ.

But could the enrichment of Gĩkũyũ be accomplished independently and on its own terms? This, of course, was an issue of some disagreement between Ngũgĩ and Ali Mazrui. Mazrui's subscription to *Mũtiiri* on behalf of his Institute of Global Cultural Studies was accompanied by a personal letter to Ngũgĩ raising the possibility of making *Mũtiiri* a Gĩkũyũ-Kiswahili bilingual journal. Noting that no one at his institute could read an exclusively Gĩkũyũ *Mũtiiri*, Mazrui suggested that the bilingualization of the journal would automatically quadruple its constituency and readership and, subsequently, multiply its own chances of survival in an otherwise unfavorable linguistic environment. Mazrui was of the opinion that in its rapid expansion in Africa, Kiswahili has sometimes threatened other African languages. Now, as a second language of a bilingual African-language publication in the U.S. – where, Mazrui assumed, Kiswahili had a wider readership than Gĩkũyũ – Kiswahili could perhaps contribute to their joint consolidation. Such cooperation between African languages, in other words, could strengthen Africa's capacity for the linguistic counter-penetration of the West.

Ngũgĩ, on the other hand, expressed the concern that a bilingual *Mũtiiri* would foster a relationship of dependency between Gĩkũyũ and Kiswahili, and this might not be in the developmental interest of Gĩkũyũ. For, to presume that what was intended essentially to be a Gĩkũyũ publication could not survive without the aid of Kiswahili would be to encourage, though inadvertently, the same psychology of linguistic fatalism of which Mazrui himself had been a critic. To Ngũgĩ, an ardent advocate of Kiswahili as a world language, Africa's linguistic power would be enhanced best if African languages separately could demonstrate self-sufficiency and self-reliance as media of intellectual and scientific discourse (see *The Power of Babel* 50).

Between Ali Mazrui and Ngũgĩ wa Thiong'o, then, we have two paradigms on the promotion of African languages – one based on linguistic strength rooted in inter-linguistic unity, and the other on linguistic credibility founded on demonstrated linguistic capacity of the individual languages. Ali Mazrui was concerned primarily with Gĩkũyũ-Kiswahili unity as a promotional and marketing strategy in a foreign linguistic situation in which both Gĩkũyũ and Kiswahili are minority languages. But even in such a circumstance, Ngũgĩ was conscious of the potential negative psychological effects that such a linguistic pairing could have on the *Mũtiiri* reader.

Underlying Ngũgĩ's various propositions on the language question is the conviction that African languages must take on the responsibility of 'speaking' for the continent. In direct reaction to this suggestion, however, postcolonial and postmodern critics have argued that imperial languages too can be appropriated to serve counter-discourse functions on behalf of Africa. What these critics of Ngũgĩ fail to appreciate, however, is that counter-discourse in English or other European languages in Africa is not the same thing as independent discourse. Counter-discourses may continue to be entrapped in the terms of reference of the dominant discourse. An independent discourse, on the other hand, is one that allows Africa to set its own terms of reference. While the power to formulate independent discourses is itself a matter of global struggle, we must take seriously the possibility that the re-centering of African languages in African societies at this historical juncture, may offer new spaces for the construction of discourses that are more independent of the West. Once again, I am inclined to agree with Ngũgĩ's claim that, as long as ideas 'are available in African languages, even anti-African ideas, the people will start developing them in ways that may not always be in accordance with the needs of the national middle classes and their international allies' (*Penpoints, Gunpoints and Dreams* 97–8). And part of the challenge that faces Africa is the construction of a space of liberation struggles that is founded on the democratic inclusion of the voices of those of the continent that are not Euro-glottal and Euro-literate.

In the final analysis, then, what is at issue here is not only the imperative for Africa to speak in its own voice, but also the question of what gets articulated in the act of speaking. Here we are back to the popular African metaphor of the hunter and the lion. In their encounters, the hunter always emerges victorious because it is he who has the power of voice to narrate the stories of the encounter with the lion. But when the lion eventually speaks, we discover that it, too, has had its great moments of triumph. So part of the struggle over languages and meanings is also a struggle to reclaim Africa's history and appropriately inscribe it in the global tapestry of human diversity. It is precisely this convergence of linguistic medium in all its literary brilliance and the wider political message of human liberation – as reflected in *Ngaahika Ndeenda, Caitaani Mũthaaraba-inĩ, Matigari ma Njirũũngi* and *Mũrogi wa Kagogo* – that arguably Ngũgĩ has demonstrated his greatest creative genius. If the potency of this remarkable genius has sometimes made Ngũgĩ and his family targets of some powerful political criminals, it is also one that is likely to continue inspiring and galvanizing young African artists and their audiences for generations to come.

27

Autobiographical Prototypes in Ngũgĩ wa Thiong'o's Early Fiction & Drama

Gĩchingiri Ndĩgĩrĩgĩ

Critics have speculated on the 'autographical dimension' in Ngũgĩ's fictional work for some time. The publication of *Dreams in a Time of War, In the House of the Interpreter*, and *The Birth of a Dream Weaver*, the memoirs covering his childhood and youth, enables us to engage in a productive meditation on the truism that all fiction is autobiographical, and the related question whether all autobiographical writing—including memoir, which covers a portion of an important person's life—is necessarily factual, as opposed to a retrospective construction. I do so by rereading the autobiographical moments in *The River Between, Weep Not, Child, A Grain of Wheat,* and *Petals of Blood*, from an arguably authoritative entry point availed by the memoirs. As Ngũgĩ tells us in *Globalectics*, 'writing was an attempt to understand myself and history, to make sense of the apparently irrational forces of the colonial and postcolonial' (17). In telling his own story, Ngũgĩ also tells the stories of his compatriots, particularly friends that he made at Alliance, who become prototypes for fictional characters. All three memoirs foreground characters we have already encountered in the early fiction and drama. The most noteworthy characters are Asinjo (*This Time Tomorrow*), Omange (*The Black Hermit*), Mzigo (*Petals of Blood*), Gatuiria (*Devil on the Cross*), and Carey Francis (*River Between, Petals of Blood*), and I focus on them in this paper. I also explore the disappearing autobiographical persona in the later fiction, and close with reflections on the author's latest turn to memoir, given his earlier reluctance because writing about his 'ordinary' life would be too boring (*Detained* 127). The memoirs point to the emergence of the exceptional writer worth celebrating.

The keen Ngũgĩ reader will easily recall variants of the author's story of an upbringing in a rural peasant household. We see variations of the indomitable biological mother Wanjiku (Nyokabi in *Weep*, Wangari in *A Grain*, Mariamu in *Petals*); the polygamous but insecure husband Thiong'o (Ngotho in *Weep*, Gĩkonyo's unnamed father in *A Grain*, Karega's unnamed father in *Petals*); and a supportive/model older brother Good Wallace (Kamau/Kori in *Weep*, Kihika in *A Grain*, Nding'ũri in *Petals*). The characters modelled upon Ngũgĩ's acquaintances in real life include the chivalrous Asinjo who rescues Wanjiro, the damsel in distress in *This Time Tomorrow* (through the device of a romantic affair that crosses ethnic lines) who recalls Ngũgĩ's classmate at Alliance (*In the House* 158), and the equally nationalistic Omange of *The Black Hermit*. Ngũgĩ reports that he visited his rural home in Limuru with both Asinjo and Omange and introduced them to a nationalistic neighbor as Luo classmates, but she pointed out to him that 'These days there's no Luo or Gĩkũyũ . . . We are all the children of Kenya' (*In the House* 158), attesting to the value of the colonial school as a crucible for cross-ethnic interactions. The seemingly awkward encounter between Njoroge and Stephen Howlands in *Weep* is a fictionalization of the first encounter Ngũgĩ had with a white agemate, named Andrew Brockett of Prince of Wales School Nairobi, during the time that he was a member of the Inter-tribal Society and Boy Scouts at Alliance (*In the House* 146). While the early works like *River Between* and *Weep Not, Child* foreground an identifiably autobiographical persona, a noteworthy development begins with *A Grain of Wheat* as Ngũgĩ's concentration shifts from lonely extraordinary heroes of the modernist novel to the collective stories of his later writing. The identifiably autobiographical story becomes distorted/diffused significantly. Discussion of the works sequentially illustrates how the autobiographical dimension progressively becomes a trace element in the fictional works.

In his reading of *Weep Not, Child*, Simon Gikandi posits that while Njoroge's life is not exactly like Ngũgĩ's, the novel's 'early affective power . . . depended on many readers' ability to establish this kind of autobiographical contract and to assume that what they were reading about in the novel could very well have been a record of the author's own life' (*Ngũgĩ wa Thiong'o* 81). The memoirs reveal that in *Weep*, the autobiographical contract was executed with minor variations. Ngũgĩ's mother and Njoroge's mother initiate the education quest in almost the same words: 'Would you like to go to school?' and he answers excitedly: 'O, mother' (*Weep* 3) / 'Yes, Yes' (*Dreams* 59). The mothers similarly warn: 'We are poor. You know that . . . So you won't be getting a mid-day meal like other children' (*Weep* 3) / 'You know we are poor . . . and you may not always get a midday meal?' (*Dreams* 59). They give the same interdiction: 'You won't bring shame to me by one day refusing to attend school' (*Weep* 3) / 'Promise me that you'll not bring shame to me by one day refusing to go to school because of hunger and other hardships?' (*Dreams* 59–60). Supporting the quest for an education in real life was Good Wallace, Ngũgĩ's older brother, and Kamau in *Weep Not, Child*. Acting as a chaperon to the young Ngũgĩ is Njambi, his landlord's daughter, whose older sister Joana is a teacher at Kamaandũra School (*Dreams* 61), just like Njoroge has Mwihaki whose older sister Lucia is Njoroge's teacher (*Weep* 47).

The classic elements of Njoroge's *Bildungsroman*—the education quest, the maturation, the self-questioning about his ability to fit in his world as it was ordered—seem to be mirror images of Ngũgĩ's life. Both attend an elementary school with a strong Gĩkũyũ-nationalist orientation; both are heavily invested in the education quest; both do well and go to Alliance High School (Siriana in the novel), easily the most elite school that admits African students; both gravitate very strongly to Christianity; both identify with the nationalist cause, but while Njoroge is expelled from Siriana because of the militant actions of his kin, Ngũgĩ lives under a cloud of fear that he would be expelled should his association with Good Wallace, the brother who joins the forest fighters and is later detained, become known. As such, Njoroge's expulsion seems to be a projection of Ngũgĩ's own fear. While Njoroge's relationship with Jacobo's daughter Mwihaki (Weep) gestures towards the romantic entanglements of youth that might lead to the stabilization of society through marriage, Ngũgĩ only elliptically mentions 'the [unnamed] girl with whom I will soon lose my virginity' (Dreams 203), and 'Lady Teacher', the mysterious temptress who probed and tested his faith (In the House 203). Njoroge's frustrated enlightenment and religious quests in Weep have parallels in Ngũgĩ's progressive questioning of the promises of colonial education, the materiality of colonialism, and the utopianism in Christianity as opposed to the 'historical' (vs eschatological) Christ who would have been on the side of the colonized (In the House 176). Because he finds the colonial world disillusioning, Njoroge rejects it in the failed suicide attempt. Unlike Njoroge, the youthful Ngũgĩ still had faith that the colonial world could be changed by agents invested in education as the practice of liberation. Like Njoroge who receives support for his education from his brother Kamau, Ngũgĩ had Good Wallace who took the risk of emerging from the forest to wish him good luck on his final elementary school exam, KAPE, the Kenya African Primary Education (Dreams 223).

In The River Between, Waiyaki's vacillation and his search for a mid-way point between Kameno and Makuyu, between modernity and tradition, appears to be a fictionalization of the fairly moderate 'Franciscan mid-way point between two extremes' that Ngũgĩ learns from Carey Francis, his principal at Alliance (In the House 183). His idea of a non-judgmental Christianity and service to community as a manifestation of Christian love also seem to come from Francis (In the House 176), who is almost totally at odds with the seemingly malevolent Cambridge Fraudsham in Petals of Blood. Similarly, Waiyaki's discomfort with the ribaldry connected with initiation dances (River 41–2) seems to have echoes in Ngũgĩ's own discomfort (Dreams 198). Waiyaki's anxiety that, in spite of being a modern, educated person, he should be found courageous in the circumcision itself (River 39, 45) echoes Ngũgĩ's own anxieties (Dreams 198–203). And just like Waiyaki who comes to recognize education as the new rite of passage (River 93, 142), so does the young Ngũgĩ (Dreams 123). In addition, Ngũgĩ admits that he encountered 'the images that launched my writing'—the landscapes fictionalized as Kameno and Makuyu and the hills and valleys that provide the setting for The River

Between—while on his visit to the hilly Nyeri countryside in his third year at Alliance (*In the House* 113).

After reading *Birth of a Dream Weaver* and learning that Ngũgĩ worked at a forestry station that resembles Githima during his school holidays (106), I find myself trying to assign his equivalent in *A Grain of Wheat*. The self-loathing Anglophile 'blackaphobic' library clerk named Wainaina (*Birth* 140) is obviously Karanja, but the autobiographical pact appears to have been broken here. The Alliance and Makerere-bound Kariuki lives in the shadow of his activist brother Kihika, and indomitable sister Mumbi, and he, like Ngũgĩ, is the only student from his area to go to Alliance in his examination year, although there are murmurs that the children of government stooges should have been given his place (*A Grain* 144, *Dreams* 244). Kariuki's marginality to the story approximates Ngũgĩ's marginality and estrangement to a family and village traumatized by the dislocations of the Emergency while he was sheltered at Alliance (*In the House* 48). His story is seemingly only one of many stories that call out for re-presentation. The only clearly autobiographical detail is that his hard-working, charming, and deaf half-brother, Gitogo, is killed in similar circumstances in both *A Grain* (5) and *In the House* (208–9). The strictly autobiographical story is not privileged in *A Grain Of Wheat* and thereafter, and Kariuki, the author's equivalent, is really marginal to the story and plot development.

In *A Grain of Wheat*, then, the author seems to be deliberately breaking the 'autobiographical contract' in earlier writing and he defamiliarizes the story participants as just ordinary, but fairly complicated and imperfect Kenyans, with stories to tell. Gikonyo is a meticulous carpenter like Ngũgĩ's older brother, Good Wallace, but he does not have the heroic escapes of the latter (*Dreams* 213), or a younger brother who looks up to him like Ngũgĩ did with Good Wallace, who appears to morph into both Gikonyo and Kihika. Unlike Good Wallace who is forced to make a fairly public choice between continuing to fight alone when his fighting unit is entrapped or living to fight another day like Matigari—the gun Wallace buried under a fig tree (*In the House* 82) anticipates the actions of the title character in *Matigari*—Gikonyo secretly betrays the oath out of inner romantic turmoil (*A Grain* 68, 110). Both engage in petty trade after detention (*A Grain* 18, *In the House* 197), but it seems almost unthinkable that the angelic Good Wallace could be the Gikonyo in the novel. The autobiographical character is not involved in any of the novel's major events.

Continuing with the autobiographical defamiliarization in *Petals*, Jacobo's daughter Mwihaki (*Weep*) returns as Waweru's daughter Mukami who is the authorial surrogate's love interest, but there is an overtly sexual relationship that the father stops leading to Mukami's suicide. Whereas Ngũgĩ was close to Good Wallace, Karega, the authorial surrogate, only has a 'vague/misty impression' of his older brother, Nding'ũri (60). Both Good Wallace and Nding'ũri are betrayed by an informer (Nding'ũri by the named Kimeria, *Petals of Blood* 266), but Good Wallace survives the betrayal and only his half-brother Gicini is caught and tried at Githunguri, though it is unclear whether he is hanged (*Dreams* 211–13). Nding'uri is caught, tried, and hanged at Githunguri, and it is Abdulla, his mixed-race compatriot who is left to carry the spirit (*Petals* 266). The indomitable Mariamu seems like a recasting of Ngũgĩ's real mother into the embodiment of the larger narrative of colonial dislocation that produced squatters. Karega's interrogation of the alienating colonial education at Siriana seems to mirror the Ngũgĩ who was uncomfortable with the curriculum until he discovered that he liked the literature, particularly Shakespeare (*In the House* 68, 216), unlike the Afrocentric students at Siriana who demand the removal of the bard from their reading lists (*Petals* 293). The climactic conflict Karega has with Munira over education as rote learning versus critical thinking recalls the different approaches students at Alliance took to the learning process—education predicated on the memorization of 'facts' versus Ngũgĩ's approach to education as mastery of underlying processes (*In the House* 35, 179; *Petals* 293).

Intriguingly, even though Ngũgi was surrounded by Shakespeare buffs like Moses Gathere and Joseph Mungai at Alliance (*In the House* 14, 155), none of them seems to come close to Chui's venality in *Petals*. In addition, Ngũgĩ had a classmate named David Mzigo who helped him with Swahili lessons, but it is unclear how the well-meaning Mzigo of *In the House* (157) becomes the grasping opportunist of *Petals*. It is also unclear why the vacillating intellectual of *Devil on the Cross* is named after Joseph Gatuiria, a fellow classmate of Ngũgĩ's at Alliance, whose only crime seems to have been the fact that he challenged Ngũgĩ to take the fairly demanding 'Additional Math' class (180). Unlike Evanson Mwaniki and Joseph Kariuki, Gatuiria, who was Ngũgĩ's college-mate at both Alliance and Makerere (*In the House* 157), was not associated with music. He published a few poems when he was a student at Makerere, but after graduation he went on to become a high ranking official in the Ministry of Finance and Economic Planning in Kenya.

The most radical difference between a fictional character and the authorial/autobiographical surrogate's memory of the historical prototype is Carey Francis. As Cambridge Fraudsham in *Petals*, he embodies the colonial high school curriculum that was standardized by Cambridge University and its exacting exit exam. In *In the House*, the education received at Alliance is presented as knowledge abstracted from local reality (63), but the narrator connects with the sublime in the literature. '[T]he glamor of the far away and long ago' provided an 'escape into wintry snow, flowers of spring, mountain chalets, and piracy on the high seas of those times and places' carried his mind 'from the anxieties of the moment' (68). This hardly sounds like the curriculum that

Karega's agemates in *Petals of Blood* would riot over, leading to the resignation of Fraudsham. Indeed, *In the House*, Carey Francis is presented as a cosmopolitan Christian, tolerant of other brands of Christianity (182), a firm believer in 'the middle way between two extremes,' and a good mentor to Ngũgĩ as he prepared to leave Alliance (183). Carey's cosmopolitanism—and his striving for a middle way—is unlike Bellowes Ironmonger or Cambridge Fraudsham of *Petals* whose intransigence is critiqued by three former Siriana students, Munira, Karega, and the Lawyer.

On one thing at least, both Munira, the central consciousness in *Petals*, and Ngũgĩ are agreed that 'Fraudsham was Siriana and Siriana was Fraudsham' (*Petals* 62); 'The fact is that the Alliance of my time was Carey Francis, and Carey Francis was Alliance' (*In the House* 181). But whereas Fraudsham was a patronizing figure to both Munira and Karega (*Petals* 34–5, 202) and an emasculating presence even to fellow white teachers (201), Carey Francis was a figure of accommodation and moderation to Ngũgĩ (*In the House* 35). In *Petals*, Fraudsham's love for dogs—exemplified by Lizzy—compensated for his betrayed love, and this betrayal is treated with derision instead of the sympathy it is accorded in the memoir (*Petals* 202; *In the House* 43). In *Petals* this love of pets seems to have become an obsession that Fraudsham expected his students to share; and hence his assumption that they would willingly participate in giving Lizzy the equivalent of a human burial. Karega's statement that '[s]omething in Fraudsham snapped … human burial' (*Petals* 202–3) reads almost word for word like Ngũgĩ's surprised reaction to Carey's response to the Russians putting Laika the dog in space (*In the House* 125). But in Ngũgĩ's recollection, Carey's love for dogs is just an eccentricity (125), not the extreme investment that propels students to riot and call for an African curriculum and principal (*Petals* 204). How, then, do we account for the humanizing of Carey Francis in the memoir? Even the Francis who berates Ngũgĩ for his flattened colonial characters and critique of Christianity in *Birth* (172) does not come close to the venal and hypocritical Cambridge Fraudsham.

After *Petals*, Ngũgĩ stops using an autobiographical register and his friends, classmates, and acquaintances disappear from fiction. And since the disappearance of the autobiographical corresponds with the emergence of the more repressive Kenyan state in the late 1970s and 1980s, a question arises: Did Ngũgĩ distort the characters to protect himself and his friends from the repressive state's agents who reportedly descended on his village of Kamĩrĩĩthũ seeking to find the namesakes of the characters in *Ngaahika Ndeenda*, his provocative play whose performance the state had banned? This might explain the re-emergence of some autobiographical element in *Wizard of the Crow*, a novel written in exile. Here, we see characters like Professor Materu and Nyawĩra, probably modelled on the radical historian and Ngũgĩ friend of long standing, Maina Kinyatti, and Wangari Maathai. Kinyatti had been imprisoned in Kenya before fleeing to exile, while Maathai's run-ins with the repressive Moi State and her activism were legendary.

The foregoing dialogic reading of the memoirs and the fiction reveals some concordances and discordances between the portraits of Ngũgĩ's friends on the one hand, and the autobiographical persona, on the other. To what extent are the memoirs the memory of an adult narrator who filters and recollects the experiences of the youth who experienced them, or a retrospective construction? My conclusion is that in both the memoir and fiction, Ngũgĩ invites his readers to enter an 'autobiographical contract' and in the process he complicates the relationship between the two genres. The memoirs are good examples of autobiographical fiction and the early fiction reads like an extended autobiography. Having downplayed the modern novel's focus on the lonely bourgeois individual, and distorted, identifiable authorial surrogates after *Petals*, Ngũgĩ invites the reader to invest in the memoirs' consolidation of the autobiographical self. If memoir and autobiography are the 'stories of a personality' who has achieved greatness, as Phillipe Lejeune argues in *On Autobiography* (4), Ngũgĩ, it seems, has become like the lizard in Achebe's *Things Fall Apart* who decided to praise himself after falling from the high Iroko tree since no one else was doing it. A collection in honor of his work is a befitting recognition.

28

Homecoming: The Idea of Return in the Works of Ngũgĩ wa Thiong'o

James Ogude

(Originally published in *City Press*, Johannesburg, September 5, 2003. Reprinted with permission.)

This paper was written for the Steve Biko Foundation in celebration of what they dubbed as the 'Co-creators of the African Imagination: Ngũgĩ wa Thiong'o and Robert Sobukwe'. Ngũgĩ delivered the Steve Biko memorial lecture at the University of Cape Town in September 2003. The idea behind my piece was to draw attention to those ideological affinities that connect these two African intellectuals and activists: Robert Sobukwe and Ngũgĩ wa Thiong'o. This short essay was first published in the *City Press*, September 5, 2003, among other essays. I still believe it is a befitting tribute to Ngũgĩ, especially in drawing attention to those intellectual and political currents from his works, which have close affinities to the South African struggle. Indeed, Ngũgĩ remains one of the most popular African writers in South Africa and his works continue to inspire recent struggles by the University students around decoloniality and a decolonized curriculum at the institutions of Higher learning in South Africa.

*

The visit of one of Africa's foremost writers and political activist, Ngũgĩ wa Thiong'o, to South Africa in honor of the late leader of the Pan Africanist Congress (PAC), Mangaliso Sobukwe, had been billed by the organizers as a homecoming. This was apt because Ngũgĩ was returning to a free South Africa in memory of a very fine son of Africa who stood stoically against those forces of domination that he has written so much about in his creative writing and essays. Ngũgĩ's writings have always been about that quest for freedom for which Sobukwe laid down his life. Ngũgĩ has always written against the repressive political structures engendered by both colonialism and neo-colonial forces in Africa. Like Sobukwe, Ngũgĩ is a staunch believer in the Pan-Africanist vision and in a united Africa working in tandem to rid itself of the ravages of colonialism and all anti-human ideologies such as apartheid.

What therefore joins these two thinkers are their loathing for human oppression and racism, their love for Africa and affirmation of the black people's dignity denied by centuries of European imperialism and racism. But they are also joined in the common belief that every nation, every community has the right to use its vernacular languages because, as Fanon would have it, whoever takes up a language assumes a culture (*Black Skin, White Masks* 17–18). To come to South Africa in honor of Sobukwe is a befitting homecoming for Ngũgĩ. For indeed, Ngũgĩ's writing spanning four decades has been undergirded by the metaphor of return. It has been about a dislocated home and the desire for its restoration.

If there is one single thing that unites Ngũgĩ's narrative with the South African experience, it is that overwhelming presence of homelessness. The sense of abandonment and exile, which marked much of the South African experience in the recent past, and continues to haunt its nascent democracy, is most passionately rendered in Ngũgĩ's narratives and essays. But his works are also defined by a desire shared by many South Africans, a desire for which heroes like Sobukwe fought tirelessly, and that is the need to reconstitute a home, a nation where man and woman can experience joy and love, liberty and freedom, regardless of their race or creed. Ngũgĩ's homecoming to South Africa should signal that undying project to restore and reconstitute a community of people that is at the heart of his works.

Significantly, the central argument in his *Homecoming* essays is the rebuilding of a national culture and the disavowal of the liberal idea of culture, which privileges bourgeois individualism over the collective consciousness, and the spirit of caring for all, *Ubuntu*, that ought to be at the heart of all human cultures. What made culture so central to Ngũgĩ's liberation narrative was its close affinity to history in colonial discourses on Africa, a cultural history that had been denigrated and distorted by years of colonial miseducation. As early as 1968, in an essay called 'The Writer and His Past' Ngũgĩ begun serious reflections on the writer's relationship with his past and how an engagement with this past was a precondition to a genuine nationalist literature. The writer's encounter with history, his people's history, would inaugurate that moment of return—the moment of reconnection. Ngũgĩ argued that it is this return that would restore the African character to his history because '[t]he African novelist has turned his back on the Christian god and resumed the broken dialogue with the gods of his people' (*Homecoming: Essays on African and Caribbean Literature, Culture and Politics* 43).

Yet Ngũgĩ was acutely aware that a fixation with the past could soon became an act of amnesia that the nationalist politicians would use to avoid contemporary problems and concerns. He rejected any attempts to reify culture and drew attention to the dialectical and historical imperatives that defined all living cultures. Culture, he insisted, in 'Towards a National Culture', 'is the sum total of a people's art, the science and all their social institution, including their system of beliefs and rituals', forged in their 'creative struggle and progress through history' (*Homecoming* 4). It is this wealth of cultural heritage that European colonialism had worked to deny and repress in Africa. Yet, Ngũgĩ is careful to add: 'In our present situation, we must in fact try to see how new aspects of life can be clarified or given expression through new art forms or a renewal of the old' (4). He was not calling for a return to some mythical past, but a creative engagement with a complex present that has been created out of a shared colonial experience and indigenous African practices alike. He was calling for an engagement with that space characterized by Fanon in *The Wretched of the Earth* as the 'zone of occult instability where the people dwell' (227)—the liminal space where Africa's many modernities are shaped through dialogue with itself and other cultures.

Thus, a time when political leaders in Africa were turning the so-called African culture into a fetish and an instrument of political control, Ngũgĩ was careful to represent the function of culture in the new nation as one tied to a progressive political agenda. At a personal level, Ngũgĩ was involved in a process of self-examination, an interrogation of his Christian past and missionary education. The process of self-examination led him to reject his Christian name, James, once again making a symbolic return to his ancestral heritage by reclaiming his father's name. Henceforth, he became Ngũgĩ wa Thiong'o, a name that has signified a breakaway from that tortured relationship with colonial education.

In rejecting the Christian tradition that had been central to his identity as a writer, Ngũgĩ was making a major homecoming and creating the space within which the radical Marxist politics he had embraced would find expression. At the creative level, the publication of *The Trial of Dedan Kimathi*, co-authored with Mĩcere Mũgo (1976) and *Petals of Blood* (1977) signaled the beginning of Ngũgĩ's radical aesthetic. This was followed by a collection of essays in *Writers in Politics* (1981) and *Barrel of a Pen* (1983) which sought to interrogate and reconfigure the dominant English literary culture in Kenya. The literature syllabus debate in Kenya in the 1970s was about what kind of texts needed to be privileged in Kenyan schools after independence and, was ultimately about the status of English and Englishness in the postcolony. Ngũgĩ was in effect grappling with what continued to be the hegemony of English in Kenyan schools and the continuing denigration of African literatures, even those written in English like his own.

In Ngũgĩ's view, the privileging of the English literary canon in African schools deprived the African child of the cultural representation of the collective consciousness of the people of the continent—their coming into being through struggle and creativity. He was rejecting the dominant thought that Western European experience and culture was a universal one, which all so-called 'civilized' communities had to emulate. And yet, even as Ngũgĩ embarked on a cultural campaign that sought to center African Literature at the core of our literary syllabus, he had forgotten that he continued to write in English at the expense of his own mother tongue. In his words, he was merely enriching the English language and its literary heritage. Ngũgĩ had to make another radical homecoming, this time rejecting English as the medium through which his future writing would take place and embracing Gĩkũyũ as his new tongue of expression.

The point is that Ngũgĩ finally began to address an audience of workers and peasants who had been central subjects of his novels and plays, but for whom his writing remained inaccessible for as long as he continued to address them in English. In an important paper, called 'Return to Roots', written soon after his release from detention in 1979, Ngũgĩ set to redefine African literature in terms of its language, echoing what in 1962 Obi Wali had characterized as the uncritical acceptance of English and French culture as the inevitable medium for educated African writing (see *Writers in Politics* 53–65). This perhaps was not something new given the Kamĩrĩĩthũ experiment with a play written in Gĩkũyũ. But the fact that it drew the ire of the authorities leading to his detention without trial had obscured a radical cultural project that would later shape the discourses on cultural production and consumption in the continent.

In the decade that followed, Ngũgĩ was to pursue the language agenda both in thought and practice, producing two novels written in his mother tongue, Gĩkũyũ. The two novels were later translated into English as *Devil on the Cross* (1982) and *Matigari* (1987). Whatever we think of Ngũgĩ's radical return to African languages, nativist or idealist as many would want to argue, and whatever its ultimate fate in the global scheme of things, Ngũgĩ was inaugurating a new cultural aesthetics that was bound to send ripples across the continent. The return to roots, Ngũgĩ argued, marked a moment of departure from colonial conventions of writing and signaled a libertarian discourse of decolonization. It is the decolonizing project that he elaborates in his most widely read text in apartheid South Africa, *Decolonising the Mind: The Politics of Language in African Literature* (1986). In it Ngũgĩ argues that the legacy of colonialism in Africa had separated the Africans from their language and colonized their minds. The root to freedom lay in the articulation of a new grammar of nationalism that would liberate the African identities from the prison house of European languages and culture.

Finally, although Ngũgĩ continued to keep Gĩkũyũ as an important part of his intellectual and literary project, he has also made a return to English language, particularly in his collection of essays. It is tempting to read Ngũgĩ's return to English as some act of political capitulation in the face of global capitalism. However, it is a statement against rather than a fatalistic resignation to the power and tyranny of modernity and its vicissitudes; the kind of tyranny that has managed to keep Ngũgĩ in exile away from his native country thereby forcing him to improvise his craft and intellectual project on the uncanny stage of a globalizing world. Ngũgĩ, like the proverbial bird, *eneke*, in Achebe's *Things Fall Apart*, has learnt to fly without perching just like his hunters have learnt to shoot without missing. Like Matigari in his novel by the same name, Ngũgĩ is still in search of a truly humane home in Africa. Will the new South Africa become the ideal home for which Ngũgĩ is searching? Only time will tell, but if his popularity in the southern tip of the continent is anything to go by, then his legacy lives on precisely because he embodies the best of those values that were championed by the makers of modern South Africa history such as Steve Bantu Biko, Robert Magaliso Sobukwe, and Nelson Mandela.

Long live the spirit of Pan-Africanism! Long live the legacy of *Mwalimu* Ngũgĩ!

29
Gūcookia Rūī Mūkaro

Kīariī Kamau*

[For English Translation from the Gīkūyū, see Appendix B]

Profeca, ingīka atīa nī guo menye kwaria Gīkūyū wega itegūtondoira? Aciari akwa matiandutire Gīkūyū, mandutire Gīthūngū. Rīū ndīna mīaka mīrongo īīrī na īīrī, na ndingīaria Gīkūyū wega. Njiguaga njonokete mūno rīrīa twīna arata akwa tūkīrīa, tūkīnyua na tūgītereta maūndū mwanyamwanya, o makīaria na Gīkūyū, no niī, no njokirie na Gīthūngū!

Kīūria gīkī kīoririo nī mūirītu ūmwe irugainī rīrīa rīarī kīrabuinī gīa Karen Country Club, mweri-inī wa Njuni, 2015, thutha wa Mwandīki ti Ngūgī wa Thiong'o kwarīria a memba a kīrabu kīu. Iruga rīu rīatabanītio nī kambuni īrīa īcabaga mabuku ma Ngūgī, East African Educational Publishers (EAEP), rī rīmwe rīa maruga maingī marīa matabarīirio nī kambuni īno gūkūngūira mīaka mīrongo ītano kuma rīrīa Ngūgī andīkire ibuku rīa *Weep Not, Child*.

Nī getha tūhote kūrikīria ūritū wa kīūria kīa mūirītu ūcio-rī, nī wega twambe tūmenye merī kana matatū makoniī kīrabu gīa Karen Country Club. Kīrabu gīkī kīanjirio mwakainī wa 1937; mwaka ūmwe Ngūgī atanaciarwo. Nī kīmwe kīa irabu cia ngobu būrūri-inī wa Kenya, na ithuothe nītūkīūī wega atī andū aingī arīa mathakaga ngobu nī andū meiguīte, na me gatū. Hamwe na ūguo, nī getha mūndū atuīke mūmemba wa kīrabu gīkī, agīrīirwo nī kūrīha ciringi ngiri magana matano (Kshs. 500,000 [marīhi ma 2017]) – ta Ndora mīrongo ītano (USD 50,000); na o mwaka akarīha kīgīna kīngī o kīmata nī getha athiī na mbere gūkorwo e mūmemba. Ūrīa ndīrageria kuga nī atī, gīkī nī kīrabu kīa itang'a, na gīkoretwo kīhana ūguo kuma kīanjīrīrio.

Tondū maarī arīmi anyinyi, aciari a Ngūgī matingiarotire atī no metīkīrio kūingīra kīrabuinī ta gīkī; kana o na kuna ngū cia mītī ya mītarakwa īrīa īrekagia honge ikabuthīra thī. Gwa kahinda ka mīaka mīingi, Ngūgī we mwene ndangīaingīrire kīrabuinī gīkī, tondū mwīcirīrie wake, na mandīko make, matingīaingīranire na meciria ma a memba aingī a kīrabu gīkī. Ningī mahinda ma hau kabere ndaakīrī na ūhoti wa kūrīha kīgīna kīa ū memba!

---

* Kīariī Kamau nī Mūrūgamīrīri Mūnene wa Kambuni ya Gūcaba Mabuku ya *East African Educational Publishers, Nairobi, Kenya*

Arĩa tũthomete mũikarĩre wake mĩakainĩ ya hau kabere, nĩtũĩ irabu iria ciamũkenagia; no ningĩ icio ticio tũrenda gũtenderia!

Maruga marĩa matabarĩirwo nĩ matangathagwo mũno tũmemeinĩ, terebiceni-inĩ, magathĩti-inĩ, o na coco-midiainĩ. Andũ a Kenya makĩhana ta marũrũngana kũnyita Ngũgĩ mbaru, agĩtĩtĩrithia gũtĩa, kwĩruta, kwaria, gũthoma, na kwandĩka thiomi cia mũndũ mũirũ.

Na tondũ Mũikarĩri Gĩturwa wa kambuni ya EAEP, Ndagĩtarĩ Henry Chakava nĩ mũmemba wa Karen Country Club, akĩũrio nĩ a memba arĩa angĩ atĩrĩ: Wahota atĩa gũtabarĩra maruga maingĩ ũguo makonii Ngũgĩ, na ndũngĩkĩmũrehe narĩ tũmũgeithie? Nake Ndagĩtarĩ Chakava akĩnginyĩria ndũmĩrĩri ĩyo; na akĩnjũria kana no hote kuona kamweke mũtaratarainĩ wa maũndũ marĩa twatabarĩire, nĩ getha tũtware Ngũgĩ Karen.

Reke njuge o na gũtuĩka nĩ ndetĩkĩrire, ndaarĩ na nganja kana a memba aingĩ a kĩrabu kĩũ no makorwo na bata wa gũthikĩrĩria mĩario ya Ngũgĩ. No kaĩ nĩndehenetieĩ!

Nĩ ũndũ wa maũndũ mwanyamwanya, mũthenya ũrĩa twathiaga nĩ twac-ereirwo kahinda ka mathaa merĩ. No ũndũ wa magegania nĩ atĩ twakorire andũ maiyũrĩte hooru, aingĩ ao marũngiĩ, othe mamwetereire.

Mũirĩtu ũcio woririe kĩũria kĩu arĩ hamwe na andũ angĩ aingĩ ethĩ; arĩa makirĩrĩirie mathaa macio merĩ metereire Ngũgĩ amarĩrie. Nayo ndũmĩrĩri ya Ngũgĩ yakĩrĩ o ĩmwe: Rekei tũtĩĩe, twĩtĩĩre, twĩrute, twarie, tũthome, na twandĩke thiomi citũ. Na akĩrĩkia agĩkindĩra na kuga: *Ũngĩmenya thiomi nyingĩ cia thĩ yothe na wage kũmenya rũthiomi rwaku, ũcio nĩ ũkombo; no ũngĩmenya rũthiomi rwaku na thutha ũcio ũmenye thiomi nyingĩ cia thĩ yothe, ũcio nĩ ũcamba.*

Kĩũria kĩa mũirĩtu ũcio; hamwe na ũkirĩrĩria ũrĩa gikundi kĩu gĩa Karen gĩakirĩrĩirie gĩetereire Ngũgĩ agĩtarĩrie ũhoro ũkoniĩ thiomi citu; na cĩũria cia bata cikoniĩ thiomi citũ iria cioririo gĩikaroinĩ kĩu; o hamwe na ũingĩ wa andũ arĩa mendaga kũrũmĩrĩra ũrutani wa Ngũgĩ, nĩ maũndũ matũmire menye atĩ rũgendo rũrĩa Ngũgĩ ambĩrĩirie mĩaka mĩrongo ĩna mĩhĩtũku, rũgendo rwa gũcokia rũĩ mũkaro, nĩ rũrĩkĩtie kũgĩa na arũmĩrĩri aingĩ.

Na arũmĩrĩri aya nĩ mathire na mbere o kwĩyumĩria kũrĩa guothe twathire na Ngũgĩ akĩaragĩria ikundi mwanyamwanya. Ndingĩhota gũtarĩria na njĩra ngindĩrĩku ũrĩa ndũmĩrĩri ĩno ya Ngũgĩ yamũkĩrirwo kũrĩa guothe twathire, no nĩ wega ngwete na njĩra nguhĩ mĩario yake kũũrĩa Kisii University. Thutha wa kwamũkĩrwo na gĩkeno kĩnene nĩ Mũrũgamĩrĩri Mũkaru wa yunibacĩtĩ ĩyo (Vice-Chancellor), Profeca John Akama, o hamwe na arutwo, arimũ na mũingĩ mũnene wa Gĩthii, Ngũgĩ agĩkĩruta ndũmĩrĩri yake. Agĩtĩtĩrithĩria athikĩrĩria ake matĩĩe, metĩĩre, merute, marie, mathome na mandĩke thiomi cia Mũndũ Mũirũ. Na agĩkĩrĩkĩrĩria agĩkindĩra na kuga: *Ũngĩmenya thiomi nyingĩ cia thĩ yothe na wage kũmenya rũthiomi rwaku, ũcio nĩ ũkombo; no*

ūngĩmenya rũthiomi rwaku na thutha ũcio ũmenye thiomi nyingĩ cia thĩ yothe,
ũcio nĩ ũcamba.

Ndũmĩrĩri ĩyo ĩkĩamũkĩrwo na ngemi nene, na ĩkĩnyitwo mbaru wega.
No ũrĩa ndirikanaga mũno nĩ mũndũ ũrĩa wahoithirie tũkĩhinga gĩikaro kĩu.
Akiuga atĩ nĩ ũndũ wa ũrĩa ahutio nĩ ndũmĩrĩri ya Ngũgĩ, e kũhoya na rũthiomi
rwa Gĩgĩthii. Agĩkĩhoya mahoya marĩ maraihu ma, no mũno ti ũraihu wa
mahoya wangambacire. Aca. Nĩ ũrĩa mahoya mau matagwetire kiugo o na
kĩmwe gĩa Gĩthũngũ kana Gĩthwaĩri; na ũrĩa cama wa ciugo icio cia Gĩgĩthii,
iria itamenyaga ũrĩa iroiga, ciangambacire! Ngĩkĩyũria atĩrĩ, angĩkorwo nĩ
ngũkambacwo ũguo nĩ rũthiomi itarataũkĩrwo nĩ ruo-ĩ, ĩ nake mũndũ ũrĩa
ũrataũkĩrwo arakambacwo atĩa?

Ngĩgĩtaũkĩrwo atĩ rũu nĩ ruo rũĩ rũrĩa Ngũgĩ akoretwo agĩcokia mũkaro.
Nĩ amu tugaga ngemi ciumaga na mũciĩ; na kanua kene gatinyuaga muma.
Tũngĩriganĩrwo nĩ harĩa tumĩte, tũtingĩhota gũkinya harĩa tũrorete.
Tũtingĩtuĩka tũkũina na tũtiirũ twene. Muma witũ no tũũnyuire na tũnua
twitũ. Kwoguo no mũhaka twĩthuthurie na twĩcokere.

Gĩkĩ nĩ kĩo kĩoneki kĩrĩa Ngũgĩ onirio mĩaka mĩrongo ĩna mĩhĩtũku,
akĩonio atĩ ahota gũte inya akinyĩrĩte inyanya. Akĩonio atĩ twateire ikinya o
rĩrĩa twetĩkĩrire gũkũngũĩra thiomi ciene, na mũno cia Athũngũ. Akĩonio atĩ
twateire ikinya o rĩrĩa twanyararire na tũgĩteanĩire thiomi citũ, tũgĩciria atĩ
itikoniĩ ũthii wa na mbere – atĩ iria ikoniĩ ũthii wa na mbere nĩ cia Mũthũngũ.
Akĩonio atĩ twateire ikinya o rĩrĩa tweyagĩire bata, na njĩra ya kũmenereria
thiomi citũ, na gũkũngũĩra cia Mũthũngũ. Akĩonio atĩ twateire ikinya o rĩrĩa
twagire gwĩtĩĩra, kwĩruta, kwaria, gũthoma na kwandĩka thiomi citũ.

Thutha wa gwĩthuthuria na gwĩcokera, akĩhĩta atĩ mandĩko make ma ng'ano,
kana mathako, marĩkoragwo me ma rũthiomi rwa Gĩkũyũ. Nĩ guo akĩandĩkire
Ngaahika Ndeenda, na akĩrũmĩrĩria na *Caitaani Mũtharabainĩ*. Thutha ũcio nĩ
andĩkĩte mabuku mangĩ maingĩ, o nginya ng'ano cia ciana.

Agĩkĩambĩrĩria gũcokia rũĩ mũkaro. Agĩtũririkania atĩ o na gũtuĩka nĩ
twarũire na tũkĩgĩa na wĩyathi kuma kwĩ Mũkoroni, wĩyathi ũcio nĩ wa
tũhũ nĩ amu Mũkoroni athiire na mbere kwoha meciria maitũ na njĩra ya
gũtũgĩria thiomi ciake, na kũnyarara thiomi citũ cia Mũndũ Mũirũ. Ngũgĩ
agĩgĩtũtĩrithĩria tũteithũkie meciria maitũ kuma mĩnyororoinĩ ya ũkombo
wa Mũkoroni, nĩ getha tũhote kũgĩa na wĩyathi ũrĩa ũrĩ wa ma.

Na rĩũ agĩkũngũĩra mĩaka mĩrongo ĩnana kuma rĩrĩa aciarirwo, ndĩ na ma
ena gĩkeno nĩ kuona atĩ rũĩ rũrĩa akoretwo agĩtungata, no rũrathiĩ na mbere
gũcoka mũkaro. Nĩ amu rĩrĩa thirikari ya Kenya ĩratabarĩire mũtaratara
mwerũ wa gĩthomo, nĩ ĩrekĩrĩire ngumĩi thiomi cia ũndũire wa andũ a bũrũri
wa Kenya. O na gũtuĩka mũtaratara ũrĩa ũrarĩ ho kabere nĩ warĩ na ũhoro o
ũcio wa thiomi citũ, ndeto ĩyo ndĩigana gũkindĩrwo na kũrũmĩrĩrwo.

Itũmi nyingĩ nĩ ikoretwo ikĩheanwo kuonania ũrĩa tũtagĩrĩire kũruta ciana
citũ thiomi citũ. No nĩ itũmi itarĩ na mũtwe kana magũrũ. Andũ angĩ nĩ

makoretwo na meciria mahinyĩrĩrĩku ma gwĩciria atĩ gūthomithia ciana citū thiomi cia ūndūire witū, nĩ gūkindĩra ūgayūkanu wa kĩndūrĩrĩ. No meciria mau matirĩ na ūma o na hanini. Andū matigĩaga na ūgayūkanu wa kĩndūrĩrĩ nĩ ūndū wa kūmenya thiomi ciao. Magayūkanaga nĩ ūndū wa gūcogerwo nĩ ateti arĩa matongoragio nĩ maūndū mwanyamwanya ta kwĩyenda, ūkoroku, na kwenda ūnene.

Angĩ nao makoiga atĩ twaruta ciana citū thiomi citū, nĩ tūgūtūma ihotome mathomoinĩ na mĩmenyereinĩ ya maūndū ma 'kĩrĩu'. Mageciria atĩ twaruta ciana citū Gĩthūngū kana thiomi iria ingĩ cia Mūthūngū, nĩ guo ciana icio ikūhĩga na ihenya, na ihote kūiganana na ciana cia mabūrūri marĩa mangĩ, na mūno ma Athūngū. No urĩa andū ta acio matoĩ nĩ atĩ athuthuria a thiomi na mĩthomithĩrie ya ciana irĩ nyinyi, nĩ marĩkĩtie kuonania atĩ mwana angĩrutwo rūthiomi rwa ūndūire wake e mūnyinyi, nĩ ahotaga kūnyita na kūmenya wega thiomi ingĩ na ihenya, gūkĩra ūrĩa ūterutĩte rūthiomi rwa ūndūire wake.

Gūtirĩ ūikagia itimū atekūmenya harĩa ekūratha. Na rĩū Ngūgĩ agĩkinyia mĩaka mĩrongo ĩnana, itimū rĩa kūratha ūhinyĩrĩrĩku wa meciria ma gūcambia thiomi citū nĩ rĩrutĩte wĩra warĩo. Andū aingĩ nĩ manyitĩte mbaru ndūmĩrĩri ĩno ya gūcokia rūī mūkaro. Ceceni nyingĩ cia tūmeme iria cirahūthĩra thiomi cia kĩndūire nĩ cianjĩrĩirio. O na ceceni cia terebiceni cia thiomi cia kĩndūire no irathiĩ na mbere kuongererekaaga. Magathĩti o na mo makĩrĩ o ho, hamwe na marĩa mandĩkagwo Intaneti-inĩ ta Mburogi *(Blogs)*.

Kwoguo tūgĩkūngūĩra mĩaka mĩrongo ĩnana ya Ngūgĩ, rekei tūkūngūĩre ūhotani ūrĩa arĩkĩtie kūhotana; ūhotani wa gūtūma tūtĩĩe, twĩtĩĩre, twĩrute, twarie, tūthome, na twandĩke thiomi citū.

Nawe ūregete kūruta ciana ciaku rūthiomi rwa ūndūire waku, ūmenye gūtiri wĩriraga agĩthiĩ ta agĩcoka. Ūgūtūma mwana ūcio agecokera na mai-thori, ta mūirĩtu ūcio wakaĩire Ngūgĩ kūūrĩa Karen Country Club.

Ngĩtiriha njuge: Tūtikahane ta kaihū gacangacangi, karĩa kerirwo gatigaga kwao gūgĩthĩnjwo; nĩ amu ciene itirĩ ndokeirwo nū! Na ningĩ tūririkane ūrĩa Gĩkūyū augire; atĩ wathi wakūra wongagĩrĩrwo ūngĩ. Rĩu nĩ ihinda ritū kuo-erera kuma harĩa Ngūgĩ akinyĩtie. Ithuothe tūcokie rūī mūkaro!

30
Muthoni's Afterlives

Grace A. Musila

My fear of South African taxi drivers goes back to an encounter in my early days in Johannesburg in the early 2000s. I was in a taxi van on Jan Smuts Avenue, going to Braamfontein, in Johannesburg. I needed to be at WITS University by 12.30 for a meeting. It was 11.15, and there was a stop near Braamfontein Centre on Jan Smuts, right across from one of the University entrances. I was confident I would be on time for my meeting, having made this trip countless times before. By the time we got to my stop, I was the only passenger left in the taxi. I asked the driver to please drop me at Braamfontein Centre, to which he responded, '*yhini hawukhulumi?*'

'I understand, but I can't speak isiZulu', I said.

'*Mna, angizwa ukhulumani sisi*', (I don't understand what you are saying, sister), he shot back, as he drove past my stop.

I suddenly remembered a Facebook status update by a well-known radio presenter on an English medium radio station, who had posted one morning: 'Today, I don't feel like speaking English, I am #unableToCan speak today. *Akhant.*'

As we drove deeper into the Johannesburg CBD towards the notorious Hillbrow precinct, well known to many foreign students as a no-go area, a cold panic started settling in my stomach at not only missing my meeting, but also being stranded in Hillbrow with all its reputed horrors. I begged him to drop me, but he just calmly kept asking why I was speaking English. Was I not Black? He stopped somewhere in Hillbrow, and dropped me off, with a firm word of advice: 'learn your language!'

When I told my friends about the encounter, they asked me why I hadn't responded in Kiswahili. This bit of wisdom has saved me many taxi crises since. In situations that hover towards an accusation of being a 'coconut'—black on the outside, white inside—I simply respond in Kiswahili '*sielewi unachosema*' ('I don't understand what you are saying'). My response works wonders. The tone of these conversations changes from aggressive to curious. We immediately switch back to English, and they inquire about the language I am speaking, where it is from, and whether it is similar to South African languages.

My encounter took me back to Ngũgĩ wa Thiong'o's reflections on the loss of African languages; and a black middle-class parents' misguided sense of pride not only in their children's inability to speak these languages, but in the fact that they speak English with accents that approximate what parents consider to be indices of whiteness. The taxi driver incident underscores the class dimension to the language question; and the ways in which English continues to be associated with cultural whiteness and class formation in post-independent Africa. To the taxi driver, I was yet another educated middle-class woman flaunting my class location and proximity to whiteness; and disavowing our kinship as Black people.

For Ngũgĩ wa Thiong'o, Alliance High School was a site of enlightenment and cultural alienation. There, in the 1950s, he was exposed to the best education available to brilliant black Kenyan students at the time. It was an education that simultaneously opened up a larger world and widened the cultural gap between him and his beloved community. Its sister school, Alliance Girls High School, equally promised brilliant girls drawn from across the country the same rewards: success and cultural passing. Over half a century later, when the 2017 Kenya Colleges and Schools Examinations results were announced, a few weeks before Ngũgĩ's eightieth birthday, Alliance Girls High School was among the top performing schools, much to its staff and alumni's joy. Retaining top positions despite the rooting out of cheating—which had displaced many other schools from the top rungs—affirmed the school's integrity as enjoined by the school motto: 'Walk in the Light'. It meant the school still honored the twin values on which it had been founded in 1948: strong Presbyterian ethics and the pursuit of excellence. As a previous headmistress repeatedly reminded the students during assembly: 'Girls, you really have the potential. I am trying to raise you to be ladies.'

Ladies with potential. Scientific potential. Commenting on the latest examination results, the headmistress would inform the girls and teachers: 'last year, one hundred and sixty-six girls sat for the KCSE exams. Out of those girls, ninety-eight have been admitted to universities to pursue science-based courses.' It was beneath her to mention the sixty-two girls who would be pursuing 'other' courses; much less the six who did not make the university entry grade. Potential was scientific. And cultivated ladies with potential was the school's mission. So, the Home Science and Agriculture departments catered to those untalented girls who had been gently but firmly discouraged from pursuing Fine Art or Music. Home Science was naturally popular. All those trips to the Asian-owned shops on Ngara Road to purchase fabric and make clothes during the clothing and textile classes; and whipping up exotic meals during the food and nutrition classes was enough incentive to endure the home management classes and the lessons on cleaning different kinds of domestic spaces, surfaces, fabrics. Cultivated domestic scientists with medicine, engineering, actuarial potential.

The girls at Alliance are Muthoni's afterlives. In *The River Between*, Muthoni may have succumbed to infection in her attempt to be a Christian and a woman, beautiful in the tribe; but her spirit lives on in the many generations of her daughters who pour in and out of schools like Alliance Girls annually. They take forward her desire in different combinations. They seek to be modern women of their communities and of the world. They desire to be beautiful in the tribe and in the economy. They learn to live with other kinds of cultural deaths that shadow their paths, because they recognize the privilege of having a shot at cultivating their potential in a country that specializes in drowning young people's futures. And so, they internalize the firm reminder that Gĩkũyũ, like all other Kenyan languages, is backward; a danger to the pursuit of cultivated ladies' potential. Even at Alliance, located in rural Kiambu, surrounded by Gĩkũyũ peasantry and elites, English would still be seen as the key to success, to the future, to unlocking potential, to crafting ladies:

> We disdained Kiswahili and crammed facts about places we would never visit so that we could pass exams and slip behind other desks in national schools that were extensions of our primary schools, schools named Lenana and Nairobi that had not long ago been Duke of York and Prince of Wales. The prize at the end was the White-Collar job behind another desk, a car in the secured parking lot, 2.8 kids in a primary school much like the ones we were in. (Kantai, 'The Redykyulass Generation')

Muthoni's daughters would master the art of cultural passing. They would learn to freeze parts of themselves that were not legible to the conveyor belt of upward mobility in Kenya, which was narrower than the biblical needle's eye; briefly defrosting these during the short school holidays, to reconnect with their communities. Inevitably, these cultural lives would be malnourished:

> Quiet as it is kept, there were no marigolds in the fall of 1941 … I even think now that the land of the entire country was hostile to marigolds that year. This soil is bad for certain kinds of flowers. Certain seeds it will not nurture, certain fruit it will not bear, and when the land kills of its own volition, we acquiesce and say the victim had no right to live. (Morrison, *The Bluest Eye* 164)

The girls whose mother-tongues leaked onto their English pronunciations would be subject to much laughter. They would wrap the shame of their mothers' languages under their tongues; and work hard to mute these cultural leaks.

One of the ironies of the reception of Ngũgĩ wa Thiong'o's work is that the one project which most candidly articulated his concerns about cultural imperialism, the abuses of state power and the fate of ordinary people, with the involvement of ordinary people—his work with the Kamĩrĩĩthũ community—is also the one project that has received comparatively less scholarly and popular public attention, relative to his other work. The irony of this lies in the fact that the difficulties he meticulously unpacks around the sustenance and preservation of African languages through literature are in part yoked to literacy, which in turn, in post-independent Africa, has tended to be a severely compromised domain, designed to produce labor fodder for the corporate market and civil service; the next Black middle class:

> Sons and daughters of the victors of anti-colonial struggle, the only reliable precedent for our ongoing invention was the colonial elite our parents had replaced ... Like Kenya's other successful experiments of the time—tea and coffee as small-holder cash crops—we were rooted locally but designed for export. We, the sons and daughters of the nationalist elite, sat behind dark and heavy wooded desks wounded with the insignia of those other children—the white kids of colonial bureaucrats. ('The Redykyulass Generation')

Like Kantai's father's generation, Ngũgĩ wa Thiong'o was enrolled into a schooling system designed to follow the footprints of the white children of colonial bureaucrats and settler farmers. He variously writes about the punishment meted out to school children for speaking Kiswahili and other Kenyan languages, instead of English. While a good number of his generation of writers remained invested in the families, communities and lives they left behind, locked out of the anglophile formal education in Kenya, subsequent generations have found themselves increasingly pressured by both the system and the families they left behind to fully embrace English and its attendant residual traces of Englishness; because that way lay the future, the key to a comfortable middle-class life. And, while he and others revolted, and subsequent generations of Kenyan writers and thinkers continue to revolt, the question remains: what about those locked out of the networks of circulation of their ideas and thoughts by illiteracy in English and inability to read in their mother tongues, even when they can speak these languages? And what do we do with the worlds we have crafted, where universal literacy remains unattainable, and when attained, it is largely geared towards taking us away from our cultural hearths? How do we answer to the accusing gaze of our ancestors across the waters, for whom literacy was forbidden, at the pain of death, and who still managed to not only write themselves into the future, but to also speak the ideas, concepts and worlds that had survived the middle passage, into the future?

> When the Wheatleys arrived at the auction they greeted their neighbors, they enjoyed this business of mingling with other townsfolk politely shifting about the platform, politely adjusting positions for a better view of the bodies for sale ... They looked at that child, that Black child standing nearly naked, by herself. Seven or eight years old, at most, and frail ... We know that the Wheatleys

named that African girl child Phillis after the slave ship (the *Phillis*) on which her transatlantic abduction through the Middle Passage was completed. The Wheatleys made an experiment of her. They allowed and encouraged this Phillis, child of a 'bitterly anonymous man and woman', to 'develop', to become literate, to write poetry, to become 'the first Black human being to be published in America'. (Sharpe, *In the Wake* 42–3)

If the debt African writing owes African oral forms over the many generations of its existence is to embody something more than the extractive economy that the same writers lament about—and Ngũgĩ wa Thiong'o's writing is seminal on this question—then it is not enough to resign ourselves to market forces, and the attendant reality that only literate Africans with a disposable income or access to a good library infrastructure will be able to access African writers' books. In surrendering to the reality of what Eileen Julien has termed 'the extroverted novel', African writers and the African publishing industry at large turn their back on the riches of orality—something Julien has written about, incidentally, albeit pursuing different arguments. In other words, surrendering to the tyranny of literacy generally, and the crisis of Africans' illiteracy in their own languages—since they live in these languages orally— is an expensive price that African writers and the publishing industry continue to pay; in effect limiting the audiences of their work to primarily middle class African readerships, and a Euro-American readership:

> **bell hooks:** One of our issues as black folks is: if the major buying audience is white and we want to reach that audience, to what extent do we compromise ourselves in trying to reach that audience? My books are commodities. I want to sell them to as many people as will buy them, right?
>
> **Ice Cube:** Well, see, I feel that I've gotten the most success by not compromising. And I say it in interviews, that I do records for black kids, and white kids are basically eavesdropping on my records. But I don't change what I'm saying. I won't take out this word or that word because I got white kids buying my records. White kids need to hear what we got to say about them and their forefathers and uncles and everybody that's done us wrong. (hooks, *Outlaw Culture* 150)

Unlike Ice Cube, whose music faces a different challenge—one of content and addressivity, as opposed to accessibility—Senegalese writer and filmmaker Sembene Ousmane grappled with questions of the split between his desired audiences and his actual audiences. In his case, film became a powerful medium with which to confront the challenges of literacy, access and language; albeit still a commercially demanding one, with its own concerns around sourcing funding and retaining the integrity of his projects. In some respects, film shifts the conversation from literacy and purchasing power to a different set of concerns. But for other writers, markets and audiences remain a challenge:

> The irony is that, more than ever, today the writers have the opportunity to do things previous writers could not imagine. We now have other outlets and collaborations that have been made possible by technology—film, TV, etc. And yet at the same time, you have the writer grappling with questions of audience and market. Unlike the high noon of the African Writers Series, where a writer like, let us say Dambudzo Marechera, was assured of an audience that spanned the continent; today the writer is preoccupied with seeking Western markets in order for his craft to be viable. Now, this comes with its own sets of problems and dilemmas. The Western market wants truths and realities translated. (Parselelo Kantai quoted in Musila, 'Writing History's Silences' 77)

Those of us lucky enough to have grown up on the African Writers Series in school libraries, before the Structural Adjustment Programs delivered different funding models that were to indelibly affect the book industry, lived with Muthoni's feverish words in *The River Between* seared into our minds: 'tell Nyambura I see Jesus. And I am a woman, beautiful in the tribe'. In East African literature, Muthoni was one of the casualties of the deadly encounter between indigenous epistemologies and colonial modernity, which, in the Kenyan context, was embedded in Christian logics:

> What does it mean to defend the dead? To tend to the Black dead and dying: tend to the Black person, to Black people, always living in the push towards our death? It means work. It is work: hard emotional, physical and intellectual work that demands vigilant attendance to the needs of the dying, to ease their way, also to the needs of the living … Wakes are processes; through them we think about the dead and about our relations to them; they are rituals through which to enact grief and memory. Wakes allow those among the living to mourn the passing of the dead through ritual … At stake is not recognizing antiblackness as total climate. [How] might we stay in the wake with and as those whom the state positions to die ungrievable deaths and live lives meant to be unlivable? These are questions of temporality, the *longue duree*, the residence and hold time of the wake. At stake, then, is to stay in this wake time toward inhabiting a blackened consciousness that would rupture the structural silences produced and facilitated by, and that produce and facilitate, Black social and physical death. (Sharpe 10, 22).

There have been many subsequent casualties to that intersection; albeit dying different kinds of deaths; including the social death of exclusion from the promises of colonial modernity and its exclusionary logics, inherited wholesale and reproduced along class lines with postcolonial fervor:

> The colonial world is a world divided into compartments … The settler's town
> is a well-fed town, an easy-going town; its belly is always full of good things.
> The settler's town is a town of white people, of foreigners … The native town
> is a hungry town, a town starved of bread, or meat, of shoes, of light … The
> look that the native turns on the settler's town is a look of lust, a look of envy,
> it expresses his dreams of possession—all manner of possession. The colo-
> nized man is an envious man. And this the settler knows very well; when their
> glances meet he ascertains bitterly, always on the defensive 'They want to take
> our place.' It is true, for there is no native who does not dream at least once a
> day of setting himself up in the settler's place. (Fanon, *Wretched* 37–8)

In a country that never reconfigured the state and the social cartography to
ensure equitable access to a dignified life that had hitherto been the exclusive
preserve of white society and their black lackeys, exclusivity and exclusion
remained the doctrine of social mobility; cultural passing the price of the
ticket.

Having grown up in a Kenya whose public life included a certain sense of
shame that attached to Kenyan languages, and speaking English with 'mother-
tongue influence', both of which marked one as rural, backward, poor, or all
of these and more, I found South Africans' use of their languages in television
drama series and soap operas remarkable. Before the democratization of the
airwaves brought local language radio and TV stations, TV dramas and com-
edies in Kenya were either in English or Kiswahili. Watching South African
TV, I was envious of the commitment and investedness that went into producing TV dramas that featured characters speaking to each other in four different languages and providing English subtitles. So, on the popular TV drama,
Isidingo, the characters from the Sibeko family would speak isiZulu, while the
Moloi family's characters would speak in seSotho. And these exchanges would
be subtitled in English.

Like many Kenyans, I consumed my quota of Mexican and Filipino 'soap-
ies' in the 1990s. These were often poorly dubbed, and actors' lips would still
be moving, long after the English audio statement was completed. We never
minded this, though; our attention was fully taken by the storylines. Now, decades later, I find myself watching Kenyan TV dramas exported to South Africa
and dubbed into South African languages. In one such drama, *Mali*, which airs
on the SABC channels, in place of the original English, Kiswahili and Sheng,
characters variously speak isiXhosa, Sesotho, Setswana and isiZulu, with
English subtitles. The joy of consuming four different languages simultaneously—lip-reading a character's Kiswahili, listening to their IsiZulu audio and
reading the English subtitles, all at the same time—adds to the pleasure of the
storylines. While the jury is still out on whether TV dramas can be considered literature, often with the same people who embrace conventional African

oral forms as literature, contesting the literariness of TV dramas, I am struck by the costs of the blind spot on ordinary people's consumption of stories in their own languages through television and radio. This is something Sembene Ousmane recognized and understood long before the rest of us. While it still leaves the question of written literature in African languages un-addressed, I continue to long for the radio and TV editions of Ngũgĩ wa Thiong'o's fiction in Gĩkũyũ and other Kenyan languages. I dream about watching a Sheng edition of *A Grain of Wheat* on the ubiquitous flat screens of Nairobi *matatus*. If the coincidence of 2018 also being the year of publication of Sheng studies scholar Chege Githiora's forthcoming book *Sheng: Rise of a Kenyan Swahili Vernacular* (2018) is anything to go by, then it might not be a long wait.

Part V

The Other Ngũgĩ

31
Kwa Grant Kamenju

Ngũgĩ wa Thiong'o

(Hotuba ya Kuipokea Digrii ya Heshima ya Uzamifu Kutoka Chuo Kikuu cha Dar es Salaam, 23 Novemba, 2013)
[For English Translation from the Kiswahili, see Appendix C]

Mwaka 2004 nilialikwa na Chuo Kikuu cha Transkei ambacho sasa kinaitwa Chuo Kikuu cha Walter Sisulu, Africa Kusini, ili kupokea digrii ya heshima ya uzamifu (au ya udaktari wa falsafa), pamoja na Nelson Mandela na Ali Mazrui. Hafla hiyo ilikuwa pia ni ya kuadhimisha kubadilishwa jina la zamani la Chuo Kikuu hicho, na kupewa jina hilo jipya. Jina lake la zamani, yaani Transkei, lilikuwa na kumbukumbu za utawala wa ubaguzi wa rangi wa kuigawa nchi. Na hilo jina la sasa lina uhusiano na shujaa wa taifa.

Nikiwa pamoja na mke wangu na watoto wawili, tuliwasili kwenye maeneo ya Chuo ambako kulikuwa kumetundikwa mabango yaliyoandikwa HOMECOMING (yaani KURUDI NYUMBANI/ KARIBU NYUMBANI) Niliguswa moyoni: Hiyo ilikuwa ni digrii yangu ya kwanza ya heshima niliyotunukiwa na chuo kikuu cha Afrika, baada ya nyingine kadhaa nilizotunukiwa na vyuo vikuu vya Ulaya na Marekani. Lakini hilo bango la HOMECOMING – ambalo ni jina la kitabu changu kimojawapo – lilikuwa na maana nyingine muhimu. Nilikuwa ninarudi nyumbani Kenya, kwa kupitia Afrika ya Kusini, baada ya kulazimika kuishi uhamishoni kwa miaka ishirini na mbili. Huko kurudi nyumbani kwa kupitia Afrika ya Kusini, kilele chake kilikuwa kiwe Kenya; watoto wangu wawili waliozaliwa uhamishoni walikuwa hawajaigusa ardhi ya Kenya.

Yaliyotokea baada ya siku kumi na moja tangu kurudi nchini kwangu kwa furaha kuu, pamoja na digrii niliyotunukiwa Afrika nikiwa njiani kurudi nyumbani, sasa ni historia. Kurudi kwangu nyumbani kukageuka kuwa ni jinamizi. Mimi na mke wangu tuliponea chupuchupu, baada ya kuvamiwa na watu wanne wenye bunduki/ bastola.

Si makosa ya Afrika ya Kusini, kwamba digrii yangu ya kwanza ya heshima kutoka Afrika pia ina kumbukumbu za ugaidi. Hii ya leo ni digrii ya kwanza ya heshima tangu usiku ule wa ugaidi.

Makamu Mkuu wa Chuo: Mimi ni mwandishi; yaani mimi ni mhunzi wa maneno (au mfua maneno). Lakini nimekosa maneno muwafaka ya kueleza jinsi heshima hii – ambayo Chuo Kikuu cha Dar es Salaam imenipa leo – ilivyo na maana kubwa kwangu. Si kwa sababu tu ya kwamba ni matumaini yangu kuwa nitaweza kuisherehekea digrii hii kutoka Afrika bila ya furaha yangu kufujika; lakini hasa ni kwa sababu ya hadhi ya Chuo Kikuu hiki katika usomi na siasa za Afrika.

Hapana shaka kwamba Chuo Kikuu cha Dar es Salaam ni mtoto wa uhuru wa kisiasa. Kilifikiriwa, kikapangwa na kikabuniwa na nchi ya kwanza huru katika Afrika ya Mashariki. Punde baadaye, Chuo Kikuu hiki kikawa ni kituo cha Fikira Mpya: kikitoa changamoto, kikijasiri, kikisaka njia. Katika zama za ubarobaro wake, Chuo Kikuu cha Dar es Salaam kilikuwa ni chemchemi ya fikira za kimaendeleo; na kiliwavutia wanataaluma kutoka sehemu mbalimbali za dunia.

Dar es Salaam kilikuwa ni chuo kikuu cha Walter Rodney, Issa G. Shivji, Dan Nabudere, Mahmood Mamdani, na Yash Tandon. Chuo Kikuu hiki kilikuwa ni nyumbani kwa *Cheche*. Kilikuwa ni nyumbani kwa mmojawapo miongoni mwa waandishi mashuhuri wa tamthilia wa Afrika, Ebrahim Hussein. Kilikuwa ni nyumbani kwa mshairi kutoka Kenya, Abdilatif Abdalla. Kilikuwa ni nyumbani kwa wana wengi – wake na waume – wa vyama mbalimbali vya ukombozi wa Afrika, hasa kusini mwa Afrika.

Chuo Kikuu hiki kikawa ni kiongozi wa fikira. Pia kilikuwa ni Tanzania ya Nyerere: Tanzania ambayo – kwa Afrika ya Mashariki, Afrika na dunia, iliyokuwa inaibuka kutoka ukoloni – ilikuwa na maono tafauti; Tanzania ambayo ilijaa matumaini ya wakati ujao; na matumaini kwa Umajumui wa Afrika, ambao msingi wake umechimbwa na watu wenyewe.

Lakini hivi leo nataka kumtaja Mkenya mwingine ambaye hapa Chuo Kikuu cha Dar es Salaam palikuwa ni nyumbani. Jina lake ni Grant Kamenju. Yeye alikuwa ni mmojawapo wa wahadhiri waanzilishi wa Idara ya Fasihi ya Chuo Kikuu hiki; idara ambayo niliwahi kuhusiana nayo kwa kuwa mtahini wake wa nje.

Kamenju ndiye aliyemvuta mmojawapo wa wanataaluma mashuhuri wa fasihi duniani, Arnold Kettle, kukubali kuja hapa kushika wadhifa wa uprofesa na uenyekiti wa Idara ya Fasihi. Nilimjua Kamenju. Nilifanya naye kazi Chuo Kikuu cha Makerere na cha Leeds. Alipokuja Chuoni hapa, Kamenju alikuja na nishati na baadhi ya fikira tulizokuwa tukizifanyia kazi tulipokuwa katika hivyo vyuo vikuu viwili. Kamenju hakuwa akijali sana kuchapisha maandishi yake. Kwa hivyo, mchango wake mkubwa haukuwa ukionekana kwa maandishi. Alikuwa ni mtu ambaye akipenda zaidi kushughulika na fikira, na kuzikabidhi kwa wengine, badala ya kubaki nazo na kuzitia kwenye Wasifu-Kazi (CV) wake.

Kamenju alikuwa ni miongoni mwa wale wanaofuata desturi ya kitaaluma simulizi. Taaluma hii ina historia ndefu – tangu zama za Socrates na wengineo; ambao fikira zao bado zingali zinaendelea kuwako hadi leo kwa sababu wanafunzi wao walizihifadhi fikira hizo kutokana na matini waliyokuwa wakiyaandika. Kamenju ameacha athari kubwa katika usomeshaji, na upangaji wa usomeshaji fasihi, katika vyuo vikuu hivi vitatu. Hata hivi leo, wanafunzi wake wa zamani – miongoni mwao akiwemo M. M. Mulokozi – wanajihesabu kwamba ni watoto wa Kamenju.

Hakuna hata wakati mmoja ambapo Kamenju aliwania kutaka kupata sifa. Amefariki, kimyakimya, bila ya kushangiliwa kuwa ni shujaa wa mapinduzi katika fasihi; mtetezi mkuu wa kuihusisha fasihi na maisha; na mwanaha-rakati wa mapambano ya ukombozi wa kiuchumi, kisiasa, kitamaduni na kiroho. Huo ndio msimamo wangu pia; na nimejitolea kuutetea katika maisha yangu, maandishi yangu, na fikira zangu. Nalishangilia jina lake leo. Na ni kwa makumbusho ya hayati Profesa Grant Kamenju ndio ninaipokea heshima hii kwa shukurani nyingi. Ahsanteni sana.

(Namshukuru ndugu Abdilatif kwa utafsiri huu ambao umeniwezesha nitoe shukrani zangu kwa lugha tukufu la Kiswahili.)

32

Wasomi, Lugha za Ulaya na za Kiafrika: Kati ya Kuweza na Kuwezwa

Ngũgĩ wa Thiong'o

[For English Translation from the Kiswahili, see Appendix D]

(Mhadhara wa hadhara uliotolewa Chuo Kikuu cha Dar es Salaam, Ukumbi wa Nkrumah, baada ya kutunukiwa Digrii ya Heshima ya Uzamifu [PhD] na Chuo hicho, 23 Novemba, 2013)

Katika mhadhara huu, nataka kuangalia na kufafanua, kwa ufupi tu, uhusiano wa kitaaluma kati ya lugha za Afrika na za Ulaya, na hasa Kiingereza. Jambo hili ni muhimu katika wakati huu, ambapo nchi nyingi za Afrika zinasherehekea miaka hamsini tangu zipate uhuru wake kutoka utawala wa kikoloni.

Msomi, au mwanataaluma wa aina yoyote ile, si kitu kipya kwa Afrika: Kila jamii, za leo au za kale, zilikuwa na wasomi au wanataaluma wake. Tunalitumia hili neno 'msomi' kwa maana ya mtu anayeshughulika na fikira. Yawezekana kwamba msomi huyo huenda akawa ana ujuzi mwingine; lakini kazi yake kuu inayojitokeza ni matokeo ya kujishughulisha kwake na fikira. Katika kundi hili wanaingia pia waganga wa kimwili na wa kiroho, wahunzi (au wafua vyuma), wajenzi, na mafundi wengineo.

Watu kama hawa walikuwa ni miongoni mwa wajenzi wa utamaduni wa Misri, Uhabeshi, Zimbabwe, Songhai, na kwengineko. Kati ya hao, alikuwamo pia mshairi, ambaye alichanganya ujuzi wa historia, maadili na utabiri. Afrika ya Magharibi, mtu kama huyo aliitwa 'griot'. Uswahilini kulikuwa na washairi wengi waliokuwa ni viongozi wa fikira, na ambao wameendelea kuweko karne baada ya karne. Kitabu alichokihariri Abdilatif Abdalla, na kuchapishwa na shirika la Mkuki na Nyota, kiitwacho *Kale ya Washairi wa Pemba: Kamange na Sarahani*, kina majina ya wachache kati ya hao. Miongoni mwao wakiwemo Fumo Liyongo wa Bauri (karne ya kumi na mbili); Zahidi Mgumi (karne ya kumi na nane); Muyaka bin Haji; Suud bin Said al-Maamiriy; Kamange na Sarahani (wote ni wa karne ya kumi na tisa); na wengineo walioishi katika karne ya ishirini. Washairi kama hawa walikuwa ni sauti za jamii zao, na pia watetezi wa haki. Ni muhimu kueleza hapa kwamba washairi-wasomi kama hao – tangu hizo zama za ustaarabu wa Misri, mpaka katika ustaarabu wa Waswahili – walitumia lugha za jamii zao. Yaani wasomi wa kabla ya kuvamiwa na utawala wa kikoloni, walikuwa wameshikamana na mizizi ya jamii zao.

Leo nataka kuzungumza, kwa ufupi tu, kuhusu msomi Mwafrika wa zama zetu. Yaani msomi aliyekwenda shule za kisasa, na kupata elimu yake kwa kupitia lugha za Ulaya. Kuna nyuso mbili za msomi kama huyu, ambazo zinapingana; na pia kuna mihula miwili aliyoipitia, ambayo pia inapingana: Wasomi Waafrika walioshiriki katika mapambano dhidi ya ukoloni, wali-zichukua hazina zilizokuwamo katika lugha za kigeni, na wakazipeleka hazina hizo katika lugha za Afrika na kuzitajirisha.

Katika nchi iliyoitwa Gold Coast (ambayo leo inaitwa Ghana) kulichap-ishwa taarifa katika gazeti lililoitwa The Gold Coast People, la tarehe 30 Novemba, mwaka 1893. Taarifa hiyo iliwahimiza wasomi Wafante wa wakati huo kushukuru kwamba 'Wafante wanaona fahari kuwa Wafante, na hawaoni aibu kujiita kwa majina yao ya kienyeji; wala kuzungumza kwa lugha zao; wala kuonekana wamevaa mavazi ya kikwao ... Badala ya kuwa Waafrika-Wazungu, walitaka kubaki kuwa wasomi Waafrika wastaarabu.'

Mawazo kama haya pia yalielezwa na wasomi wa Afrika ya Kusini wa karne ya kumi na tisa (wasomi wa Lovedale, na kadhalika). Hapa Afrika ya Mashariki tuna mfano wa mshairi wa Tanzania, Shaaban Robert, na ule msemo wake maarufu, 'Titi la Mama litamu lingawa la Mbwa, lingine halishi tamu.'

Baada ya Ghana kupata uhuru wake, mwaka 1957, Kwame Nkrumah hakuchelewa kuanzisha Kituo cha Lugha za Afrika; na kuanzisha mpango wa kuwatayarisha walimu kufundisha lugha za Afrika. Na vile vile akaanzisha magazeti ya lugha za Kiafrika.

Katika hotuba yake ya ufunguzi wa Kongamano la Kwanza la Kimataifa la Wanataaluma wa Afrika, lililofanyika Accra mwaka 1962, Kwame Nkrumah alieleza matumaini yake kwamba kongamano hilo litakuwa ni hatua muhimu ya kulifanya bara la Afrika kujithamini, na kuthamini historia na utamaduni wake; na kwamba lugha za Afrika zitachukua nafasi muhimu.

Nkrumah alilirudia tena swala hilo mwaka mmoja baadaye, alipokuwa aki-fungua Taasisi ya Taaluma za Afrika ya kwanza. Kwake yeye, swala la taaluma na uendelezaji wa lugha za Afrika halikuwa ni swala la kuwekwa pembeni; bali aliamini kwamba lugha za Afrika ni lazima zichukue nafasi ya kati, kwa sababu zilikuwa ni kiungo muhimu katika taaluma, maendeleo na uhusiano wa Afrika na Waafrika wanaoishi nje ya Afrika. Nkrumah hakutaka Afrika ijitenge kilugha na sehemu nyingine za dunia, kwani aliijua nafasi na faida ya lugha nyingine za dunia – kama vile Kiarabu, Kiingereza, Kifaransa na Kireno.

Wakati ambapo watu wengine waliziona lugha za Afrika kuwa ni duni katika pepo ya Kiingereza, Nkrumah aliziona lugha za Afrika kuwa zina thamani na nafasi sawa na lugha nyingine duniani katika kuijenga pepo ya pamoja. Kitu muhimu ni kwamba Nkrumah hakusema kwa maneno tu, lakini alihakiki-sha kwamba kuna nyenzo za kufanyia kazi hiyo na kulitimiza lengo hilo kwa vitendo. Lakini serikali za kijeshi zilizoipindua serikali ya Nkrumah ziliibadil-isha sera hiyo, na huku baadhi ya Waghana wa tabaka la kati wakishangilia.

Waghana hao hawakutaka kuzuiliwa kuipanda ngazi ya kuwapeleka kwenye pepo ya lugha ya Kiingereza.

Nchini Kenya, mapambano dhidi ya ukoloni yalipelekea kuanzishwa kwa magazeti ya lugha za Kiafrika. Jomo Kenyatta aliwahi kuwa mhariri wa gazeti mojawapo kama hilo, lililoitwa *Mũiguithania*. Baadaye aliandika kitabu kwa Kikikuyu, kiitwacho *Kenya Bururi wa Ngũĩ*; yaani, Kenya: Nchi ya Migogoro. Hiki kilikuwa ni nyongeza ya kitabu chake alichokiandika kwa Kiingereza, *Facing Mount Kenya*. Serikali ya kikoloni ikayapiga marufuku magazeti hayo ya lugha za Kiafrika, na baadhi ya wahariri wake wakalazimika kukimbilia uhamishoni, na wengine wakafungwa jela.

Baada ya uhuru wa Tanganyika, mwaka elfu moja na mia tisa na sitini na moja, Mwalimu Julius Nyerere akakifanya Kiswahili kuwa lugha ya taifa. Hatimaye, Kiswahili kikawa na kwao. Naye akaonyesha mifano kwa vitendo. Baadhi ya hotuba zake muhimu alizitoa kwa Kiswahili; na baadhi ya maandishi yake yakatafsiriwa kwa Kiswahili. Na hata akazitafsiri kwa Kiswahili tamthilia mbili za William Shakespeare – *Juliasi Kaizari* (Julius Caesar) na *Mabepari wa Venisi* (Merchants of Venice).

Wasomi kama hawa waliutumia ujuzi wao wa Kiingereza kuzizidishia uwezo jamii zao – tafauti kabisa na Waafrika wa tabaka la kati la baada ya uhuru! Hawa ni wale ambao baadhi yao wameshika madaraka ya serikali, na ambao wamekuwa ni mateka wa lugha za Ulaya!

Miaka kadhaa iliyopita, nafikiri miaka mitatu iliyopita, bunge la Kenya huru lilipiga kura kuzipiga marufuku lugha za Kiafrika zisizungumzwe katika maeneo rasmi, kwa mfano, maofisini. Kichekesho ni kwamba bunge hilo halingekuwako kama si kwa sababu ya wafanyakazi na wakulima wadogo wadogo wanaozungumza lugha hizo za Kiafrika kuingia misituni na bara-barani ili kupambana dhidi ya serikali ya kikoloni. Bila ya shaka, bunge hilo halikuona kwamba mizizi yake inatokana na lugha za Kiafrika, bali inatokana na lugha ya Kiingereza na lugha nyingine za Ulaya. Sheria hiyo haijapitishwa kwa sababu tu Rais hakuitia sahihi.

Lugha imekuwa ni medani ya mapambano ya fikira. Lakini ninalotaka kuli-zungumzia hapa ni kwamba lugha ni uwanja wa vita vya mapambano baina ya utumwa na harakati za kujikomboa na kujipa uwezo. Historia ya lugha, ame-andika Tom Paulin, mara nyingi huwa ni hadithi ya kutamalaki na kupora; ni hadithi ya kuziteka ardhi na kuziweka katika mamlaka ya walioziteka; au kuwalazimisha watu kufuata utamaduni fulani.

Lugha, haidhuru iwe inatumiwa ndani au nje ya maeneo ya taaluma, ime-kuwa ni uwanja wa vita – katika hali zote – baina ya mtawala na mtawaliwa, hasa katika enzi za ukoloni. Katika hali kama hizo, lugha imekuwa ni silaha ya kutamalaki au ni silaha ya kupinga kutamalakiwa, sawa na silaha kama upanga. Kwa hakika, vita vikali zaidi vimepiganwa, na vinaendelea kupiganwa, katika eneo hili.

Mshairi mmoja wa Kiingereza, Spenser, aliyeishi zama moja na Shakespeare, na ambaye aliandika kitabu maarufu, *The Faerie Queene*, aliueleza vizuri umuhimu wa kutumia silaha ya lugha katika kutamalaki. Katika mwaka elfu moja na mia tano na tisiini na tisa, aliandika kwamba, 'imekuwa ni kawaida kwa anayetamalaki kuidharau lugha ya anayemtamalaki, na kumlazimi-sha kwa kila njia huyo anayemtamalaki kujifunza lugha yake (mtamalaki).' Spenser aliyaandika maneno haya katika kitabu chake *A View of the Present State of Ireland*. Katika kitabu hicho alitetea kupigwa marufuku mfumo wa majina ya watu wa taifa la Ireland – kitendo ambacho lengo lake lilikuwa ni kuzifuta kabisa kumbukumbu za taifa hilo. Udhibiti wa mfumo wa majina ya wananchi wa Ireland ulikuwa ni njia kuu iliyotumiwa na Waingereza kuita-malaki Ireland.

Kama alivyoeleza Tony Crowley katika kitabu chake, *Wars of Words: The Politics of Language in Ireland 1537–2004*, wavamizi mbalimbali wa Ufalme wa Uingereza walipitisha sheria kadhaa zilizokuwa na madhumuni ya kuilinda lugha ya Kiingereza isiingiliwe na kuathiriwa na lugha ya ki-Ireland na ya ki-Gaeli (Gaelic). Mfululizo wa sheria hizo ulianza na Sheria ya Kilkenny ya mwaka 1363, baada ya Uingereza kuiteka na kuikalia Ireland. Kwa mfano, amri mojawapo ya sheria hiyo ilitishia kwamba serikali itamnyang'anya ardhi yake Mwingereza yoyote au mwananchi yoyote wa Ireland ambaye atazungumza na mwenzake kwa lugha yao, kinyume na sheria hiyo. Kwa hivyo, Spenser aliyaandika maneno yake hayo kutokana na sheria hiyo, ambayo inaonyesha haikufaulu, kama ilivyotarajiwa. Kwani kama ilikuwa na athari yoyote, Spenser asingekuwa na haja ya kutaka sheria hiyo itekelezwe baada ya zaidi ya miaka mia mbili kupita.

Yeye Spenser mwenyewe alikuwa ni Mwingereza mlowezi (au setla) katika sehemu ya Munster. Mmojawapo wa majirani zake alikuwa ni mlowezi mwen-zake kutoka Uingereza, Walter Raleigh – ambaye ndiye aliyeanzisha makao ya walowezi Virginia, Marekani.

Inawezekana kwamba hakukuwako na uhusiano wa moja kwa moja baina ya yaliyotokea Ireland wakati huo, na yale yaliyowakumba Waafrika wali-ochukuliwa kwa nguvu kutoka Afrika na kwenda kufanywa watumwa katika mashamba ya Marekani yaliyomilikiwa na walowezi waliokuja baada ya kina Walter Raleigh. Hata hivyo, katika mashamba hayo Waafrika waliotiwa utum-wani hawakuruhusiwa kuzungumza kwa lugha zao. Hata mawasiliano ya kutumia ngoma pia yalikatazwa. Vile vile, hawakuwa na ruhusa ya kutumia majina yao ya Kiafrika. Na Waafrika waliopatikana wakizungumza lugha zao waliadhibiwa; na hata wengine kuuliwa. Lengo la yote hayo lilikuwa ni lile lile: Kuwasahaulisha uhusiano wao na kwao walikotoka.

Japani nayo ilifanya kama hivyo baada ya kuitamalaki Korea: iliwalazimisha Wakorea kutumia lugha ya Kijapani, na mfumo wa Kijapani wa kupeana majina. Sera hiyo ilitupiliwa mbali baada ya Japani kushindwa katika Vita vya Pili vya

Dunia. Lakini athari ya sera hiyo ingalipo. Mpaka hivi karibuni, ndani ya Japani kwenyewe, wenye asili ya Korea walilazimika kuwa na majina ya Kijapani.

Katika bara la Afrika, baada ya kulivamia na kulitamalaki, Wafaransa, Waingereza na Wareno, walifuata sera kama hizo. Ingawa wakoloni hao hawakuzipiga marufuku lugha za Kiafrika, lakini waliziteremshia hadhi yake ya kuwa ni lugha zenye uwezo, maarifa na kuwa ni kitambulisho cha wenye lugha hizo. Hata kama waliziruhusu lugha hizo kutumiwa katika mfumo wa elimu, ilikuwa ni katika hatua za mwanzo mwanzo tu, kabla ya wanafunzi kugeuzwa na kuwa wasemaji wa Kiingereza au Kifaransa. Siijui sheria yoyote ya utawala wa kikoloni iliyopiga marufuku majina ya Kiafrika. Lakini kutokana na athari za mamlaka ya kitamaduni, karibu kila Mwafrika aliyepata elimu ya kisasa ameliambatanisha jina la Kizungu katika jina lake la Kiafrika. Sera za kikoloni kuhusu lugha zilikuwa zinaendeleza sera za vita vya kutamalaki, kwa kutumia mbinu za kilugha.

Kulikuwa na Mwingereza mmoja, jina lake ni Macaulay. Yeye alikuwa ameajiriwa na kampuni ya British East India, ambayo ndiyo ilikuwa inatawala India. Yeye ndiye aliyependekeza sera za kutumia Kiiingereza kuwasomeshea raia wa India, badala ya Kihindi au Kisankrist. Alisema, 'Ni lazima tuwe na Wahindi ambao kwa rangi ya ngozi ni Wahindi, lakini kwa akili ni Waingereza. Kikundi hiki kitakuwa kati yetu na umma tunaoutawala.' Fikira kama hizo ndizo zilizopelekwa katika makoloni mingine ya Waingereza: Kikundi, au tabaka, ambalo kwa ngozi ni Waafrika, lakini katika mabongo yao ni Waingereza.

Bara la Afrika linaendelea kuteseka na kudhalilika kutokana na kutamalakiwa kilugha. Uhuru wa kisiasa tulioupata labda umeikomboa miili yetu tu, lakini haukuyakomboa mabongo yetu. Na hayo ndiyo matokeo ya kutamalakiwa kilugha kwa muda mrefu.

Kutokana na hali hiyo, hivi leo katika bara la Afrika kuna mgawanyiko mkubwa baina ya Waafrika wenye elimu, wa tabaka la kati, na Waafrika wengine kwa jumla. Na hilo ndilo lililokuwa lengo la ukoloni. Tukiurudia ule mfano tulioutoa – wa kwamba lugha ni silaha ya kivita – imekuwa ni kama kwamba majemadari Waafrika wameshikwa mateka katika kambi ya adui. Na nisemapo 'majemadari', simaanishi serikali zetu tu; bali ninamaanisha tabaka zima la wasomi. Na hakuna hata mmoja katika sisi anayeweza kujigamba kwamba hakuathirika na huko kukubali kushindwa kwetu. Au kwa kuendesha maisha yetu ya kisomi na kitaaluma na huku tukiendelea kuwa mateka.

Kwa sababu hiyo ya kuwa sisi ni mateka, tunalazimishwa kulitazama bara la Afrika kama kwamba sisi ni wageni hapa. Nyanja kadha wa kadha za elimu yetu kuhusu Afrika zimejikita katika ule mfumo wa kikoloni wa aliyeko nje akiangalia ndani. Tunakusanya elimu na maarifa mingine ya humu barani Afrika, na kwa msaada wa Waafrika wenyeji, halafu tunaificha elimu na maarifa hayo katika lugha ya Ulaya kwa faida ya wale tu wanaoifahamu lugha hiyo. Yaani tunaendelea kuvikusanya vito vya thamani vya kisomi na kuviweka katika majumba ya makumbusho na makavazi ya lugha za Ulaya. Jamii ya wasomi Waafrika – walioko nje na ndani ya bara la Afrika – wamesalimu amri, na wameikubali hali hii kwamba ni hali ya kawaida.

Katika mwezi wa Septemba mwaka jana, kulikuwa na kongamano kubwa mjini Leeds, Uingereza. Kongamano hilo lilihudhuriwa na zaidi ya wataalamu mia tano kutoka Afrika na Ulaya. Nikawauliza wataalamu waliohudhuria: Ni wangapi kati yao walioandika angalau kitabu kimoja tu kwa lugha yoyote ya Kiafrika? Hakuna hata mmoja aliyeinua mkono! Je, aliyeandika makala mamoja tu kwa lugha ya Kiafrika? Hakuna hata mmoja aliyeinua mkono! Je, aliyeandika ukurasa mmoja tu kwa lugha ya Kiafrika? Hapo kukainuliwa mikono mitatu! Mikono mitatu tu!! – katika kongamano kubwa kama hilo, lililohudhuriwa na wasomi na wataalamu wa kiwango cha juu wanaojishughulisha na taaluma za bara la Afrika.

Niliuliza maswali kama hayo nchini Nigeria na Kenya, Zambia na Ghana, mbele ya hadhira ya Waafrika mashuhuri. Matokeo hayakuwa tofauti na haya!

Labda hoja yangu itaeleweka vizuri zaidi lau tutaliuliza swali hilo kwa namna tofauti: Unaweza kumfikiria Profesa wa Historia au Utamaduni wa Italia, ambaye hafahamu hata neno moja la Kitaliani? Au Profesa wa Historia ya Ufaransa asiyejua Kifaransa. Au Profesa wa Kigiriki au Kilatini ambaye hazifahamu lugha hizo? Bila ya shaka utajibu kwamba hilo si jambo la kawaida. Lakini, inapohusu taaluma za Afrika, hali hiyo imegeuzwa na kuwa ya kawaida. Huu ni mzaha, kama si upumbavu! Bara kubwa kabisa duniani – kubwa kuliko mabara ya Ulaya, Amerika na China yakikusanywa pamoja – kutendewa hivi!

Hali hii ni lazima ibadilishwe. Na hili litawezekana tu iwapo kutakuwako na ushirikiano baina ya asasi za taaluma – ambazo zitakubali na zitakuwa tayari kufuata mbinu tofauti za kutafutia elimu; na wachapishaji – ambao watakubali kuwa na mikakati tafauti ya uchapishaji; na wasomi – ambao watakuwa tayari kuzidisha juhudi zao ili kulifanikisha lengo hili.

Lakini kuna mshirika mwingine ambaye ni muhimu pia. Naye ni serikali: serikali zenye sera za kuziendeleza na kuzikuza lugha za Afrika. Tusisahau kwamba wanaoziendesha serikali hizo, wao wenyewe wamefinyangwa na asasi za kitaaluma. Labda, kama wakati walipokuwa wanafunzi misimamo yao ya kuongoza serikali ingekuwa imekabiliwa na changamoto, huenda wangeibuka kuwa majemadari walio tayari kuongoza wakiwa ni watu huru wanaotaka kutafuta mbinu nyingine za kupigana na kuelewa, badala ya kuwa ni mateka. Lakini hakuna mabadiliko makubwa yanayoweza kupatikana ikiwa serikali zinashinikizwa kufanya shughuli zake bila ya kutoka nje ya mipaka iliyowekwa na wanaotamalaki.

Kuna dalili chache za matumaini ya kwamba mambo huenda yanabadilika, na kwamba Kiswahili kiko mstari wa mbele. Kufaulu kwa Kiswahili nchini Tanzania ni matokeo ya wasomi wa aina ya kwanza tuliowataja: Yaani wale waliochukua kutoka lugha za Ulaya kile walichoweza, na kukihifadhi katika lugha za Afrika. Tumeshamtaja Mwalimu Julius Nyerere. Kama tunavyojua, yeye alihitimu katika vyuo vikuu viwili maarufu vya wakati wake – Makerere na Edinburgh. Aliposhika uongozi wa taifa hili, aliweka sera – kwa nadharia na kwa vitendo – za kukipa Kiswahili hadhi na uwezo. Urithi mkubwa wa Nyerere ni wa lugha: Kutuachia mfano wa kuonyesha bila ya shaka kwamba lugha za Kiafrika zina uwezo wa kukua na kukuza fikira, kama lugha nyingine za dunia. Heshima tunayoweza kumkumbuka nayo ni kukiendeleza na kuki-kuza Kiswahili mpaka kiwe moja ya lugha za dunia. Baadhi ya watu wana fikira ya kwamba lugha ya taifa inaweza kujengwa tu juu ya makaburi ya lugha nyingine za Afrika. Kuwa na lugha moja tu ya taifa kumelinganishwa na dhana ya ki-Ulaya ya taifa – dhana ambayo ilibuniwa katika karne ya kumi na saba, mwanzoni mwa ubepari wa kisasa na ukoloni.

Pia si jambo la kushangaza kuona kwamba Tanzania imezaa shirika la uchapishaji ambalo limekuwa na msimamo thabiti wa kuchapisha vitabu kwa lugha za Afrika, zaidi maandishi ya Kiswahili ya kiwango cha juu. Shirika hilo ni Mkuki na Nyota, la Walter Bgoya. Na shirika la Henry Chakava, East African Educational Publishers, nalo limechapisha tafsiri za Kiswahili za vitabu vya karibu waandishi wote maarufu wa Afrika, ambavyo viliandikwa kwa Kiingereza na Kifaransa.

Lakini, je, asasi za taaluma kwa jumla zinafuata nyayo hizi?

Hata hapa kuna dalili za matumaini: Hatua ndogo, ingawa yenye athari kubwa, imechukuliwa katika uwanja wa falsafa kutokana na kuchapishwa kitabu kinachoitwa *Listening to Ourselves*, ambacho kimehaririwa na msomi mwenye asili ya mchanganyiko wa Karibea na Kanada, anayeitwa Chike Jeffers. Kimechapishwa na State University of New York (SUNY). Kitabu chenyewe ni mkusanyiko wa insha kuhusu falsafa, ambazo zimeandikwa kwa lugha mbal-imbali za Afrika ya Mashariki na Afrika ya Magharibi – kwa mfano, Kiwolof, Kijaluo, Kiigbo, Kiacan, Kiamhara, Kikikuyu – na tafsiri zake kwa Kiingereza. Waandishi wa insha hizo, miongoni mwao akiwemo hayati Emmanuel Eze, ni wanataaluma Waafrika maarufu wanaoshughulika na falsafa; na ambao wanashikilia nyadhifa za uprofesa katika vyuo vikuu vya nje ya Afrika. Hii ni mara yangu ya kwanza kuona maandishi kwa lugha za Afrika, yaliyoandikwa na wanafalsafa wa zama zetu.

Msomi mwenye asili ya Karibea amelifanyia bara la Afrika jambo ambalo ni la kwanza kufanywa. Alikuwa na nia ya kufanya jambo kama hili, na kuingia katika orodha ndefu ya Wakaribea wenziwe waliolifanyia kazi bara la Afrika; kwa mfano, Marcus Garvey, CLR James, George Padmore, W.E.B. Du Bois, Walter Rodney, kwa kuwataja wachache tu.

Kitabu hiki cha Jeffers kinatukumbusha lugha nyingine, ambayo haija-tumiwa kwa mapana yake katika kuzipa uwezo lugha za Afrika. Lugha yenyewe ni Tafsiri. Katika kitabu changu, *Something Torn and New*, nimeeleza kwamba tafsiri ni lugha ya lugha mbalimbali. Hakuna utamaduni hata mmoja duniani ambao haukufaidika na tafsiri. Kwa hivyo, hapana shaka kwamba tafsiri baina ya lugha za Afrika zenyewe kwa zenyewe, na tafsiri baina ya lugha za Afrika na lugha nyingine za dunia, zitazifaidi tamaduni za Afrika na tamaduni nyingine za dunia. Vyuo vyetu na vyuo vikuu vyetu vinapaswa kuwa ni viwanda vya shughuli za kutafsiri maandishi ya lugha za kigeni kwa lugha zetu za Afrika.

Lakini mambo haya yanahitaji mshikamano na ushirikiano mkubwa baina ya wasomi, wanataaluma, wachapishaji, na wanaotayarisha sera za elimu. Wasomi, walioko ndani na nje ya Afrika, ni lazima waongoze njia na kushika nafasi zao za heshima za tangu jadi. Katika tamaduni na historia zote za dunia, msomi amekuwa ni msaka njia. Na katika tamaduni zote, wasomi kama hawa imewabidi kulipa bei ghali, wakati mwengine hata kwa kupoteza roho zao. Na mimi nimelipa – ingawa si malipo makubwa hivyo. Lakini nimelipa: kufungwa gerezani, na hata kulazimika kuishi uhamishoni. Wasomi wa zama zetu wasiyakimbie mapambano. Wasiukimbie uwanja wa vita.

Lakini na serikali na asasi zetu nyingine nazo ziache kuvizika vichwa vyao kwenye mashimo ya huu unaoitwa utandawazi. Utandawazi ulianza tangu karne ya kumi na saba wakati mwili wa Mwafrika ulipolazimishwa kufanya kazi ya kitumwa katika mashamba. Na kazi hiyo ya kitumwa ikapelekea kwenye utumwa wa kikoloni. Hivi leo, utandawazi unategemea maliasili ambayo bado yanapatikana katika bara kubwa kabisa duniani – Afrika. Serikali zetu nyingi, na wanataaluma na wasomi wetu wengi, wanaishi katika njozi kwa kufikiria kwamba ili kuishi katika utandawazi, ni lazima wapotelee kwenye lugha ya Kiingereza.

Watu kama hao inawabidi waukumbuke ukweli huu: Wao walitupa lafdhi ya Kiingereza; na sisi tukawapa njia za kutuingilia katika bara letu. Katika karne za kumi na saba na kumi na nane, waliuchukua mwili wa Mwafrika. Katika karne ya kumi na tisa na ya ishirini walipata njia ya kuchukua shaba yetu, dhahabu yetu, almasi yetu; na sasa mafuta yetu. Hivi leo, wakati ambapo tumeshughulika kuzifanya lafdhi zetu za Kiingereza kuwa bora zaidi, wao wanashughulika kutumia njia bora zaidi za kupora mali ya bara letu.

Tusipoteze wakati wetu na nyenzo zetu kwa kujibidiisha kuboresha lafdhi zetu za Kiingereza. Badala yake tutumie wakati wetu mwingi zaidi, na nyenzo tulizonazo, ili kuulinda utajiri wa Afrika kwa kila hali. Lugha ni silaha ya kivita.

Tuyakumbuke maneno ya Shaaban Robert: Titi la Mama litamu lingawa la Mbwa, lingine halishi tamu.

Tuseme hivi: Ukijua lugha zote za dunia, lakini huijui lugha yako ya mama, wewe ni mtumwa; umewezwa! Lakini ukijua lugha yako ya mama, na halafu ukaongezea lugha nyingine za dunia, wewe unajiweza; yaani umejiongezea uwezo. Lazima tuchague baina ya kujiweza na kuwezwa. Na natumai Afrika itajichagulia kujiweza badala ya kuwezwa.

Ahsanteni sana kwa kunisikiliza.

33
Asia in My Life

Ngũgĩ wa Thiong'o

(Originally published in the Global South Project, http://www.
globalsouthproject.cornell.edu/asia-in-my-life.html. Reprinted with permission.)

The links between Asia and Africa and South America have always been present but in our times, they have been made invisible by the fact that Europe is still the central mediator of Afro-Asian-Latino discourse. We live under what Satya Mohanty in his interview in *Frontline* (April 2012), aptly calls the long intellectual shadow of the Age of European Empire.

In my case, I had always assumed that my intellectual and social formation was tied to England and Europe, with no meaningful connection to Asia and South America. There was a reason. I wrote in English. My literary heroes were English. Kenya being a British colony, I had learnt the geography and history of England as the central reference in my widening view of the world. Even our anti-colonial resistance assumed Europe as the point of contest; it was we, Africa, against them, Europe. I graduated from Makerere College in Uganda in 1964, with a degree in English; then went to the University of Leeds, England, for further studies, in English. Leeds was a meeting point of students from the Commonwealth: India, Pakistan, Australia, and the Caribbean. We saw each other through our experience of England. Our relationship to England, in admiration, resentment or both, was what established a shared space.

After I wrote my memoir of childhood, *Dreams in a Time of War*, published in 2006, I looked back and saw how much India had been an equally important thread in my life. I had not planned to bring out the Indian theme in my life: but there it was, staring at me right from the pages of my narrative. The thread starts from home, through school, college and after.

I did not grow up in a Christian home, but we celebrated Christmas, everybody did; it was a time of carnival, with children, in their very best, trooping from house to house to indulge their fancy in terms of food. We were vegetarians throughout the year, though not out of choice, and to many, Christmas day was the first time they would taste meat. For me Christmas meant the occasion for eating *gĩtoero*, a curried broth of potatoes, peas, beans, and occasionally a piece of lamb or chicken, but the centerpiece of the dishes was *cabaci* sometimes called *mborota*. Even today, Christmas and feasts in Kenya mean plentiful of *cabaci*, *thambutha* and *mandathi*, our version of the Indian chapati, paratha, samosa. The spices, curry, hot pepper and all, so very Indian, had become so central a part of Kenyan African cuisine that I could have sworn that these dishes were truly indigenous.

It was not just Christmas: daily hospitality in every Kenyan home means being treated to a mug of tea, literally a brew of tea leaves, *tangawizi*, and milk and sugar, made together, really a masala tea. Not to offer a passing guest or neighbor a cup of tea is the height of stinginess or poverty; and for the guest to decline the offer, the ultimate insult. So African it all seemed to me that when I saw Indians drinking tea or making curry, I thought it the result of African influence. Where the Indian impact on African food culture was all pervasive, there was hardly any equivalent from the English presence; baked white bread is the only contribution that readily comes to mind.

This is not surprising. Imported Indian skilled labor built the railway line from the Coast to the Great Lake, opening the interior for English settlement. Every railroad station, from Mombasa to Kisumu, initially depots for the building material, mushroomed into a town mainly because of the Indian traders who provided much needed services to the workers initially but in time, to the community around. If European settlers opened the land for large-scale farming for export, the Indian opened the towns and cities for retail and wholesale commerce.

Limuru where I come from had a thriving Indian shopping center built on land carved out from that of my maternal grandfather's clan. The funeral pyres to burn the bodies of the Indian dead were held in a small forest that was also under my maternal grandfather's care. Cremation is central to Hindu culture: it asks Agni, the fire god to release the spirit from the earthily body to be re-embodied in heaven into a different form of being. The departed soul traveled from *pretaloka* to *pitraloka* unless there were impurities holding it back. My mother did not practice Hinduism, but to her dying day, she believed and swore that on some nights, she would see disembodied Indian spirits, like lit candles in the dark, wandering in the forest around the cremation place. She talked about it as a matter of regular material fact and she would become visibly upset when we doubted her.

It was not all harmony all the time. The Indian community kept to itself, there was hardly any social interaction between us, except across the counters at the shopping center. Fights between African and Indian kids broke out, initiated by either side. The Indian *dukawalla*, an employer of Africans for domestic work and around the shops, was, more often than not, likely to hurl racially charged insults at his workers. Some of the insults entered African languages. One of the most insulting words in Gĩkũyũ was *njangiri*. A *njangiri* of a man meant one who was useless, rootless, like a stray dog. *Njangiri* came to Gĩkũyũ from *Jangaal*, the Sanskrit/Hindi word for wild: it would have been what the Indian employer was likely to call his domestic help. In the colonial times, in my area at least, I do not recall the tensions ever exploding into inter-communal violence.

The post-colonial scene presents a different picture. Time and again Indians and Indian owned stores have been targets of violence especially in times of crisis, mostly victims of looting. I am not sure if it's the fact of their Indianness or the fact of their being a most visible part of the affluent middleclass. In such a case the line between the racial and class resentment is thin. Different in that sense is the case of Idi Amin's Uganda, where hundreds of Asians were expelled from a country that had been their home for almost a century. In both the colonial and post-colonial era, social segregation, forced in the case of the colonial era, or a consequence of habit and history, has exacerbated tensions.

The colonial school system segregated Asian, European and African from each other and it was not until Makerere College that I had social interaction with Indians. Makerere was an affiliate of the University of London in Kampala, Uganda, where, until the advent of Idi Amin, racial relations were benign. Before its college status, Makerere used to be a place of post-secondary schooling for African students from British East Africa, but as Independence approached, the college opened its doors to a sizeable Indian student presence. That is when we started learning about each other's different ways of life at a more personal basis. We shared dorms, classes, and the struggles for student leadership in college politics and sports. Leadership emerged from any of the multi-ethnic and multi-racial mix. Doing things together is the best teacher of race relations: one can see and appreciate the real human person behind the racial and ethnic stereotypes.

The lead role of an African woman in my drama, *The Black Hermit,* the first major play ever in English by an East African black native, was an Indian. No makeup, just a headscarf and a kanga shawl on her long dress, but Suzie Oomen (now Suzie Tharu) played the African mother to perfection, her act generating a standing ovation lasting into minutes. I dedicated my first novel, *Weep Not, Child,* to my Indian classmate, Jasbir Kalsi, probably as homage to our friendly but fierce intellectual rivalry in our English studies. Ghulsa Nensi led a multi-ethnic team that made the costumes for the play while Bahadur Tejani led the team that raised money for the production.

It was not simply at the personal realm. Commerce, arts, crafts, medical and legal professions in Kenya have the marks of the Indian genius all over them. Politics too, and it should never be forgotten that Mahatma Gandhi started and honed his political and organizing skills in South Africa where he spent twenty one years of his life from 1893 leaving for India in 1914. The South African scholar, Masilela Ntongela, places Gandhi squarely as one of the founding intellectuals of what Masilela calls the New African Movement. The honorific Mahatma, the great soul, was first applied to him in South Africa for by the time he left for India, he had already developed his Satyagraha and

Ahimsa ready for use in his anti-colonial struggles that eventually led to Indian independence in 1947, an event that had a big impact on anti-colonial struggles in Africa. What India achieved could be realized in Africa! Gandhi kept in touch with politics in Africa, Kenya in particular, and wrote a letter of protest when the British imprisoned one of the early Kenyan nationalists, Harry Thuku, in the 1920s. Gandhi created the tradition of South African Asians at the front line of struggle in South Africa. Ahmed Kathrada was one of the ten defendants in the famous Rivonia trial that would lead him to Robben Island where he spent eighteen years alongside Mandela and others. What Gandhi started Mandela completed. When I met Mandela in Johannesburg soon after his release and becoming President of the ANC party, I came out from the hour-long one on one conversation, struck by the charisma of his simplicity, reminiscent of what people say about Gandhi.

The birth of the Trade Union Movement in Kenya was largely the work of Gamal Pinto and Makhan Singh. Imprisoned by the Kenya colonial authorities repeatedly, Makhan Singh would never give up the task of bringing Indian and African workers together. He was the first prominent political leader to stand in a court of law and tell the British colonial state that Africans were ready to govern themselves, a heresy that earned him imprisonment and internal exile. Kapenguria is usually associated with the trial and imprisonment of Jomo Kenyatta but Makhan Singh preceded him. There have been some Indian political martyrs, the first being the Indian workers executed for treason, by the authorities in the very early days of colonial occupation. Gamal Pinto, a hero of the anti-colonial resistance, would be a prominent victim of the post-colonial negative turn in Kenyan politics. Though under a fictional name, Gamal Pinto has been immortalized in Peter Nazareth's novel, *In a Brown Mantle,* one of the best literary articulations of the political drama of the transformation of African politics from the colonial to the neo-colonial.

The recent explosion of Chinese interest in African might obscure the fact that there has always been a small but significant migrant Chinese presence, South Africa mostly, but also in Zimbabwe. Fay Chung whose grandparents migrated to Rhodesia in the 1920s became an active participant in the anti-colonial struggle, at one time running for her life into exile in Tanzania, was a big player in the founding of Zimbabwe. She founded Zimfep which invited Kamĩrĩĩthũ theater to Zimbabwe, a visit was scuttled by the Moi regime by simply banning the theater group and forcing one of its leaders, the late Ngũgĩ wa Mĩrĩĩ, to flee to Zimbabwe, and under Zimfep, launched the Zimbabwe Community Theater Movement, ensuring the continuity and expansion of the Kamĩrĩĩthũ spirit.

Mao Tse Tung never visited Africa but his thought has been part of the intellectual debate in the post-colonial era. His class analysis of Chinese society was seen as providing a more relevant model for analyzing African post-colonial social realities than the European Marxist model, and Kwame Nkrumah's book, *Class Struggle in Africa*, has Mao's marks all over it. The notion of the Comprador bourgeoisie dependent and serving foreign capital and hence contrastable from the national bourgeoisie with its primary reliance on national capital has become an analytic model in Political theory and development studies.

The intellectual history of the continent would be the poorer without the journal, *Transition,* now based in Harvard, but founded by Rajat Neogy way back in 1962. Neogy, a brilliant and creative editor, was Uganda born and educated: he believed in the multi-cultural and multifaceted character of ideas, and he wanted to provide a space where different sides could meet, clash, and mutually illuminate. *Transition* became the intellectual forum of the New East Africa, and indeed Africa, the first publisher of some of the leading intellectuals in the continent, including Wole Soyinka, Ali Mazrui and Peter Nazareth. *Transition* published my short story, 'The Return' (collected in Secret Lives and Other Stories), a turning point in my literary life. The story that captured what would later become so central a part of my aesthetic explorations in my novels, principally *A Grain of Wheat* et al., was the sole basis of my inclusion in the 1962 conference of African writers of English expression.

Peter Nazareth and Bahadur Tejani, early contributors to *Transition*, would later set the tradition of Afro-Indian writing with their novels, a tradition taken to new heights by Moyez G Vassanji. More than even black African writers, these three have been among those who have explored extensively and intensively the often problematic African-Indian relations. My own work, *Wizard of the Crow*, published in 2006, in which I tried to bring Eastern philosophies into imaginative discourse with African realities, was following in the footprints already made by these writers on the sands of the cultural scene in Africa.

It may be argued that in the specific cases of East and South Africa where there has always been a sizeable Asian immigrant presence, Afro-Asian dialogue was inevitable. But, in general, Africa and Asia have met through the political entities like the Bandung conference; the non-alignment movement; the Afro-Asian Peoples solidarity organization; and at the intellectual practice, the long years of the Afro-Asian writers movement which staged conferences in various capitals of Asia and Africa.

I have always felt the need for Africa, Asia and South America to learn from each other. This south-to-south intellectual and literary exchange was at the center of the Nairobi Literature debate in the early sixties, and is the centerpiece of my recent theoretical explorations, in *Globalectics: Theory and the Politics of Knowing.* The debate brought about a literature syllabus that centered the study of Indian/Asian, Caribbean, African-American and South American writers alongside those of the European tradition. The result was not to the liking of the neo-colonial regime in Kenya who accused me and my colleagues of replacing Shakespeare with Marxists revolutionaries from Asia, the Caribbean, Afro-America and Latin America, among them being Lu Xun, Kim Chi Ha, VS Naipaul, George Lamming, Kamau Brathwaite, CLR James, Alejo Carpentier, Richard Wright, and Ralph Ellison. Shakespeare was of course safe but we had committed the crime of placing him among other writers and changing the name of the department from English to Literature, which we thought the more appropriate designation of the study of literature without borders.

As the editor of the Gĩkũyũ language journal *Mũtiiri*, I have published the Gĩkũyũ translations of some of the poetry of Ariel Dorfman and Otto Rene Castillo. Professor Gitahi who did the translations directly from Spanish into Gĩkũyũ did his doctoral work on the Latin American literature. Gĩtahi was a product of the literature syllabus of the reorganized literature department of Nairobi University. His translation has facilitated direct Spanish-Gĩkũyũ language conversation.

I would like to publish numerous translations from the languages of Asia and South America and you can call this a challenge to African, South American and Asian translators. More important I would like to see similar efforts at enabling conversations between African, Asian and South American languages. This also calls for a new category of literary scholars who have studied a combination of languages from Asia, Africa and South America.

It is time to make the invisible visible in order to create a more interesting—and ultimately more creative and meaningful—free flow of ideas in the world. Satya Mohanty is quite right when he points out that 'One of the many advantages of the present moment is that the long intellectual shadow of the Age of European Empire seems to be receding a bit, and we have remarkable opportunities to work across cultures to learn from one another.'

Mohanty's call for the cultural interaction and interchange across borders—beyond the Eurocentric campus and our current notions of Comparative Literature—echoes in a forceful way and fresh manner the vision assumed and contained in the call for the abolition of the English Department made in Nairobi in 1969, the first steps in what would later become post-colonial theories and studies. Mohanty's call for cross-regional comparative literary studies is a necessary and timely intervention on the path towards a genuine world literature.

34
Ndaĩ ya Wendo

Ngũgĩ wa Thiong'o

[(Originally published in *Mũtiiri: Njaranda ya Mĩikarire*, No. 1. Reprinted with permission. www.mutiiri.com/njaranda/11994/mahua.shtml)
For English Translation from the Gĩkũyũ, see Appendix E]

Gwata ndaĩ
Ĩno ya wendo
Gwata ũgwatĩrĩre

Kana ũhe kĩgacwa
Kũrigwo ti kũrigara
Na mũgĩ nĩ mũtaare

Nderirwo nĩ mũkũrũ atĩ
Mwanake na mũirĩtu
Magĩgatua kwendana
Nĩ ta mũndũ na kĩĩruru gĩake

Teng'eria kĩĩruru
Gĩgakũũrĩra
Kĩũrĩre kĩĩruru
Gĩgakũrũmĩrĩra

No niĩ nawe
Twanaruona
Tũkarũmenya
Twanakanyuĩra
Rĩako rita nĩ tũrĩũĩ

Na tondũ wa kũmenya
Atĩ mũteng'erio
Na mũteng'erenia
Gũtirĩ ũtahũma rĩ

Reke niĩ nawe
Tũhĩmbanĩrie ngoro
Ituĩke kĩĩruru kĩmwe
Twĩyũage mbura na riũa ho

Kana tũtuĩke mũtirima wa ũrĩa ũngĩ
Getha kũrĩ heho kana rũhuho
Tũtirimanagie kahoora
Tũkĩgwatanagia ndaĩ ya wendo.

Appendixes

Appendix A
Review of *Wizard of the Crow*: Ngũgĩ's Homecoming Gift to Kenyans

Cabral Pinto (Willy Mutunga)

In 2004, Ngũgĩ wa Thiong'o came home after 22 years in exile. Ngũgĩ told Kenyans that his homecoming gift to them was the novel *Wizard of the Crow*, then in its Gĩkũyũ version. Fundamental changes in a society, including revolution, undertaken and carried out successfully by its people, and led by a patriotic political leadership, constitute one part of the core story and message of *Wizard of the Crow*.

Ngũgĩ demystifies dictatorship by focusing on its cardinal ingredients. And the dictators Ngũgĩ talks about are men. Some of these ingredients of dictatorship, for example, are murder, rape, and corruption; there is the greed of the dictator who struggles to centralize, own and control all the resources of his country, decadent masculinity, staunch heterosexuality and male chauvinism; and there is also homophobia, religious confusion, political illnesses, patronage and reliance on foreign military and foreign economic, social, cultural and political support, not to mention poverty, unemployment, disease, environmental degradation and low quality and unpatriotic education. Though fictionalized, one can identify the Ruler in the novel as Kenyatta, Bokassa, Mobutu, Banda, Mugabe, Moi and other African dictators all rolled up in one.

The nemesis of dictatorship is resistance. This resistance is led by an organization, the Movement of the Voice of the People. This movement is led by multi-ethnic and multi-racial youth. The central committee of the movement has six male youth and five female youth. The chair of the committee is a woman. The key cadres of the movement are also youth who organize and direct the People's Assembly. These youth are university educated and most of them are unemployed. The movement has a base in the mountains and caves of the Aburiria. The base has farms, an army, library, hospital, and an art museum. Aware of the insecurity of bases because of military exercises carried out by local and foreign troops and the militarization of outer space, the movement relies on the bases of the people, which have no specific location. The ideology and politics of the movement is staunchly anti-dictatorship and anti-anything that dictatorship stands for.

In the resistance movement, Ngũgĩ glorifies the leadership of women and youth. The stories about Kamiti, the wizard of the crow, as narrated throughout the novel by AG, are some of the stories young Kenyans heard in the 1950s about Kimathi Wachiuri, the leader of the Land and Freedom Movement and its armed wing, the Land and Freedom Army. Nyawira in *Wizard of the Crow* symbolizes the role women played in the Land and Freedom Movement and women's lack of recognition by historians and men of the movement. Nyawira also embodies the qualities Kenyans associated with the leaders and freedom fighters of the Mau Mau. The implied message is that leaders and freedom fighters like those of the Mau Mau have to come back for the resistance to have any meaningful impact.

A resistance movement has its life in the mobilization of the people to support its cause, ideology and politics. The novel has great stories of this mobilization. And the mobilization endures its sacrifices as the dictatorship becomes brutal and murderous. This mobilization, however, exposes the weaknesses of the dictatorship and its insecurities and confusion. The movement, in its mobilization, also recruits allies from the belly of the dictatorship. Intelligence about the dictatorship becomes a life and death struggle of the movement. Again, there are parallels from other resistance movements that actually took place.

Religion in Aburiria is a contested terrain. Aburiria is a fanatically religious country. Religion not only exposes the insecurity and hypocrisy of the dictatorship, but also reinforces the political position that no resistance movement in Aburiria can ignore this religious phenomenon. Indeed, contestation of political power in Aburiria is about which religion and healing powers are more potent and have the support of the people. Again, parallels can be drawn from real-life African resistance struggles.

Revolutionary optimism is the other part of the core message of *Wizard of the Crow*. After the collapse of the Berlin Wall, which also signaled the end of the Soviet Empire, the dominant ideology of the world disorder has been that the world has no alternative but to put up with that world disorder. That is the ideology of neo-liberalism fueled by the engine of globalization, of which the World Bank, the IMF and the WTO are a part. Militarism remains the tool of ensuring the world disorder is permanent and unchangeable. International, continental, regional and national resistance to global disorder is in evidence the world over. Aburiria is no exception. Although the ongoing propaganda is that alternative systems of government were buried in the rubble of the crushed Berlin Wall, revolutionary optimism is the life blood of any resistance that takes place in any country in the world. Without revolutionary optimism, the first step towards liberation from dictatorships, the world over, cannot be made. In the *Wizard of the Crow* this revolutionary optimism is excellently portrayed in the resistance bases set up by the Movement for the Voice of the People. In these bases, an alternative Aburiria is exemplified and glorified.

What or who is the wizard of the crow? The core messages and the leadership of the Movement of the Voice of the People and the movement itself collectively constitute what and who the wizard of the crow is. The wizard of the crow individualized in the character of Kamiti, who ultimately becomes a member of the central committee of the movement, does not negate, but underscores, this answer of what or who the wizard of the crow is.

Appendix B
Directing the River Back to its Course

Kīariī Kamau

Professor, what can I do to be able to speak fluent Gĩkũyũ? My parents never taught me Gĩkũyũ, they taught me English. Now I am twenty-two years old, and I cannot confidently converse in Gĩkũyũ. I feel very embarrassed every time I am with my friends – eating, drinking and having small talk – they are speaking in Gĩkũyũ, and I, responding in English!

This question was posed by a young lady at an evening function at the Karen Country Club, in June 2015, after Ngũgĩ wa Thiong'o had addressed members of the Club. The function had been organized by Ngũgĩ's publishers, East African Educational Publishers (EAEP), as part of an elaborate program that had been planned by the publishers to celebrate the 50th Anniversary of Ngũgĩ's *Weep Not, Child*.

In order for us to appreciate the weight of that lady's question, it is important to shed a bit of light on the nature of the Karen Country Club. This Club was inaugurated in 1937, a year before Ngũgĩ was born. It is one of the most exclusive golf clubs in Kenya, and it is common knowledge that most golfers are affluent and prominent. In addition, for one to become a member of the Club, one has to pay 500,000 Kenya shillings (membership rates as at December 2017), which is about 50,000 US dollars, and a substantial annual subscription fee. There is no doubt that this is a preserve of the affluent. And it has been so from its inception.

Being peasant farmers, Ngũgĩ's parents could not have dreamt of being admitted into such a Club, or even allowed to fetch firewood on the vast bush, where branches of the many cedar trees at times break and fall to the ground, but are left to disintegrate on their own. And for many years, Ngũgĩ himself could not have joined, or visited the Club, because his ideological leaning, and his writing, were not compatible with the thinking of most members of the Club. In addition, during those early days, Ngũgĩ probably did not have the wherewithal to pay for, and sustain, membership in such a club. In any case, those of us who have read about Ngũgĩ's lifestyle during those early days will agree that he was never excited whiling away a social evening in such clubs. But that is a story for another day!

The various functions that had been organized to mark that fiftieth Anniversary of *Weep Not, Child* were widely broadcast on radio, television, newspapers and social media. Kenyans warmly embraced Ngũgĩ's message as he emphasized the need to respect, learn, speak, study and write in African languages. And since Henry Chakava, the chair of EAEP, is a member of the Karen Country Club, others members of the Club presented him with a challenge: how could he organize so many functions for this anniversary and fail to bring Ngũgĩ over to the Club, if only to let us greet him? Chakava took up the challenge and delegated me with the responsibility of slotting Ngũgĩ's visit and talk at the Club.

Let me admit that, although I agreed to organize the visit and talk, I had doubts whether members of the exclusive Club would be interested in listening to Ngũgĩ at all. But alas, how misguided I was! Owing to our tight schedule, on the appointed date we were late for two full hours. But the most surprising thing was that by the time we arrived, the hall was full to capacity, and many members did not get sitting space, so they were standing, all waiting for Ngũgĩ. The lady who posed the question that opened my essay was among many youthful members of the audience, who had also patiently waited for those two hours, to listen to Ngũgĩ's message. And Ngũgĩ's message was simple: Let us respect, learn, speak, study and write our own tongues. He concluded his talk by making the following observation: 'If you learn all the languages of the world, and fail to learn your own tongue, that is enslavement; but if you first learn your own tongue, and later learn many other world languages, that is empowerment.'

The young lady's question, coupled with the patience the Karen audience showed as they waited for Ngũgĩ to tell them about our indigenous languages and related questions, as well as the large number of listeners who were keen to embrace Ngũgĩ's message, all pointed towards the fact that the author's crusade for indigenous languages, which he had started forty years earlier, had already attracted a huge following.

This following continued to expand, everywhere we visited, as Ngũgĩ addressed various congregations. It is not possible to describe in detail how Ngũgĩ's message was received everywhere we visited, but it is important that I give a brief snapshot of his talk at Kisii University. After getting a warm reception from the Vice-Chancellor, Prof. John Akama, together with his staff, students and general audience from Kisii, Ngũgĩ delivered his lecture. He implored his audience to respect, be proud of, learn, speak, study and write in African languages. As he concluded, he emphasized again, as to other audiences: 'If you learn all the languages of the world, and fail to learn your own tongue, that is enslavement; but if you first learn your own tongue, and later learn many other world languages, that is empowerment.'

Ngũgĩ's message was enthusiastically received by the Kisii audience. But one person who captured my attention in a special way was the one who led us in the final prayer as we came to the official close of the function. Owing to

the way she had got enamored by Ngũgĩ's message, she declared that she would
pray in the Ekegusii language. She went ahead to deliver a fairly lengthy prayer.
But it was not the length of the prayer that captured my attention. No. Rather,
it was the way she stuck to pure Ekegusii, without a single word of English or
Kiswahili straying into the prayer, and the way her musical Ekegusii words
captivated me, in spite of the fact that I am not familiar with the language.
Then I asked myself: If indeed I could be so captivated by words of a language
I was not familiar with, what impact did the same words have on those who
were familiar with the tongue?

Then it dawned on me that that this was the river that Ngũgĩ has all along
been trying to redirect to its rightful course. For we say that charity begins at
home, and one cannot delegate the taking of an oath to another person. If we
forget our starting point, we shall lose sight of our destination. We refuse to
take to the dance floor with borrowed attire. We must take our oath of fidelity
(to our tongues) with our very own mouths. We must therefore interrogate
our inner selves.

This is the revelation that Ngũgĩ received about 40 years ago, when he
realized that he might lose the bird in hand in pursuit of two in the bush.
It was revealed to him that people lost direction the moment they embraced
the celebration of foreign tongues, especially European ones. It was revealed
to him that we lost direction the moment we despised and abandoned our
own languages, in the misguided notion that they do not represent modern
development – and thought that European languages are the ones that represent modern development. It was revealed to him that we lost direction the
moment we auctioned our dignity, through demeaning our own tongues and
celebrating European tongues. It was revealed to him that we lost direction the
moment we failed to respect, learn, speak, study and write our own tongues.

After intense interrogation of his inner self, he vowed that he would be writing his subsequent creative works in Gĩkũyũ. And he wrote *Ngaahika Ndeenda*,
followed by *Caitaani Mũtharabainĩ*. After that he has written many others in
Gĩkũyũ, including storybooks for children. With these works, Ngũgĩ began
the process of redirecting the river back to its rightful course. He reminded
us that, although we fought for and got independence from the colonialist,
that freedom was meaningless because the colonialist continued to enslave our
minds through making us celebrate his language, while despising our own. He
therefore emphasized to us the need to decolonize our minds, as a sure route
of acquiring real independence.

As he celebrates his eightieth birthday, I am certain that Ngũgĩ is jubilant on
realizing that his effort of redirecting the river back to its rightful course has
not been in vain. For in the first place, when the government of Kenya recently
launched a new curriculum for primary and secondary schools, it placed a lot
of emphasis on indigenous languages. Although the teaching and learning of

indigenous language was there even in the previous system of education, the program was neither emphasized nor enforced.

A number of reasons have always been given to show why we should not bother to teach our children our own tongues. But these are lame excuses, lacking in any form of justification. Some people hold simplistic arguments to the effect that teaching our children our indigenous languages is promoting tribalism. Yet such thinking is as misguided as it is ridiculous. People do not practice tribalism because they speak their indigenous languages. They do so due to incitement by politicians whose stock-in-trade is selfishness, greed and self-aggrandizement.

Others argue that by teaching our children our indigenous languages, we shall suppress learning abilities and impede efforts towards embracing 'modernity'. They think that by teaching our children English and other western languages, we shall empower them to learn fast and hence compete favorably with other children, especially those from the West. Yet, what they fail to understand is that linguists and experts in early childhood education have scientifically proven, that if a child learns its indigenous language at a young age, it is has better and faster ability to learn and understand other languages.

No one shoots an arrow without a target in mind. And, as Ngũgĩ clocks eighty, the arrow that he directed towards simplistic mindsets that thrive on demeaning our own tongues has already hit its target. Many people have embraced his effort of redirecting the river back to its rightful course. Many radio stations that broadcast in indigenous languages continue to spring up every day. The same case applies to television stations that broadcast in indigenous languages. The same tread can be seen in newspapers, including online ones, as well as blogs.

Therefore, as we celebrate Ngũgĩ's eightieth birthday, let us also celebrate the victory that he has achieved, the victory of making us respect, be proud of, learn, speak, study and write in our tongues. But woe unto you who have refused to teach your children their indigenous language, for you might regret this decision when it is too late. And you might make your child curse in tears, feeling lost, like that lady who posed a question to Ngũgĩ at the Karen Country Club.

As I conclude, let me note that we should not be like the truant child that leaves a feast at its own homestead, hoping to eat at the neighbors, only to end up hungry; a borrowed item can always be reclaimed by the owner; we need to protect our own! At the same time, let us remember the meaning of the Gĩkũyũ saying that, when prowess diminishes (due to age), it is replenished (through younger blood). In other words, we should take up the gauntlet and gracefully receive the baton from Ngũgĩ and continue the effort of redirecting the river back to its rightful course!

Appendix C
For Grant Kamenju

Ngũgĩ wa Thiong'o

Acceptance speech on the occasion of the award of an Honorary Ph.D. from the University of Dar es Salaam, at the 43rd Graduation ceremony, Saturday 23 November 2013.

In 2004, I was invited by what is now Walter Sisulu University in South Africa to receive an honorary doctorate, along with Nelson Mandela and Ali Mazrui. The occasion also marked the transition of the University from its former name of Transkei, reminiscent of apartheid-era bantustanism, to become associated with its present memory of a nationalist hero.

Accompanied by my wife and two children, we arrived at the Campus to banners of Homecoming. It was touching: it was my first honorary degree from the African continent after several others from Universities in Europe and America. But the Homecoming banner, a reference to my book of the same title, had another significance. I was returning home to Kenya via South Africa after literally twenty-two years of forced exile. The homecoming via South Africa was to going to find its climax in Kenya; my two children born in exile had never touched Kenyan soil.

Well, what happened, eleven days into my triumphant return to my beloved country, with an honorary degree from the continent along the way, is now history. My homecoming turned into a nightmare at home with my wife and I barely escaping from four gunmen. So, no fault of South Africa, memories of my first honorary doctorate on the continent also carry memories of terror. This is the first honorary doctorate on the continent since that night of terror.

Mr. Vice-Chancellor: I am a writer, wordsmith really, but I don't have the words to describe what this honor that the University of Dar es Salaam has conferred upon me today means to me. It is not only because, hopefully, I will be able to celebrate a doctorate from Africa with undiluted joy; but also, quite frankly, because of the place of Dar in the African intellectual and political imagination.

Dar is definitely a child of political independence. It was thought up, planned and imagined by the first independent African state in East Africa. Soon Dar became the center of new thought; challenging, daring, path finding. In its heyday Dar became the Mecca of progressive thought attracting scholars from all over the world and Africa. Dar was the university of Walter Rodney,

Issa G. Shivji, Dan Nabudere, Mahmood Mamdani, and Yashon Tandon. It was home to *Cheche* [the radical magazine]. It was home to probably one of the leading African playwrights of all time, Ebrahim Hussein. It was home to the Kenyan poet, Abdilatif Abdalla. It was home to many sons and daughters of the different liberation movements in Africa, particularly Southern Africa. Dar became a leader of thought. Dar was also Nyerere's Tanzania, which, for East Africa, Africa and the world emerging from colonialism, was an alternative vision of tomorrow, hope, really, for a people-based Pan-Africanism

But tonight I want to mention one other Kenyan who found a home in Dar. His name was Grant Kamenju. He was one of the founding lecturers of the literature department to which I became formally linked as an external examiner. Kamenju was instrumental in attracting one of the world literary scholars, Arnold Kettle, to a Professorship and chair of the department. I knew Grant Kamenju. I worked with him at Makerere and Leeds. He brought to Dar some of the new energy and thinking that we had developed during our sojourn in the two institutions. Kamenju was careless about publishing, so his enormous output was never reflected in what appeared in journals. He was a great worker in ideas, glorying more in passing on his ideas than having them add to his CV. He was in the tradition of the great oral tradition of the academy going all the way back to Socrates and in others whose thoughts survive today only because their students preserved the notes they took. Kamenju's impact on the teaching and organization and reorganization of the teaching literature in the three universities is enormous. Even today, his former students among them M.M. Mulokozi regard themselves as Grant Kamenju's children.

Kamenju never ever sought personal glory. He passed on, unnoticed, an unsung hero of the literature revolution and a relentless advocate of the relevance of literature to life, to the struggles for economic, political, Cultural and spiritual emancipation. It's a view I share and for which I have dedicated my life, writing, and thought. I sing of him today. It is in memory of the late Professor Grant Kamenju that I gratefully accept this honor.

Appendix D
Intellectuals, European & African Languages: Between Enslavement & Empowerment

Ngũgĩ wa Thiong'o

Public Address Delivered at Nkrumah Hall, the University of Dar es Salaam, during the Award of an Honorary Ph.D., 23 November 2013*

I want to look at the genealogy of the African intellectual relationship to African and European languages, English in particular. This is particularly relevant today when most of Africa is celebrating their fiftieth years of independence from colonial rule.

The intellectual is not a new creation in Africa, every society has had its intellectuals, intellectual here defined as a worker in ideas. They may do other things but their primary social significance and visibility was as workers in ideas. African healers, seers, artisans, including builders, would be in this category. The intellectual was an integral part of the old Egyptian, Ethiopic, Zimbabwean, and Songhai civilizations. A most important component of this pre-colonial intellectual was the poet who often combined the role of the historian, moralist and seer. In West Africa they call him the *griot*. Swahili civilization is replete with poets, leaders of thought, spanning centuries. A book edited by Abdilatif Abdalla and published by Mkuki na Nyota, *Kale ya Washairi wa Pemba*, lists quite a few including Fumo wa Liyongo. In total, Liyongo wa Baury in the twelfth century, Muyaka bin Haji in the eighteenth century, and Suudbin Said Al-Maamiriy in the nineteenth century. These poet-intellectuals largely saw themselves as voices of the people and seekers of justice. It may seem needless to say, but it is important to emphasize that these intellectuals, from Egyptian to Ungozi/Uswahili times, used the languages of their society. The pre-colonial African intellectual was rooted among their community.

Today I want to focus at the modern African intellectual, particularly. I am talking of course of the intellectual who has been to a modern school and for whom European languages have been means of his education. There have been two faces and phases of these African intellectuals, and these phases are almost contradictory.

---

* This is an earlier version by the author of the Kiswahili text.

The intellectuals of the anti-colonial struggle used European languages to get what they carried and then took it back to African languages, enriching them. They went into European languages as scouts. In Gold Coast, today Ghana, a statement was published in *The Gold Coast People*, of November 30, 1893, called upon the Fante intellectuals of the time to be thankful that the 'Fantis are proud to be Fantis and are not ashamed to be known by their native names, heard speaking their liquid language, and seen arrayed in their flowing robes' (quoted in Kimble, *A Political History* 528). Instead of Europeanized Africans, they wanted to become 'native civilized Africans' (see Hopkins 'R. B. Blaize'). Similar sentiments were expressed by nineteenth-century South African black intellectuals emerging out of the Lovedale Mission. In East Africa we have the example of Shabaan Roberts with his famous poetic quip that *Titi la Mama litamu lingawa la Mbwa, lingine halishi tamu* ('A mother's milk is the sweetest, even if she is a dog. No other tastes as sweet').

At Ghana's independence in 1957, Kwame Nkrumah moved quickly to establish an African language bureau; he helped train teachers to teach African languages. He established newspapers in African languages. In his opening address at the First International Congress of Africanists in Accra in 1962, Kwame Nkrumah hoped that the conference would be a major step towards an Africa-centered view of itself, its history and culture, with African languages at the center. He came back to the same theme when a year later he opened the first Institute of African Studies. For him a study and development of African languages was not a side issue. African languages were central in African scholarship, development and its relationship to the diaspora and the world. He did not call for linguistic self-isolation, for he saw the role of other languages like Arabic, English, French and Portuguese. Where others saw African languages as merely a lower rung in the ladder to an English heaven, Kwame Nkrumah saw African languages as equal partners in the construction of a common heaven. The key thing is that he put resources into his commitment. Alas, the military coups that followed reversed the policy, with some Ghana middle class cheering: nothing was going to deter them from climbing the ladder to an English heaven.

The anti-colonial struggle in Kenya gave rise to a vigorous nationalist press in African languages. Jomo Kenyatta was once editor of an African language paper; *Muguithania*. Later he wrote a book in Gĩkũyũ, *Kenya Bururi wa Ngui* ('Kenya the Land of Conflicts'). This was in addition to his famous book, *Facing Mount Kenya*, which was written in English. As part of its war machine, the colonial state banned the African language press, forcing some of the editors into exile and others into prison. At independence in 1961, Julius Nyerere of Tanzania established Kiswahili as the national language. At long last Kiswahili had a home. Nyerere translated Shakespeare into Kiswahili. He led by example, giving some of his major speeches in Kiswahili or having his works translated into Kiswahili. These intellectuals used their access to English for self-empowerment.

Very different from the post-independent African middle class, some of whom hold reins of power; these became captives of European languages. Some years ago, I think three years ago in independent Kenya, parliament voted to ban African languages in official premises. The irony was that this parliament was only possible because an African language speaking peasantry and working people had organized in the mountains and in the streets to oust the British colonial state. Obviously, this parliament did not see itself rooted in an African language past, but that of English and other European languages. It is not yet law only because the President never signed it.

Language has been a battlefield of ideas, but I want to talk of language as a war zone in the struggle between enslavement and empowerment. 'The history of a language', Tom Paulin has written in *A New Look at the Language Question*, 'is often a story of possession and dispossession, territorial struggle and the establishment or imposition of a culture' (6). Language in and outside the academy has been a zone of war in every situation of the dominating and the dominated, particularly the colonizer and the colonized. In such situations, language has been as much the tool of conquest and resistance as the sword. Indeed some of the fiercest battles have been fought and continue to be fought in this zone. Not that language is the prime mover but it is often seen as a necessary consequence of conquest, the element needed to cement conquest.

It was an English poet, Spenser, a contemporary of Shakespeare, and the celebrated author of *The Faerie Queene*, who best summed up the centrality of language in enabling and completing conquest when in 1599 he wrote that 'it hath ever been the use of the conqueror to despise the language of the conquered, and to force him by all means to learn his'. This was in his book *A View of the Present State of Ireland* in which, he also advocated the abrogation of the Irish naming system, as part of a program whose end was the erasure of memory of an Irish nation. Control over the naming system was key to the English conquest and taming of the Irish. According to Tony Crowley, there were several acts enacted by the various occupants of the English Crown, aimed at protecting English language against the subversive encroachment of Irish or Gaelic, beginning with Statute of Kilkenny in 1366, following the Anglo-Norman conquest and settlement of Ireland (*Wars of Words: The Politics of Language in Ireland, 1537–2004*). Among other things the statute threatened to confiscate any lands of any English or any Irish living among them who would use 'Irish among themselves, contrary to the ordinance' (quoted in Crowley 15). Spenser then was writing within the spirit of that earlier enactment which could not have been working too well if two hundred and something years after he found it necessary to reinforce it.

Spenser was himself an English settler in Munster: One of his neighbors, also an English settler, was Walter Raleigh who led the first English settlement in Virginia. There may not be a direct cause and effect relationship, but it cannot be lost on us that following the capture of Africans on the continent and the turning of them into plantation slaves in the America settled by Raleigh's successors, African languages, including the drum, their naming systems, were banned on the plantations. Africans caught speaking their languages were punished, some even losing their lives. The aim was the same as in Spenser's doctrine: make them forget any connections with wherever they had come from.

Japan had the same ideas after their colonial conquest of Korea: they imposed Japanese language and naming system. Within Japan itself, until recently, all Japanese-Koreans had to take on Japanese names. In Africa, and following their conquest of the continent, the French, British and Portuguese pursued similar policies. If they did not actually ban African languages and naming systems, they nevertheless marginalized them as languages of power, knowledge and identity. Even where they allowed African languages in the education system it was only as a primary step before they were turned into English and French speakers. I am not aware of any law banning African names in the continent, but through cultural engineering, following the Gramscian idea on the hegemony of culture, every educated African today appends a European name, however ridiculous or ill-fitting, to his African name. The colonial language policies were a continuation of those of war by linguistic means.

The Africa continent continues to suffer the consequences of linguistic conquest. Political independence may have freed the body, but it certainly did not free the mind, which is precisely the result and the long-term effect of linguistic conquest on the conquered. The result for Africa is a gigantic disconnect between the educated middle class and the general population, which was always the intention of the colonial enterprise. If you think of languages at war, it was as if the African generals became captives in the enemies' camp. By generals I don't just mean the government alone. I am thinking of the entire intellectual class; and none of us can say we have escaped the consequences of our acceptance of defeat, or our attempts to lead the intellectual and academic battles as captives.

As captives, we are forced to look at the continent as if we are outsiders. Our various fields of knowledge of Africa are in many ways rooted in that entire colonial tradition of the outsider looking in, gathering and coding knowledge with the help of native informants, and then storing the final product in a European language for consumption by those who have access to that language. Today, we still collect intellectual items and put them in European language museums and archives. The intellectual community in and outside Africa has come to accept this as the norm in method.

Last September, at a conference in Leeds University attended by more than five hundred scholars from Africa and Europe, I posed the question: how many of the scholars present had ever written a single document in an African language? Not a hand was raised when it came to books. Not a hand was raised when it came to even a single paper in an African language. When it came down to a page, three hands were raised. Three hands at a conference of top-notch scholars and experts on Africa. I have posed similar questions in Nigeria and Kenya before predominantly African audiences. The results were similar.

Perhaps my point would be clearer if we posed the question the other way: can you think of a Professor of Italian history, culture, who does not know a world of Italian? Or a Professor of French history who did not have a word of French? A Professor of Greek and Latin without a word of Latin and Greek? Abnormal you would say; but the abnormal and even the ridiculous have been turned into a norm in the case of the biggest continent in the world, bigger than all Europe, Americas and China put together.

Surely this has to change: and this change can only come about as a result of cooperation between an academy, willing to countenance other ways of knowing; and publishers, willing to countenance other ways of publishing; and intellectuals willing to put in the necessary effort. But another partner is necessary: governments with pro-African language policies. However we should remember that the people who run those governments are also products of the academy. Perhaps if the orthodoxy they have about governance had been challenged at the academy, when they were students, they might have emerged as generals willing to lead, not as captives, but as free agents, willing to find other ways of fighting and knowing. But little can change when governments are under enormous pressure to operate within the boundaries of conquest and defeat.

There are tiny glimpses of hope that things may be turning round, and Kiswahili is at the forefront. The triumph of Kiswahili in Tanzania is the result of the intellectuals of the first type: those who got from European languages whatever they had and stored it an African language. We have already mentioned Nyerere in this respect. He was a graduate of two of the leading institutions of the time (Makerere and then Edinburgh) at the time when he translated Shakespeare into Kiswahili, and later established the policy of empowering Kiswahili through active pro-Kiswahili policies and resources. The limitation of this policy was the assumption that a national language can only be built on the graveyard of other African languages. Monolingualism as synonymous with nation state is rooted in the European idea of the nation state that, ironically, was forged at the beginnings of the modern capitalist and colonial enterprise in the seventeenth century.

Not surprisingly, Tanzania has also produced a publisher who has been very consistent in his commitment to publishing in African languages, Kiswahili mostly. I am talking of Walter Bgoya's Mkuki na Nyota, making possible not only the revival of Swahili classics. Henry Chakava of East African Education Publishers (EAEP) has also brought out the Kiswahili translations of nearly all the major African writers in English and French.

But is the academy as a whole following suit?

Even here are glimpses of hope: A small step, though a giant in its potentiality, has been taken in the area of philosophy, in a book, *Listening to Ourselves*, edited by the Caribbean-Canadian intellectual, Chike Jeffers, published by SUNY press. The book contains essays on philosophy in different African languages, Wolof, Dholuo, Igbo, Akan, Amharic, Gĩkũyũ, from East and West Africa. The contributors, who include the late Emmanuel Eze, are some of the leading African scholars in philosophy, holding professorial ranks in universities outside Africa. Each piece, though, carries an English translation. Once again, as far as I know this is the first time I have come across pieces written by modern African philosophers in African languages. It has taken a person of Caribbean origins to do a first for Africa. It has been his dream to do this, thus taking his place in a long line of others who have dreamt and acted for Africa: Marcus Garvey, C. L. R. James, George Padmore, W. E. B. Dubois and Walter Rodney to cite a few.

Jeffers' work points to yet another language that has not been widely used in a conscious way to empower African languages. Translation, I have argued in my book, *Something Torn and New*, is the language of languages. There is hardly any culture that has not gained from translation. Translation between African languages and between African languages and other languages of the world would be a win-win situation for Africa and world cultures. Our colleges and universities should also be hives of translation activities from other languages into African languages.

All this calls for a grand alliance of scholars, academies, publishers, and makers of educational policies. Intellectuals in and outside Africa must lead: they have to live up to their venerable tradition. The intellectual of all cultures and histories has been a pathfinder. And in all cultures, these intellectuals have had to pay a price, sometimes with their own lives. I have had to pay a price, not too big, but a price all the same; prison, exile, even. The intellectuals of our times must not run away from the fight, from the zones of war.

But governments and institutions cannot continue to hide their heads in the sand of globalization. Globalization begun with the black body, way back in seventeenth century: plantation slavery. Plantation slavery mutated into colonial slavery. Globalization today is dependent on resources still available in the biggest continent in the world: Africa. Many governments, academics and intellectuals have the illusion that globalization demands that they get lost in English. They should remember this: they gave us an English accent; we gave them access to the continent. In the seventeenth and eighteenth centuries, it was their access to the black body; in the nineteenth and twentieth centuries, it was their access to copper, gold, diamonds, and now oil. Today while we are very busy perfecting our English accent, they are very busy perfecting their access to the resources of the continent.

It's time we spent less time and resources to perfect our English accent and spent more time perfecting all the means at our disposal to protect the wealth of Africa. Languages are part of the fight. Remember Shabaan Roberts: *Titi la Mama litamu lingawa la Mbwa, lingine halishi tamu* (The breast of a mother is sweetest, even if she is a dog; no other tastes as sweet').

Appendix E
A Riddle of Love

Ngũgĩ wa Thiong'o

[(Originally published in *Mūtiiri: Njaranda ya Mĩikarire*, No. 1.) Translated from Gĩkũyũ by Simon Gikandi]

Take this riddle
Of love
And hold it tight

Or take a forfeit
For being wrong is not ignorance
And the wise one is well advised

I was told by an elder that
When a man and a woman
Choose to love each other
It is like a person and their shadow

You chase the shadow
It disappears from you
You think the shadow is lost
But it is behind you

But you and I
Have seen it all
And know it well
Drinking from the same cup
We know its weight well

And because we know
That the chaser
And the chased
Eventually get tired

Let you and I
Merge our hearts
Make them one shadow
Where we can feel the rain and sun

We will be each other's support staff
In the cold or wind
Supporting each other slowly
Sharing the riddle of love.

References

References

Bibliography of Ngũgĩ's Primary Works

In date order. Others mentioned in the articles are found in Works Cited.

Weep Not, Child. London: Heinemann, 1964.

The River Between. London: Heinemann, 1965.

A Grain of Wheat. London: Heinemann, 1967.

The Black Hermit. London: Heinemann, 1968 [1963].

This Time Tomorrow: Three Plays. Nairobi: East African Literature Bureau, 1970.

Homecoming: Essays on African and Caribbean Literature, Culture and Politics. London: Heinemann, 1972.

Secret Lives and Other Stories. London: Heinemann, 1975.

The Trial of Dedan Kimathi. With Mĩcere Gĩthae Mũgo. Nairobi and London: Heinemann, 1976.

Petals of Blood. London: Heinemann, 1977.

Caitaani Mũtharaba-inĩ. Nairobi: Heinemann, 1980. Translated as *Devil on the Cross.* London: Heinemann, 1982.

Ngaahika Ndeenda: Ithaako rĩa Ngerekano. With Ngũgĩ wa Mĩriĩ. Nairobi: Heinemann, 1980 [1977]. Translated as *I Will Marry When I Want.* London: Heinemann, 1982.

Detained: A Writer's Prison Diary. Nairobi and London: Heinemann, 1981. Reissued in an extended edition as *Wrestling with the Devil: A Prison Memoir.* New York: The New Press, 2018.

Maitũ Njugĩra, unpublished.

Writers in Politics: Essays. London: Heinemann, 1981. Revised and enlarged as *Writers in Politics: A Re-Engagement with Issues of Literature & Society.* Oxford: James Currey; Nairobi: EAEP; Portsmouth, NH: Heinemann, 1997.

Njamba Nene na Mbaathi ĩ Mathagu. Nairobi: Heinemann, 1982. Translated as *Njamba Nene and the Flying Bus* by Wangũi wa Goro. Nairobi: Heinemann, 1986.

Barrel of a Pen: Resistance to Repression in Neo-Colonial Kenya. London: New Beacon; Trenton, NJ: Africa World Press, 1983.

Bathitoora ya Njamba Nene. Nairobi: Heinemann, 1984. Translated as *Njamba Nene's Pistol* by Wangũi wa Goro. Nairobi: Heinemann, 1986.

Decolonising the Mind: The Politics of Language in African Literature. London: James Currey; Nairobi: EAEP; Portsmouth, NH: Heinemann, 1986.

Matigari ma Njĩrũũngi. Nairobi: Heinemann, 1986. Translated as *Matigari* by Wangũi wa Goro. Oxford: Heinemann, 1989.

Writing against Neocolonialism. Wembley, UK: Vita, 1986.

Njamba Nene na Cibu King'ang'i. Nairobi: Heinemann, 1986.

Moving the Centre: The Struggle for Cultural Freedoms. London: James Currey; Nairobi: EAEP; Portsmouth, NH: Heinemann, 1993.

Penpoints, Gunpoints, and Dreams: Towards a Critical Theory of the Arts and the State in Africa. Oxford: Oxford UP, 1998.

Mũrogi wa Kagogo. Vol. 1 (Bks. I & 2), Vol. 2 (Bks. 3 & 4) and Vol. 3 (Bks. 5 & 6). Nairobi: East African Educational Publishers, 2004. Translated as *Wizard of the Crow*. New York: Knopf/Pantheon Books, 2006.

Something Torn and New: An African Renaissance. New York: Civitas Books, 2009; also published as *Re-membering Africa*. Nairobi: East African Educational Publishers, 2009.

Dreams in a Time of War. New York: Pantheon, 2010.

Globalectics: Theory and the Politics of Knowing. New York: Columbia UP, 2012.

In the House of the Interpreter. New York: Pantheon, 2012.

In the Name of the Mother: Reflections on Writers & Empire. Oxford: James Currey, 2013.

Birth of a Dream Weaver: A Writer's Awakening. New York: The New Press, 2016.

Secure the Base: Making Africa Visible in the Globe. Kolkata: Seagull Press, 2016.

Wrestling with the Devil: A Prison Memoir. New Edition of *Detained*. New York: New Press, 2018.

Works Cited

A list of Ngũgĩ's primary works is in the Bibliography. Others of his works cited in the articles are included below.

Alemseged Tesfai. 'Drama'. Mimeograph. Trans. Tekeste Yonas. N.p.: EPLF, 1983.

Arnold, Matthew, *Culture and Anarchy*. Oxford: Oxford UP, 2006.

Banham, Martin, James Gibbs and Femi Osofisan, eds. *African Theatre in Development*. Oxford: James Currey, 1999, 38–53.

Brecht, Bertolt. *The Mother*. Trans. Lee Baxandall. New York: Grove Press, 1965.

Biondi, Martha. *The Black Revolution on Campus*. Berkeley: U of California Press, 2012.

Boyce Davies, Carole. 'Beyond Unicentricity: Transcultural Black Presences'. *Research in African Literatures* 30.2 (1999): 96–109

—— 'The Caribbean Creative/Theoretical'. In *The Caribbean Woman Writer as a Scholar: Creating, Imagining Theorizing*. Ed. Keshia N. Abraham. Coconut Creek, FL: Caribbean Studies Press, 2009. xi–xiii.

Boyce Davies, Carole, Meredith Gadsby, Charles Peterson and Henrietta Williams, eds. *Decolonizing the Academy: African Diaspora Studies*. Trenton, NJ: Africa World Press, 2003.

Brathwaite, Kamau. *History of the Voice: The Development of Nation Language in Anglophone Caribbean Poetry*. London: New Beacon Books, 1984.

Brecht, Bertolt. *The Mother*. Ed. Lee Baxandall. New York: Grove Press, 1965.

Cooper, Carolyn. 'Drawing Sister P's Tongue'. http://jamaica-gleaner.com/gleaner/20111225/cleisure/cleisure3.html

—— *Noises in the Blood: Orality, Gender, and The 'Vulgar' Body of Jamaican Popular Culture*. Durham, NC: Duke UP, 1995.

—— *Sound Clash: Jamaican Dance Hall Culture at Large*. New York: Palgrave, 2004

—— 'Interview'. *New Journal of Afrikan Culture, Politics and Consciousness* www.proudfleshjournal.com 4, 2004.

—— Ed. *Global Reggae*. Mona, Jamaica: University of West Indies Press, 2012.

Crowley, Tony. *Wars of Words: The Politics of Language in Ireland, 1537–2004*. Oxford: Oxford UP, 2008.

de Villiers, John. 'Birth of a New East African Author' (1964). Reprinted in Sander and Lindfors, *Ngũgĩ wa Thiong'o Speaks*. 7–9.

Fanon, Frantz. *The Wretched of the Earth*. New York: Grove Press, 1963; London: Penguin Books, 1967.

—— *Black Skin, White Masks*. Trans. Charles Lam Markmann. New York: Grove Press, 1967.

Freud, S. (1909). 'Family Romances'. *The Standard Edition of the Complete Psychological Works of Sigmund Freud*, Volume IX (1906–1908).

wa Gacheru, Margaretta. 'Ngũgĩ wa Thiong'o Still Bitter Over His Detention'. In Sander and Lindfors, *Ngũgĩ wa Thiong'o Speaks*. 90–97.

Gikandi, Simon. *Ngũgĩ wa Thiong'o*. Cambridge, UK: Cambridge UP, 2000.

Githiora, Chege. *Sheng: Rise of a Kenyan Swahili Vernacular*. Woodbridge: James Currey/Boydell & Brewer Ltd, 2018.

Goethe, Johann Wolfgang von. *Kunst und Alterthum* (1829)

hooks, bell. **Outlaw Culture: Resisting Representations**. New York and London: Routledge, 2006.

Hopkins, A. G. 'R. B. Blaize, 1845–1904: Merchant Prince of West Africa'. *Tarikh* 1.2 (1966): 70–79.

Julien, Eileen. 'The Extroverted African Novel'. In *History, Geography, and Culture*. Vol. 1. *The Novel*. Ed. Franco Moretti. Princeton, NJ: Princeton UP, 2006, 667–700.

Kantai, Parselelo. 'The Redykyulass Generation'. http://binyavangafavorites.blogspot. co.za, 29 June, 2007.

Kimble, David. *A Political History of Ghana*. Oxford: Clarendon Press, 1963.

Lejeune, Philippe. *On Autobiography*. Translated by Katherine Leary. Minneapolis: University of Minnesota Press, 1980.

Lovesey, Oliver, ed. *Approaches to Teaching the Works of Ngũgĩ wa Thiong'o*. New York: Modern Languages Association, 2012.

Lukács, Georg. *The Historical Novel*. Trans. Hannah Mitchell and Stanley Mitchell. Preface by Fredric Jameson. Lincoln, NB: University of Nebraska Press, 1983.

Matzke, Christine, *En-gendering Theatre in Eritrea: The Roles and Representation of Women in the Performing Arts* (unpublished PhD thesis), University of Leeds, 2003.

Marcuson, Alan, Mike Gonzalez and Dave Williams. 'James Ngũgĩ Interviewed by Fellow Students at Leeds University'. In Sander and Lindfors, *Ngũgĩ wa Thiong'o Speaks*, 25–33.

Mazrui, Alamin. 'The English Language in the Post-Cold War Era: Africa in a Comparative Context'. In *The Scholar Between Thought and Experience*, Binghamton, NY: Institute of Global Cultural Studies, 2001, 159–86.

Mazrui, Ali A. 'The African Renaissance: A Triple Legacy of Skills, Values, and Gender'. *Africa Beyond 2000: Essays on Africa's Political and Economic Development in the Twenty-first Century*, ed. S. Saxena. Delhi: Kalinga Publishers, 2001, 29–60.

Mazrui, Ali A. and Alamin Mazrui. *The Power of Babel: Language and Governance in the African Experience*. Oxford: James Currey, 1998.

Mignolo, Walter. 'Delinking: The Rhetoric of Modernity, the Logic of Coloniality and the Grammar of De-coloniality'. *Cultural Studies* 21.2 (March 2007): 449–514.

Mohanty, Satya. 'Literature to Combat Cultural Chauvinism'. Interview with Rshmi Dube Bhatnagar and Rajender Kaur. *Frontline* (April 2012).

Morrison, Toni. *The Bluest Eye*. New York: Vintage, 2007 [1970].

Mũkoma wa Ngũgĩ. *The Rise of the African Novel: Politics of Language, Identity, and Ownership*. Ann Arbor: University of Michigan Press, 2018.

Musila, Grace. 'Writing History's Silences: Interview with Parselelo Kantai'. *Kunapipi* 34.1 (2012): 71–80.

Mwangi, Evan. 'Contextualizing Untranslated Moments in Ngũgĩ's Prose and Drama'. *Ngũgĩ wa Thiong'o*, ed. Oliver Lovesey, 93–113.

Ngũgĩ wa Thiong'o. 'Life, Literature and a Longing for Home', *The Guardian* 27 May 1989, 5.

—— 'Europhonism, Universities and the Magic Fountain: The Future of African Literature and Scholarship'. *Research in African Literatures*, 31.1 (2000): 1–11.

—— 'The Myth of Tribe in African Politics'. *Transition* 101 (2009): 16–23.

—— 'The Language of Scholarship in Africa'. *The Leeds African Studies Bulletin*, 74 (2012): 42–7.

Ngũgĩ wa Thiong'o, Henry Owuor-Anyumba and Taban lo Liyong. 'On the Abolition of the English Department'. Appendix to *Homecoming: Essays on African and Caribbean Literature, Culture and Politics*, Ngũgĩ wa Thiong'o. London: Heinemann Educational Books, 1972.

NourbeSe Philip, Marlene. 'Afterword: The Absence of Writing or How I Almost Became a Spy'. *Out of the Kumbla: Caribbean Women and Literature*, eds. Carol Boyce Davies and Elaine Savory Fido. Trenton, NJ: Africa World Press, 1990, 271–8.

—— 'Discourse on the Logic of Language'. In *She Tries Her Tongue, Her Silence Softly Breaks*. Middletown, CT: Wesleyan UP, 1989. 29–34.

Opiyo, Odhiambo Levin. 'Exiled Ngugi wa Thiong'o was Subject of Talks'. *Sunday Nation*, 23 April 2017. www.nation.co.ke/oped/opinion/Exiled-Ngugi-wa-Thiong-o-was-subject-of-talks/440808-3900242-0e825wz/index.html.

Owens, Richard. 'Gael Turnbull: The Bricklayer Reconsidered – Editing Gael Turnbull's Collected Poems'. *Jacket* 36 (2008). http://jacketmagazine.com/36/turnbull-by-owens.shtml.

Paulin, Tom. 'A New Look at the Language Question'. Field Day Pamphlet, no. 1. Derry: Field Day Theatre, 1983.

Plastow, Jane. 'The Eritrea Community-Based Theatre Project'. *New Theatre Quarterly* 13.52 (1997): 386–95.

—— 'Alemseged Tesfai: A Playwright in Service to Eritrean Liberation'. In *African Theatre in Development*, 1999, 54–60.

—— 'Teatro Asmara: Understanding Eritrean Drama through a Study of the National Theatre'. *Journal of African Cultural Studies* 29.3 (2016): 311–30.

Quijano, Aníbal. 'Coloniality and Modernity/Rationality'. *Cultural Studies* 21.2 (2007): 168–78.

Said, Edward. *Beginnings: Intention and Method*. New York: Basic Books, 1975.

—— *Orientalism*. London: Penguin; New York: Vintage, 2003 [1978].

—— *Reflections on Exile and Other Essays*. London: Granta Books, 2012.

—— 'The Politics of Knowledge'. In *Reflections on Exile and Other Essays*, 2012, 372–86.

Sander, Reinhard and Bernth Lindfors, eds. *Ngũgĩ wa Thiong'o Speaks*. Oxford: James Currey, 2006.

Sharpe, Christina. *In the Wake: On Blackness and Being*. Durham & London: Duke UP, 2016.

Spenser, Edmund. *A View of the Present State of Ireland*. 1633 [1596].

Spivak, Gayatri Chakravorty. 'Can the Subaltern Speak?' In *Colonial Discourse and Post-Colonial Theory: A Reader*, eds. Patrick Williams and Laura Chrisman. New York: Columbia, 1994.

Walcott, Derek. 'Sea is History'. *The Poetry of Derek Walcott*. Selected by Glyn Maxwell. New York: Farrar, Straus and Giroux, 253–6.

Walmsley, Anne. 'No Licence for Musical'. *Index on Censorship* (Feb. 1, 1983). 22–4.

Warwick, Paul. 'Theatre and the Eritrean Struggle for Freedom: The Cultural Troupes of the People's Liberation Front'. *New Theatre Quarterly* 13.51 (1997): 221–30.

Wordsworth William. 'Preface to Lyrical Ballads', 1802.

Personal interviews (**Conducted by Ndirangu Wachanga**)

Anyidoho, Kofi (2014) Johannesburg, South Africa

Banham, Martin (2010) Leeds, United Kingdom

Bukenya, Austin (2010) Kampala, Uganda

Chakava, Henry (2016) Nairobi, Kenya

Currey, James (2014) Johannesburg, South Africa

Davies, Carole (2014) Johannesburg, South Africa

Diawara, Manthia (2015) Madison, Wisconsin

Farred, Grant (2014) Ithaca, New York

Gikandi, Simon (2015) Princeton, New Jersey

Wangui wa Goro (2014) South Africa

Jeyifo, Bioudun (2015) Syracuse, New York

Kgositsile, Keorapetse (2014) Johannesburg, South Africa

Mazrui, Ali (2013) Binghamton, New York

Mũkoma wa Ngũgĩ (2017) Chicago

Ngũgĩ wa Thiong'o (2010) Irvine, California

—— (2012) Madison, Wisconsin

Notes on Contributors

Anne Adams is Professor Emerita, Cornell University. She specializes in the areas of continental African women's writing and Afro-German cultural studies. Professor Adams served as director of the W.E.B. Du Bois Memorial Centre for Pan-African Culture, in Accra, Ghana, 2005–2010. Her publications on African literature include *Ngambika: Studies of Women in African Literature* (with Carole Boyce Davies), *The Legacy of Efua Sutherland: Pan-African Cultural Activism* (with Esi Sutherland-Addy), and *Essays in Honour of Ama Ata Aidoo: A Reader in African Cultural Studies. She* is currently preparing an anthology of essays by Afro-Germans.

Ann Biersteker is the Associate Director of the African Studies Center at Michigan State University. She has published two books on Kiswahili poetry and *Masamo ya Kisasa,* a widely used Kiswahili textbook, as well as a wide range of articles on African literature.

Carole Boyce Davies is a professor of English and Africana Studies at Cornell University. She has held distinguished professorships at a number of institutions, including the Herskovits Professorship of African Studies and Professor of Comparative Literary Studies and African American Studies at Northwestern University. She is the author of many books, including *Black Women, Writing and Identity: Migrations of the Subject,* and *Left of Karl Marx: The Political Life of Black Communist Claudia Jones.* In addition to numerous scholarly articles, Boyce Davies has also co-edited acclaimed critical anthologies, including *Ngambika: Studies of Women in African Literature, Out of the Kumbla: Caribbean Women and Literature.*

Charles Cantalupo is Distinguished Professor of English, Comparative Literature, and African Studies at Penn State University. In 1994, he organized the conference, Ngũgĩ wa Thiong'o: Texts and Contexts at Penn State Schuylkill and he was the organizer, with Ngũgĩ, of the 2000 Conference Against All Odds: African Languages and Literatures into the 21st Century in Asmara, Eritrea. Cantalupo has edited two collections of essays on Ngũgĩ and is the author of three other books of literary criticism, three books of poetry, three books of translations of Eritrean poetry, and a memoir, *Joining Africa.*

Henry Chakava is the Chairman of East African Educational Publishers Ltd., and is a pioneer publisher in Africa. A recipient of several national and international awards, Chakava has published and promoted some of the leading African writers and has contributed enormously to the growth of the education sector in Africa. He is the author of *Publishing in Africa: One Man's Perspective.*

Rhonda Cobham-Sander is Professor of English and Black Studies at Amherst College, Massachusetts. She is the author of *I and I: Epitaphs for the Self in the Work* *of V.S. Naipaul, Kamau Brathwaite and Derek Walcott*, and editor of *Watchers and Seekers an Anthology of Black Writing in Britain* as well as articles in *Callaloo, The Massachusetts Review*, and *Research in African Literatures*. Her works have been anthologized in a number of edited collections.

James Currey edited Heinemann's African Writers Series from 1967 to 1984 and added some 250 titles. Among them were frequent titles by Ngũgĩ. When James Currey Publishers was started in 1985, one of the first titles was Ngũgĩ's *Decolonising the Mind*. More than thirty years later, it is still one of their best-selling titles.

Grant Farred teaches at Cornell University. His most recent work is *Martin Heidegger Saved My Life*. His forthcoming books include *The Burden of Over-representation: Race, Sport and Philosophy* and *Entre-nous: Between the World Cup and Me*.

Margaretta wa Gacheru has been writing about the arts in Kenya for many decades, working for leading publications including the now defunct *Weekly Review* and *Nairobi Times* and *The Daily Nation*. She holds a Ph.D. in Sociology from Loyola University Chicago and Master's degrees from the University of Nairobi, Northwestern University, and Loyola and National Louis University in Education, Chicago. She is the author of *The Transformation of Contemporary Kenyan Art (1960–2010)*.

Eddah W. Gachukia is a career educationalist, and serves as the Academic Director of the Riara Group of Schools. She is the Vice-Chair, Riara University Governing Council. She has a Ph.D. from the University of Nairobi. Dr. Gachukia has served on many Governing Boards nationally and internationally. She has also served on the Boards of numerous Secondary Schools in Kenya. Dr. Gachukia has published works in literacy criticism, gender and development, education and child development and related issues.

Simon Gikandi is Robert Schirmer Professor of English at Princeton University, where he is affiliated with the Departments of Comparative Literature and African American Studies and the Program in African Studies. Gikandi is the first vice-president of the Modern Language Association of America (MLA) and will be its president in 2019. He served as editor of *Publications of the Modern Language Association of America (PMLA)*, the official journal of the MLA, from 2011 to 2016. In 2018 he was elected to the American Academy of Arts and Sciences.

Chege Githiora is a widely travelled writer and academic who publishes in Gĩkũyũ, English, Kiswahili and Spanish. He is the author of *Diccionario Swahili-Español, Marũa Ma Maitũ, Afro-Mexicans: Discourse of Race and Identity in the African Diaspora*. He currently teaches Swahili language, linguistics, translation and African Studies at the University of London's School of Oriental and African Studies (SOAS).

Ime Ikiddeh (1938–2008) was, until his death, a Professor of English at the University of Uyo in Akwa Ibom State. He held several academic positions at the Universities of Ghana, Ife (Nigeria), and Calabar (Nigeria). He also served in various administrative capacities in the Government of Akwa Ibom State and the Federal Government of Nigeria. Ikiddeh was a class mate of Ngũgĩ at the University of Leeds.

Emilia Ilieva is a Professor of Literature at Egerton University, Kenya. Some of her publications in the areas of African literature have appeared in, among other journals, *Vostok, Research in African Literatures, World Literature in English, African Literature Today,* and the *Journal of Third World Studies.* Prof. Ilieva has translated Ngũgĩ's novel, *Petals of Blood,* into Bulgarian.

Tsitsi Jaji is a poet and academic born and raised in Zimbabwe, and now based in the U.S., where she is an Associate Professor of English and African & African American Studies at Duke University. She is the author of *Beating the Graves* (2017), *Carnaval* (2014) and *Africa in Stereo: Music, Modernism and Pan-African Solidarity* (2014).

Kĩariĩ Kamau is the Managing Director and Chief Executive of East African Educational Publishers (EAEP). He holds a Master of Arts degree from the University of Nairobi. Kĩarie is also a member of the Council of Management of the Oxford-based African Books Collective, and Council member of the Kenya Publishers Association. His published works include *Notes on Chinua Achebe's A Man of the People* and *Promoting Local Authorship in Kenya.*

Susan N. Kiguli is a poet and Associate Professor of Literature at Makerere University, Uganda. She holds an MA from Makerere and a Ph.D in English from The University of Leeds. Her research interests fall mainly in the area of oral poetry, popular song and performance theory. Kiguli has been an advocate for creative writing in Africa, including serving as a founding member of Femrite, a judge for the Commonwealth Writers' Prize, and an advisory member of the African Writers Trust.

Peter Kimani is the author of three novels: *Before the Rooster Crows, Upside Down,* and, most recently, *Dance of the Jakaranda.* Kimani was one of three international poets who composed a poem for Barack Obama's inauguration in 2009. He is a founding faculty member of the Graduate School of Media and Communications at Aga Khan University in Nairobi, Kenya, and is currently the Visiting Writer at Amherst College.

Bernth Lindfors is a Professor Emeritus of English and African literatures at the University of Texas, Austin. A pioneer scholar of African Literature, he published and edited a number of books on anglophone African literatures and African American performers. His most recent works include *Early Soyinka* (AWP, 2008) *Early Achebe* (AWP, 2009) and *Early West African Writers* (AWP, 2010).

Alamin Mazrui is a Professor of Swahili language and literature at Rutgers University. His research focuses on the political sociology of language in Africa and the African diaspora, African literature in English and Kiswahili, the politics of cultural production in East Africa; cultural discourses on human rights in Africa; and Islam and Identity in Africa and the African diaspora. His many books include *Swahili beyond the Boundaries: Literature, Language, and Identity (2009), English in Africa: After the Cold War* (2007), and (with Ali A. Mazrui) *The Power of Babel: Language and Governance in the African Experience (1998).*

Mĩcere Gĩthae Mũgo is Emeritus Meredith Professor for Teaching Excellence at the Department of African American Studies, Syracuse University. She is a renowned playwright, author, activist, poet and literary critic. Her many publications include *Visions of Africa;* with Ngũgĩ wa Thiong'o, *The Trial of Dedan Kimathi, My Mother's Poem and Other Songs,* and *Orature and Human Rights.*

Grace A. Musila is an associate professor in the English Department, Stellenbosch University, South Africa. She is the author *A Death Retold in Truth and Rumour: Kenya, Britain and the Julie Ward Murder*. She also co-edited *Rethinking Eastern African Intellectual Landscapes* with James Ogude and Dina Ligaga. She writes on Eastern and Southern African literatures and popular culture.

Willy Mutunga was Kenya's Chief Justice and President of the Supreme Court from 2011 to 2016. He served as the Commonwealth Secretary-General's special envoy to the Maldives, and a distinguished scholar-in-residence at Fordham Law School's Leitner Center for International Law and Justice. Justice Mutunga played a pivotal role in the constitution-making processes in Kenya from the 1970s to the 1990s.

Roland D. Nasasira is a journalist living in Kampala, Uganda. He has been a writer and correspondent for the *Daily Monitor*, among other leading publications. He studied at the Multitech Business School in Kampala.

Gĩchingiri Ndĩgĩrĩgĩ is an Associate Professor of English at the University of Tennessee, Knoxville. In addition to numerous publications on Ngũgĩ wa Thiong'o's fiction, and drama and theater, he has published essays on Joseph Kamaru, Lorraine Hansberry, Nuruddin Farah, Chimamanda Adichie, and Josiah Mwangi Kariũki. He was Guest Editor of *Mũtiiri* #8 and the editor of *Unmasking the African Dictator*, a collection of essays.

Ngũgĩ wa Thiong'o is one of the leading novelists and theorists of post-colonial literature globally. He is Distinguished Professor of English and Comparative Literature at the University of California, Irvine.

Kĩmani Njogu holds a Ph.D. in linguistics from Yale University (1994) and taught for many years at Kenyatta University before resigning to become an independent scholar based at Twaweza Communications, Nairobi. He is recipient of the Pan-African Noma Award for Publishing in Africa. *Ufundishaji wa Fasihi: Nadharia na Mbinu*, coauthored with Rocha Chimera won the 2000 Noma Award for Publishing in Africa.

James Ogude is the Director at the Centre for the Advancement of Scholarship, University of Pretoria. He previously served as Professor of African Literature and Cultures in the School of Literature and Language Studies at the University of the Witwatersrand. His research interests include the African novel and the postcolonial experience in Africa. He is the author of *Ngũgĩ's Novels and African History: Narrating the Nation*.

Odhiambo Levin Opiyo graduated with a distinction from the London School of Journalism. He currently writes history articles for the *Sunday Nation*, and was involved in researching atrocities committed by the Colonial Government against the Kipsigis, for a lawsuit against the British government.

Jane Plastow is a professor of African Theatre at the University of Leeds, UK. Professor Plastow's research focuses on African theatre, African literature, education, development studies and politics. She has spent much of over thirty years teaching, researching, directing and facilitating African theatre projects, predominantly in East Africa and the Horn of Africa. She is the author of *African Theatre and Politics: The evolution of theatre in Ethiopia, Tanzania and Zimbabwe – A comparative Study*.

Reinhard Sander is Professor of English at the University of Puerto Rico, Rio Peidras. He is the author of *The Trinidad Awakening*, the editor of *From Trinidad: An Anthology of Early West Indian Writing*, and the co-editor of *Ousmane Sembène: Dialogues with Critics and Writers*, and *Ngũgĩ wa Thiong'o Speaks*.

Sultan Somjee is a Kenya-born, Canada-based ethnographer and writer. He worked closely with Ngũgĩ wa Thiong'o at the *Kamĩrĩĩthũ* project. He studied product design and is interested in how stories are told in products about people's lives as they are reflected on the individuals, their families, and ethnic and faith groups.

Ndirangu Wachanga is Professor of Media Studies and Information Science, University of Wisconsin-Whitewater. Wachanga is the authorized documentary biographer of Professor Ali A. Mazrui, Professor Ngũgĩ wa Thiong'o, Professor Mĩcere Mũgo, Abdilatif Abdalla, and Chief Justice Willy Mutunga. His documentary, *Ali Mazrui: A Walking Triple Heritage*, won the 2015 New York African Studies Book Award. He is a Swahili commentator for the British Broadcasting Corporation.

Index

Lightning Source UK Ltd.
Milton Keynes UK
UKHW011828211118
332699UK00001B/1/P